IN SEARCH OF DR. THORNDYKE

THE CHEMISTRY AND TECHNOLOGY
OF NAPHTHALENE COMPOUNDS

Dr. John Evelyn Thorndyke. (From a 1908 drawing by
H. M. Brock in *Pearson's* Magazine; reproduced by permission.)

IN SEARCH OF DR. THORNDYKE
THE STORY OF R. AUSTIN FREEMAN'S GREAT
SCIENTIFIC INVESTIGATOR AND HIS CREATOR

by

Norman Donaldson

Bowling Green University Popular Press
Bowling Green, Ohio 43403

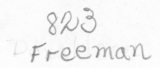

823
Freeman

Library of Congress Catalogue Card Number: 72-147819
Printed in the United States of America.

Distributed in the British Isles by
Lythway Press Limited, Portway
Combe Park, Bath, England.

to

Vincent Starrett
and the late
P. M. Stone
two good friends of
R. Austin Freeman

"When in doubt, stick to Dr. Thorndyke."

CHRISTOPHER MORLEY

"The great scene would have been a court-room
battle between Thorndyke and Spilsbury, and for
my money Thorndyke would have won hands down."

RAYMOND CHANDLER

CONTENTS

List of Illustrations

PREFACE

I first read the Thorndyke stories as a schoolboy in England, and, as R. Austin Freeman's admirers will hardly need to be told, I never could find enough of these enchanting volumes to satisfy me. A few years ago circumstances brought me to the United States and, when I discovered the excellent (though incomplete) set of Freeman's books in the library of Ohio State University, I hastened to renew my acquaintance with old favorites.

This volume, conceived shortly afterwards, was originally planned as the first study to appear on Thorndyke, to parallel the many "biographies" and studies of Sherlock Holmes. In the process I discovered just how difficult it is to separate Thorndyke from his creator, and inevitably my book has become the dual history of Freeman and his superlative detective. Also included is a bibliography of the first editions of all of Freeman's books.

Freeman, who was to become, according to Howard Haycraft, the dean of scientific detective story writers, "if not, indeed, of all detective story writers," did not publish his first Thorndyke story until he was forty-five years old. In his late twenties his health had been broken by disease and his career as a colonial surgeon, naturalist and surveyor irretrievably wrecked. Years of ill-health followed and it was not until the creation of Thorndyke in 1907 that the outlook brightened. Through it all Freeman remained rather a shadowy figure, shunning publicity and unknown to all but a small circle. I am all the more grateful on that account to those in England and the United States who have made this book possible, and whom it is now my pleasant duty to thank.

In Chicago, Mr. Vincent Starrett was not only a gracious host but, by sharing his personal memories of Freeman and passing on to me copies of their correspondence, helped enormously to my understanding of Freeman's activities in the twenties. He also supplied miscellaneous letters and notes originally belonging to the late P. M. Stone. Also in Chicago, but since removed to Dallas, Mrs. Dolores Lovell, who, with her late husband Arthur, handled the P. M. Stone library when it was dispersed, was most helpful on several biblio-graphical matters, especially those relating to periodical publication of Freeman's short stories.

In San Diego, Mr. E. T. Guymon, Jr., owner of the most com-plete private library of detective stories in the world, went to endless trouble to verify a number of doubtful and missing particulars in the Freeman bibliography. (His library [now in process of being passed over to his *alma mater*, Occidental College, Los Angeles] includes a complete set of Freeman's books, many of them inscribed to him by the author, as well as the manuscripts of *The Red Thumb Mark* and *The Eye of Osiris,* the only manuscripts by this author I have located to date.)

In Austin, Mr. F. W. Roberts, Director of the Humanities Re-search Center at the University of Texas, present home of the Ellery Queen Collection, generously took time from his busy schedule to answer questions and graciously supply copies of inscriptions.

In Waltham, Massachusetts, Mr. Percival Mason Stone, the Freeman specialist, was fatally ill at the time I was compiling my research, but his wife Adele passed on several pieces of useful inform-ation. Mr. James Keddie, Jr., whom I visited in nearby Wellesley Hills, was most generous in extending to me the resources of his ex-cellent Freeman collection.

My former colleague, Dr. James E. Rush, encouraged me in the early stages of the writing of this book and has made several valuable suggestions.

In England, Mr. C. J. A. Freeman, the author's elder son, kindly sent me a lengthy account of his father, including all he knew of his early years, as well as interesting background notes on some of the stories. Mr. Ronald F. Jessup, author of several admirable archaeo-logical works, who describes himself as almost the last survivor of the Freeman circle, took immense pains to insure that, whatever *opinions* I expressed about his old friend, the *facts* (so far as he could verify them) would be accurate. Ideally he, not I, should have written this book.

Dr. Carlos P. Blacker, now Chairman of the Simon Population Trust, was a colleague of Freeman's in the Eugenics Society Council and his pleasant recollections are quoted in this volume. Dr. Blacker also took the time to reread Freeman's *Social Decay and Regeneration* and to supply an informed commentary in the light of all that has happened in the world since it was written.

Mr. P. A. Sabine, Chief Petrographer of the Geological Survey, was most helpful in matters concerning phonolite (the volcanic rock which provides the vital clue in *The Shadow of the Wolf*) and in related areas of petrological detection.

I have enjoyed a lengthy correspondence with Mrs. T. H. Johns (née Winifred Mary Pitcairn) which began as a request for information about her father and has continued for its own sake. I have to thank the British Medical Association and Mr. Claude Berry, editor of the West Briton Newspaper Co., for information which aided my search for the Pitcairn family.

My two prime informants for Freeman's military service were Mr. S. Lewis Stevenson and Mr. H. C. Bryan, both of whom retain a remarkably clear (and affectionate) memory of their old commanding officer after fifty years.

Mr. E. S. Turner, an authority on Sexton Blake stories and their nineteenth-century predecessors, was of great assistance in our joint attempt to unravel the Freeman-Aldine mystery discussed in Chapter II. Miss Alison Hodgson shared with me her knowledge of King's Bench Walk, ancient and modern, and Miss Gwenda Jones, Buckinghamshire Librarian, kindly answered questions regarding the Aylesbury locale of *The Cat's Eye*.

For his encouragement and help so freely given in various ways I am grateful to my old friend Tom Mollard, Librarian at Downham Market, Norfolk.

I must thank the host of people, all residents or former residents of Gravesend, who responded to my call for information about Freeman and his family. Their assistance is manifest on many of the pages which follow. Mrs. Dorothy Moriarty (née Bishop), Miss Rose Standfield and Mr. James S. Warrack remembered Freeman from his earliest Gravesend years at the beginning of the century; others who helped were Mr. A. C. Smith of *The Gravesend and Dartford Reporter*; The Rev. Edward Howland; Mr. A. Bradley; Mr. C. G. Bickers;

Mr. E. Altenhein; Mr. William A. Lear; Mr. E. N. Moore, borough librarian; and Miss D. Nichols, who typed Freeman's last book.

It is a special pleasure to acknowledge the continuing help of Mr. Paul R. Lorch and his wife Irene. Although Mrs. Lorch's memories of Freeman in the twenties, when she was a young girl, are naturally dim, she has developed quite an enthusiasm for Freemanian research and has, with her husband, supplied me with many useful photographs, maps and plans.

My wife, Betty, not only typed my manuscript but prevented many an obscure or inelegant phrase from reaching the printed page.

The following have kindly permitted me to make quotations from copyright material: Constable and Co. Ltd.; Hodder & Stoughton Ltd.; University of London Press, Ltd. and A. P. Watt & Son (Freeman's literary executors). Photographs were supplied by The Science Museum, South Kensington and by the B.B.C. Television Centre.

In a recent letter, a gentleman who had heard of my projected book wrote: "I think Freeman is the greatest of all detective writers; I read all the Thorndyke books I can get hold of and am only sorry they are so scarce, because I invariably find them so fresh and interesting." He was, of course, re-echoing Christopher Morley's exhortation: "When in doubt, stick to Dr. Thorndyke."

If this volume leads new readers to sample the delights of the Thorndyke stories and indirectly persuades the publishers to bring out new editions of the old favorites, it will have been fully justified.

CHAPTER I

Traveler in the Realms of Gold

At twenty-six, Austin Freeman was an athletic young man of average height, but with slender proportions which gave him the appearance of being tall. The most striking features of his lean sun-tanned face were keen observant eyes, a sharp aquiline nose and a dark neatly-trimmed moustache. Dressed in white drill tunic and trousers, with close-fitting knee-length boots and sun-helmet, he presented a striking figure as he strode through the streets of Cape Coast Castle at seven o'clock one sunny morning towards the hospital compound, where, clustered around the gate, thirty West African natives awaited his arrival. These were the carriers of his personal possessions as well as of the medical, photographic and navigational equipment needed for his various duties. He had observed the main expedition of about three hundred march north-ward out of the Gold Coast town at day-break towards the distant and mysterious Bontúku to the accompaniment of fifes and drums;

1

and now, after enjoying the luxury of a final breakfast in civilized surroundings, he took charge of the rear-guard. It was December 8th, 1888, and this is Freeman's account of the scene:

> It was certainly a very curious and miscel-
> laneous crowd that I encountered as I approached the
> gate, for it contained specimens of nearly all the na-
> tionalities of West Africa, and afforded examples of
> every variety of costume in common use among the na-
> tives.   And when one observed how extraordinarily
> simple were their preparations for the journey, it was
> impossible to avoid a certain sense of humiliation and
> an acknowledgment of the superiority of primitive man
> amidst his own surroundings; for, while the white man
> required his tent to sleep in, his changes of clothing and
> bedding, and his stores of preserved food, here was a man
> whose entire outfit for a journey, the duration of which
> was quite unknown to him, consisted of a   ragged
> singlet and a large cotton pocket-handkerchief. He had
> "gone one better" than Diogenes, for he dispensed with
> the tub, and after all had so much accommodation to
> spare that he could carry some of the impedimenta of
> his helpless white brother.[1]

When all the loads had been apportioned, not without some protest, the little caravan moved off in single file "through the hot glowing streets of Cape Coast, between walls of dazzling white, and over roads of sparkling quartz."   Freeman's attitude was one of adventurous anticipation, and the sun, though now high in the sky, did not oppress him.

> I think the fear of out-door exercise in the sun is one of
> the many hygienic mistakes that prevail in West Africa,
> and the almost universal obesity and want of "condition"
> that is observable among Europeans there, is largely
> attributable to the prevalence of this delusion. As a matter

of fact, if the body be well covered with white drill, and the head protected by a thick, wide helmet, there is little to fear from the West African sun; and the lightness of the clothing which so little impedes the movements of the body and the free action of the skin, which so greatly assists respiration, renders moderate exercise pleasant and invigorating.[2]

The road, rich in red iron oxides, stretched across rolling dark-green bush country. Colorfully-plumaged birds, all the names of which Freeman seems to have known, abounded in the bushy masses of mimosa to either side.

Later that morning, Freeman's party joined up with the main body of the expedition waiting beneath a village shade-tree. The unit was under the command of Inspector Lethbridge of the Gold Coast Constabulary. Freeman held the position of Medical Officer, surveyor and naturalist, and there was one other European, Assistant-Inspector Ewart, who had charge of the native escort.

In his account, Freeman mentions the two white officers infrequently, and when he does, he is likely to report some bit of imprudence in their dealings with the natives. By contrast, Freeman's relations with the black members of the party were excellent. He held a high opinion of many of them; others he does not hesitate to reprove, although even with these his strongest epithet is "rascal."

Freeman had learned of the expedition on his return to headquarters in Accra after six months' leave in England. Its aims, and Freeman's reasons for wanting to take part in it can best be told in his own words:

> The object of the expedition, which was not at the time made generally known, was to take over the kingdom of Jáman as part of the British Protectorate. This step was taken by the Government in consequence of the appearance at Cape Coast of certain persons who stated that they had been sent by King Ajiman of Jáman to entreat that his country might be taken under British protection: and one

of them, a sturdy, handsome young man named Koffi Dabbi, afterwards accompanied the expedition as guide.

In addition to this mission there was some business of a somewhat delicate character to be transacted with the new King of Ashanti, Osai Kwaku Dua III (or Prempeh, as he has since been more generally called), the nature of which was briefly as follows —Prempeh had recently been elected King of Ashanti, but had not yet been placed on the gold stool. Now this gold stool was, in function, similar to the ancient coronation chair in Westminster Abbey, or perhaps I should rather say, to the "Scone stone" which is built into it. Until the king had been enthroned on the gold stool his title was not officially recognised, and he was unable to draw from the royal treasury at Bántama. But the ceremony of "stooling" a new king was one that involved considerable expense, and this Prempeh was not in a position to meet. From this dilemma he asked the British Government to extricate him by lending him four hundred pounds; but he desired that the loan should be made secretly and all knowledge of it kept from his people, who might, perhaps, have objected to the arrangement. To this request the Government had decided to accede, and the officer in charge of the mission was commissioned to signify this to the king and pay the money.

It will thus be seen that this expedition held out numerous and great attractions to persons interested in geographical research, and, as the post of medical officer was still vacant, (the surgeons previously appointed having been withdrawn in consequence of sickness) I volunteered for the special service and, to my great satisfaction, was accepted, and ordered to join the expedition at Cape Coast without delay. I had fortunately provided myself with surveying and astronomical instruments and was thus in a position to carry out the Governor's special instructions to me, which were to the effect that I should fix the positions of all important towns by astronomical observation,

construct a map of the route, and collect information relating to the natural history and resources of the country.[3]

Freeman modestly refrains from pointing out that the tasks
allocated to him would have been beyond most young physicians
fresh out of medical school, being indeed, numerous and varied
enough to demand the combined services of a botanist, a zoologist,
a mineralogist and a navigator, as well as a physician to deal with
routine sickness. The authorities probably did not realise until afterwards that, in Freeman, they had obtained all these specialists rolled
into one, with a passable historian, sociologist and, not least important, diplomat, thrown in.

How the young physician had mastered so many skills in so
many disciplines by the age of twenty-six is not entirely clear. He
was reticent about his early years even in conversation with his
closest friends, few of whom now survive. We do not even know
which schools he attended prior to his medical training. His
army records hint at private schools and tutors, but his modest
origins hardly suggest the availability of sufficient funds for such an
expensive education, and it is probable that, during some of his boyhood years at least, he attended the public elementary schools near
his home.

As far back as we can trace, the Freeman family were London-
ers. Austin's grandfather, Richard Freeman, born in 1800, was a
hotel-keeper who died in Middlesex Hospital on 2nd September,
1876. His son and namesake entered the tailoring business and married Ann Maria Dunn. Austin, their son, originally named only
Richard, was born on April 11th, 1862 in his parents' modest home
at 27 Thayer Street, near Manchester Square, Soho, in the West
End of London. This is a mile or two south of the area, running
from Hampstead, down Hampstead Road and across to Islington,
which were to become the setting for so many of his books. Richard Freeman is described on his son's birth certificate as a journey-
man tailor. Austin Freeman's elder son Mr. Clifford John Austin
Freeman supplies the following account of how his father gradually

made his way into his chosen profession:

Richard Freeman (Austin's father) worked for a man who had what was described as a select tailoring business, which meant that it was run from a private house and not a shop. The customers called at the house much as if they were consulting their doctor. Richard Freeman was probably a sort of manager or receptionist in this business. Whatever he was, his employer thought well of him and was friendly with the family. He arranged for young Richard to take the name of Austin, and on his death left the business either to Richard Austin or to the family. So Richard, the tailor who had become an outfitter, became the tailor master and managed the business.

It was expected that young Austin would be a tailor and become the tailor master, but he hated tailoring and was interested in natural history and medicine, and so was set to work in a chemist's [pharmacist's] shop, where he qualified as an apothecary, and so could have managed a chemist's shop; but he preferred medicine and entered as a student at Middlesex Hospital.

This private communication from his son is the only information we have about Austin Freeman's origins. He did admit to 1862 as his year of birth, but the precise date is not to be found in any printed source, and he was equally reticent about other personal matters.

The fact is that Austin Freeman was ashamed of his father's trade. Although he admired the arts almost equally with the natural sciences, and revered an expert craftsman above an aristocrat, he was not willing to extend this category to include tailors, however masterly, and never hinted at his family's connection with them.

At eighteen, then, Freeman embarked on a medical career at Middlesex Hospital. What sort of student he was we do not know. Certainly he did not allow the curriculum to narrow his interests; a passable natural historian before beginning his medical studies, he did not allow new concerns to supplant the old. Hampstead Heath at that time was a much more rural, far less urbanised stretch of land than it has since become. While walking between lodgings and the hospital, he would jot down his observations of nature in a small notebook he always carried. His first appearance in print may well have been a short communication—just two hundred words—on the subject of moles in *Naturalist's World*[4], an obscure monthly published in Ilkley, Yorkshire. "In the early part of last June," he wrote, "I received two specimens of a variety of *T. europœa* which I believe is somewhat uncommon. . ." and goes on to describe the animals. As they had been sent all the way from Suffolk, Freeman must, even in 1885, have achieved some slight notice as an amateur zoologist and no doubt belonged to one or more natural history societies.

After qualifying as a physician and surgeon in 1887[5] he was faced with a serious financial problem. To buy a practice was quite beyond his means. The future would have been difficult, even as a bachelor, but on April 15, 1887, he had married the daughter of a master plumber of Gothic Villa, St. Pancras Road. Miss Annie Elizabeth Edwards was a Catholic, and the couple were married in St. Mary's Church, near the bride's home. (Austin Freeman, who declared himself "C. of E." on his army papers, was indifferent to religious matters. "A healthy atheist" was a friend's description of him recently, but perhaps "a healthy agnostic" would be nearer the truth.)

In retrospect young Freeman's decision to enter the Colonial Service, made during his final year at the hospital, seems unavoidable; something in the way of a regular salary was necessary. Had he been able to foresee the future, he certainly would have found some other solution, for instead of financial security it led to years of ill-health and improverishment. It also led—ultimately—to Thorndyke, a fact for which we are all grateful, but so far as worldly riches go, Freeman would have probably fared better as a humble Ġ. P., pursuing his natural history and other interests in his spare time and living out his life in obscurity.

In June, within a few weeks of his marriage, Freeman landed

at Accra on the Gold Coast to take up the position of Assistant Colonial Surgeon. The future capital of Ghana was then "a primitive place: just a large native town of mud-walled, grass-thatched houses, with here and there an area of beehive-shaped palm-leaf Hausa huts."[6] Freeman was quartered in one of several large stone-walled houses built by the Dutch many years earlier to house slaves who were shackled to the walls. Gigantic rats infested the houses, and Freeman shot two with his rifle in the sitting room on his first night in the building. Outside, scavenger pigs roamed the streets in herds of twenty or thirty. "It was a pestilential year," wrote Freeman; "I found the entire white population of the town on the sick list, and one of [my] first duties was to make a post-mortem on a shipmate who had been brought ashore suffering from blackwater fever. [My] sanitary report for that year showed a European mortality of 40 per cent (and was not given wide publicity by the authorities)."[7]

Freeman's first year on the Coast was evidently a tedious one, tending the sick, conducting autopsies, and, most likely, acting as police surgeon. By the time his first home leave became due in the summer of 1888 he was quite ready for it. On his return to headquarters at Accra he heard of the opportunity of joining a Bontuku-bound party and sailed to Cape Coast immediately on the *S. S. Niger* to join the awaiting party. The sole native commissioned officer, Abdulai Futa by name, was "a very intelligent trustworthy little man" who subsequently became a great crony of his. Non-commissioned officers and men of the Hausa Constabulary numbered one hundred; the remaining two hundred were carriers for the enormous freight which had to be taken along; not only personal baggage and provisions, but "tents and hospital stores, [and] presents for native kings and chiefs, which consisted of folding chairs, umbrellas, cotton cloths and (I am ashamed to add) over seventy loads of excessively bad gin." Moreover, many cases of cartridges and war-rockets were taken along, just in case.

After a march of twenty-four miles, the first day ended with a cup of tea, a smoke and a gossip beneath the shade-tree at Dunkwa. Freeman's faithful servant, Joseph, prepared the folding bed,

covered it with a white sheet, and draped mosquito netting over it.
The sleeping quarters thus provided appeared "positively luxurious"
to Freeman.

> When I awoke the next morning and raised my mosquito
> curtain I was somewhat disconcerted to find that my win-
> dow was entirely blocked up by a mass of woolly heads
> and black shoulders. A small crowd, consisting chiefly of
> women and children, had collected round it, and craning
> their necks into the room, had been watching me as I slept.
> They maintained their position and their interest in
> my doings while I arose, took my bath and washed; and
> watched with great curiosity the various garments with
> which I subsequently invested my person.[8]

On the second day, the countryside began to change from open
bush to sparse forest, and the intermittent shade was welcome.
Freeman's keen attention never flagged. He noticed everything and
his powers of observation were well served by his thorough knowledge of all things botanical and zoological. Butterflies, wasps and
beetles receive a friendly word: "the surface of every pond and
stream was gay with merry parties of whirling beetles (*Gyrinus*)
whose glittering bodies flashing in the sun as they spun round and
round in their mazy dance." Freeman understandably devotes over
a full page of description to the oil-palm, "one of the handsomest
and most graceful plants met with in Africa." In this description
Freeman postulates how the wreaths of fern leaves came to be suspended from nearly every palm tree crown.

Two or three days later, after more rapid marching, a day's rest
was declared and Freeman took the opportunity to hunt for game.

> With this idea in view I arose at half-past four, and taking
> my gun and collecting-box, crossed the Pra in the canoe
> and plunged into the dense forest on the north side. I soon
> found that shooting was out of the question as I could not
> see above a dozen yards in any direction, and no game ap-

peared in that narrow radius, so I devoted my energies to a
search for insects and mollusca, to the unspeakable disgust
of my orderly who accompanied me, and of this "small
deer" [*sic*] I obtained quite a fine "bag." When I was tired
of grubbing among the roots of trees and tearing up pieces
of moss for the sake of the *Pupae* and other minute shells
which lived in them, I adjourned to the little village of
Brofo Edru, where I lit a fire, and with the assistance of
my orderly, Onitchi Gara, boiled some water in a clay pot
(which Onitchi borrowed in the village) and made some
tea, which I presently consumed together with the solid
provisions from Onitchi's haversack, with great satisfaction
to myself and to the audience of men, women and children
who squatted in a semicircle round me.

This refection concluded I bestowed a threepenny
piece and my blessing on the village chief (I think from his
manner he would rather have had two threepenny-pieces)
and returned to Prasu, where I spent the remainder of the
day in idleness.[9]

For several days after this the march northward proceeded through
the country of Adansi. Not a living soul was to be encountered, for
the inhabitants had been at war with the powerful Ashantis and had
all been captured, killed or driven away. Village after village was
found deserted. Each clearing was overgrown with coarse grass and
tangled vegetation eight or ten feet high. Shapeless masses of red
clay showed where houses had once stood and a few bleached bones
indicated the fate of those who had been caught within them.

Marching through this wilderness was wearisome. The path,
long-since overgrown, had almost entirely disappeared. A network
of roots underfoot and a tangle of creepers hanging from above
hindered progress. Foul-smelling swamps lay across the path.
While fording one of the deepest and most pungent of these,
Freeman was being carried on the back of one of his bearers.
When the unfortunate man slipped, Freeman suddenly found himself
lying up to his neck in the loathsome ooze, with "my quondam

bearer sitting on my stomach."

But perhaps the worst feature of this road was its exasperating tortuosity. Sometimes after a long day's march my astronomical observations would show that we had not advanced a dozen miles as the crow flies, and very often we of the rear-guard could hear, and sometimes even see, through the bush, the advance guard which was fully half an hour in advance of us.

It is not at all difficult to see how this extraordinary tortuosity has been brought about. Twice in every year, at the commencement and end of the rainy season, the forest is swept by a series of tornadoes, and at that time the lofty unstable trees may be heard falling in all directions, and of course a considerable number fall across the paths. Now, if they are of small or moderate size and create no very serious obstruction, no notice is taken of them; but if they happen to be of such large dimensions as to seriously impede the progress of travellers carrying burdens, one of two courses is adopted. Either a fire is made on the path by the fallen tree, when the latter ignites and slowly smoulders away; or, more commonly, a detour is made round the prostrate giant, and the path resumed farther on. In the course of time the tree is destroyed by the termites, and its *débris* washed away by succeeding rains until no trace of it remains except the loop in the path that was made to avoid it. This becomes a permanent bend in the road, for curiously enough the natives never appear to think of the simple expedient of striking across the chord of the loop and resuming the straight road. In this way, in the course of years, loop after loop is added to the paths until it becomes a continuous series of serpentine curves.[10]

More than any other feature of the wearisome march, Freeman enjoyed the quiet evenings in camp:.

After dinner and the post-prandial smoke and gossip (the post-prandial glass was tabooed on the march, and water was practically our only drink, a fact to which I think the good health we enjoyed is largely attributable) I usually retired to my tent, where a lamp had been lit and things made comfortable for the night. Very few people, I believe, who have not lived under canvas for a lengthened period, have any idea how cosy and luxurious an abode a tent can be made, if the occupant is willing to accept it in its native simplicity and refrain from encumbering it with unnecessary furniture and equipments. Mine was an ordinary regulation bell-tent with a double roof, and was furnished with the excellent camp kit made by Messrs. Pigott, the whole of which stows away in a canvas bag which can be carried by one man. When set up and furnished, my tent had a most inviting and home-like aspect and was as commodious a residence as a traveller could wish for. Occupying one side was the little folding bedstead with its mosquito net suspended from the tent pole. On the other side a writing-table was rigged up by standing two baggage cases on end and laying my drawing-board across them. The wash-stand, and a dressing-table consisting of another baggage case, were placed outside the tent. A small folding chair stood by the writing-table, and the luxurious deck-chair was placed just within the doorway. I disposed of the evenings in writing up my journal, in looking over and taking notes of my specimens, and in plotting my survey of the day's route. On clear nights my altazimuth was brought forth and I took one or two observations to fix the latitude of the camp, and, these business details being settled, the rest of the evening was spent sitting at the door of my tent in the enjoyment of a soothing pipe and the perusal of the oft-read pages of one of the few volumes that I carried in my trunk.

The morning was usually a period of tribulation.

At about half-past five the bugler took up his stand in

front of my tent, and I firmly believe turned the muzzle of his infernal instrument into my doorway as he blew a blast that abruptly put an end to my dreamless slumber: upon which I turned out shivering and wretched into the darkness of the chilly cheerless morning, performed my ablutions outside the tent—which was meanwhile being taken down—and drew on my cold damp clothing. Next came breakfast, which was tastefully laid out on the top of a box and was consumed hurriedly by the light of a lantern, and then the "fall in" was sounded and the expedition slowly filed out of the village clearing just as the first glimmer of dawn was appearing in the sky. Then commenced the labours of the day, which in my case were not light, for during the whole of the march I walked compass in hand, keeping a dead reckoning of our direction. The method of surveying which I adopted on this journey, and by which the route on the map accompanying this volume was laid down was as follows. On starting out of camp in the morning, I observed and noted down the time. I then walked for fifteen minutes, holding the compass in my hand and mentally averaging the direction indicated by it. At the end of the fifteen minutes I halted and noted in my road book the average direction and the time: and so on throughout the day, noting the average direction every fifteen minutes.

If any stream was encountered the time at which it was reached, its width, the direction and rapidity of its current and the nature of its bottom were duly noted; and if any obstruction, such as a fallen tree, arrested the progress of the column, the time taken up in passing it had also to be entered so as to avoid error in plotting the route. The method was most laborious when the marches were long—and we often marched from day-break to sunset—and may seem somewhat inaccurate, but it was the only one that was possible, for any kind of triangulation was quite out of the question by reason of the thickness of the vegetation, and even back and fore sights were impossible in such dense wood and on such a tortuous road. But the results were much more accurate than would have been expected, for the route survey was constantly checked by astronomical observations, and by its means the principal error, that of distance, was completely eliminated.[11]

(Freeman was quite proud of his surveying procedure; his map, constructed by its means, was first published in 1893.[12] Twenty years later he adapted the same method to the streets of London, and employed it in his early Thorndyke novel, *The Mystery of 31, New Inn.*)

It was during the tedious and arduous part of the march just described that starvation threatened the party: The countryside of the area was barren of food. All the plantains and papaws had been stripped from the trees by earlier wayfarers, and at village after village hopes of finding sustenance were dashed. Though for over two days the carriers had not eaten, they continued to make good progress with their heavy loads without complaints, but matters were becoming grave. On the third day, after a five hour march, suddenly the men broke ranks: first the advance guard, then the main escort, the carriers, the band and the rear guard one after the other. As they had moved forward in line, all at once a large plantation of well-stocked plantains had come into view, and the men abandoned themselves to a well-earned "blow-out." Under the circumstances, the breach of the discipline was overlooked by the officers, fires were lighted to cook the fruit, and the rest of the day given over to eating and to recovery from the effects thereof.

A day or so after these events the party found themselves once again passing through inhabited parts. At Bekwe they met the king of the region for an official "palaver." He was a young man with "a vivacious and intelligent manner" dressed in traditional style in a toga-like garment, and wearing gold ornaments around his neck, wrists and ankles.

His head was encircled by a narrow green silken fillet and numbers of gold ornaments were stuck in his hair. He was supported (literally) by two chiefs, one on either side, in much the same manner as indiscreet wassailers at home are supported by policemen during their progress to the lock-up; and when he extended his hand for us to shake, it was presented by the chief, who supported it, as though it was paralyzed. This curious fashion prevails throughout Ashanti. On ceremonial occasions it appears to be the correct thing for men of position to adopt an entirely passive attitude, all movements being executed for them by their attendants. When I was about to rise from my chair to salute the King of Bekwe several of his chiefs rushed forward to assist me, and when I endeavoured to resume my seat I was seized by the same courteous officials and gently lowered into it.[13]

The palavers were held at Bekwe, after which the expedition pushed on towards Kumasi. At this point in his account Freeman pauses to give us his impressions of the primeval forest of Ashanti, through which their route lay for over a month. The forest exerted a profound effect on Freeman and he brooded upon its characteristics long after he had left Africa and through the unhappy years in England which preceded publication of his Ashanti book. [Note—It had been my intention to reproduce here his lengthy description of the forest and his speculations upon its various characteristics but this has been rendered unnecessary by the recent reissuance of Freeman's book by Frank Cass & Co., London, 1967.[14]] In a style strongly reminiscent of Thorndyke's, Freeman ponders the root structure of the giant Bombax trees. The roots lie almost entirely on the surface of the ground and, where they join the straight vertical trunk, form immense triangular buttresses up to twenty feet high, between which it would be possible to pitch a tent. Freeman was first tempted to associate the peculiar structure of the Bombax with the absence of earthworms in the forest, but later realised that both phenomena were related to a single climatographical feature, namely, the region's heavy rainfall. Freeman's concluding remarks on the forest reveal his sensibility as well as sense, and are worth our attention:

> Beautiful as the forest unquestionably is, there is yet
> in its aspect and in its whole atmosphere something un-
> speakably solemn and sad. The deathlike silence that pre-
> vails around, broken only at long intervals by the cry of
> some animal or bird, or the distant rustle of the foliage
> overhead, the absolute stillness of the air, the motionless
> vegetation, the reeking dampness, the gloomy twilight that
> never brightens, the giant trees wreathed with fantastic
> creepers, impart to the scene a strangeness that oppresses
> the mind and fills it with awe. The traveller who wanders
> through its dim recesses soon feels the sense of its beauty
> lost in that of its mournful grandeur, and there steals over
> him a profound feeling of solitude and a deep conscious-
> ness of the solemnity, majesty, and utter loneliness of this
> great ghostly wilderness.[15]

As the march approached Kumasi, a city of some interest in
those days and a place seldom visited by Europeans, solemn and
melancholy feelings would have to be put aside. The nature of their
reception perplexed the British officers not a little. Approaching the
city, the travellers found a road had been cleared for them that day
through the herbage. Abdulai Futa, their sole native officer, advised
the Europeans that this round-about road was not the regular route
into the city. Far from paying them a compliment, the King
apparently wished to prevent the party from seeing a certain pit,
close to the regular road, into which the bodies of sacrificial
victims had been dumped. (Kumasi was notorious for the gruesome
practice of human sacrifice, although Freeman considered the
accounts to have been exaggerated.)

On arriving at a large clearing in the forest, the party met a
King's messenger who instructed them to wait until His Majesty
was ready to receive them; and they did wait, in great ill humor, while
the sun beat down and ants crawled over them. At last the contingent was able to proceed, with the band playing and the officers re-

clining in hammocks, "for it would have been unspeakably shocking
to the Royal personages of Kumasi to see the emissaries of the Great
White Queen enter their city on foot, like common baggage carriers." Large numbers of inhabitants, including the King's troops,
poured out of the city to greet them, discharging their guns in all
directions "with the utmost impartiality, causing an uproar that was
perfectly deafening."

Now when an African indulges in a *feu-de-joie* it is by
no means the harmless affair that blank-firing is at home.
In the first place, he generally rams three times the proper
charge of powder into his crazy barrel, and then fills it up
with stones, slugs, pieces of iron or anything else of a suitable size that comes handy.

Consequently, to the shouts and yells of the multitude and the unceasing din of exploding firearms was
added the whistling of slugs above our heads, and as these
irregularly-shaped missiles are extremely erratic in their
flight, we most devoutly wished that the hospitable
Ashantis had adopted some other mode of testifying their
joy at our arrival. As our procession approached the envir-
ons of Kumasi it was taken in tow by certain officials who
were facetiously described to us as "guides," by whom it
was led by the most circuitous route round the outskirts
of the city, somewhat after the fashion of a travelling
circus.[16]

Along the sides of the road sat a number of chiefs, each of them
under an umbrella the size and ornateness of which signified the importance of the person below. Chiefs of higher rank commonly displayed umbrellas six to eight feet across and eight to ten feet high.
The King was surrounded by a large crowd of men and boys, all
seated, including an orchestra of elephant tusks, drums of various
sizes and an antelope's horn.

Under a large and gorgeous canopy on the King's left

hand stood a roomy armchair of native manufacture, studded with bright-headed nails and enriched with silver ornaments, and on this stood the celebrated gold stool, the coronation seat of the Kings of Ashanti. On this the King takes his seat on his formal appointment to his royal office and it is said he occupies it thereafter once in every year; on all other occasions it occupies a place of honour upon a chair which is reserved for its use. The King (Kwaku Dua III or Prempeh) was seated on a similar chair under his own umbrella and not under the canopy. He was a fairly good-looking young man rather inclined to be stout, with a smooth, sleek, reddish-brown skin. . . .

After having saluted the King I was presented to the Queen Mother, an extremely lean and frostily dignified old lady, whose head was shaven and highly polished, apparently with some oily substance; and the rest of her jet-black and somewhat emaciated person appeared to have been similarly treated, for she shone as though she had received a skillfully applied coat of "Day and Martin." On this occasion my desire to exhibit a cordial and affable manner again led me into difficulties, for when the Queen Mother presented to me her small, soft, shapely hand I took it in mine and, as I made my bow, bestowed upon it a gentle and affectionate squeeze such as could not have hurt a baby; upon which, to my surprise and discomfiture, the old lady closed one eye and pursed up her mouth into the form of an ill-made buttonhole, murmuring at the same time something that I feel could not be construed into a benediction.[17]

The fate of King Prempeh and of the Golden Stool, here described by Freeman, were matters which agitated the entire British Empire in the years following.

It should be explained that the stool in Ashanti has a certain deep significance as a symbol of authority. Indeed it is more than that. The stool of a chief is a link with his ancestors. When a chief-elect is to be installed in office, he is taken into the stool-house "where the blackened stools of his ancestors are kept. There more than in any other place the spirits of his ancestors are believed to be present. Upon the blackened stool of the most renowned of his ancestors the chief is lowered and raised three times. He is then enstooled. He has been brought into a peculiarly close relationship with the dead."[18] Thereafter the chief's person is sacred. His bare feet must not touch the ground. He must take care not to stumble, and if he does a sacrifice is mandatory to avoid a calamity.

Most sacred of all was the Golden Stool of Ashanti. It was believed to have descended from the skies and landed in the lap of Ashanti's fourth ruler Osai Tutu one day early in the eighteenth century. Succeeding rulers added various golden ornaments to it, and it became the repository of all the power of Ashanti, and of the soul of the nation. Freeman believed the King sat on it once a year. Another authority[19] says he never sat on it. Either way, it was revered, kept off the ground and guarded at all times by the Ashanti nation. Freeman and his two companions were possibly the only Europeans ever to see it in its complete state. Its future history makes one of the most interesting chapters of Ashanti history. Rather than risk its loss in the struggle against the British in 1895 (according to Rattray's account) the Ashantis gave in without a struggle. Prempeh was banished to the Seychelles Islands but the stool was saved. Thereafter it disappeared, having been hidden away until better days should come.

In March, 1900, Sir Frederic Hodgson, as the Government's representative, made in Kumasi one of the most inept speeches in British Colonial history. His dull-witted pomposity leaps at us from the printed page:

> ". . . What must I do to the man, whoever he is, who has failed to give to the Queen, who is the paramount power in this country, the stool to which she is entitled?"
> "Where is the Golden Stool?"
> "Why am I not sitting on the Golden Stool at this moment?"

"Why have you relegated me to this chair?"
"Why did you not take the opportunity of my coming to Kumasi to bring the Golden Stool, and give it to me to sit upon?"

Outraged silence greeted this outburst. It is easy to believe that Hodgson spoke in ignorance, but such ignorance, if it proceeded from indifference to native values, is impossible to condone. At any rate, the Ashantis left the meeting to prepare for war, and more bloodshed followed. The Golden Stool remained hidden for many years. In 1920 the building of a road near Abuabugya brought to light the box containing it. The headman of the village, under cover of darkness, hid the relic in one of the houses, but he was later persuaded by "one Seniagya, a professing Christian," to strip the Stool of its golden ornaments. The word reached the Kumasi chiefs, and soon the entire Ashanti people was in mourning. The desecrators were rushed to prison by the British to protect their lives while a national council was convened to try them. Five men were sentenced to death for a crime which, in Ashanti eyes, amounted to sacrilege. The British Government intervened and ordered a new hearing. Even stronger evidence was brought forward at the second trial and the Government agreed that the guilty charge was fully made out. However, the Chief Commissioner refused to confirm the death sentence, and the men were banished from Ashanti instead.[20]

The Queen Mother's muttered curse may have packed some native magic; a bout of malaria overtook Freeman a few minutes afterwards and, leaning on the shoulder of his faithful servant Joseph, he was forced to withdraw to the house set aside for him. Headache and fever laid him low for three days. Even with this, however, his acute faculties of observation did not desert him. Visits to his hut by various lizards, ants and rats and even a couple of birds, merited comment in his accounts. Christmas Day came and went with little improvement in the invalid's condition but the following morning he was able to walk about. Kumasi disappointed him; so much had been destroyed and not rebuilt. The destruction had taken place in the Anglo-Ashanti War of 1873-74 and Freeman "could not help reflecting on the strange and regrettable fact that [it] had been accomplished by a nation that yearly spends millions on the conversion of the heathen and the diffusion of civilisation."

The party spent six days in Kumasi before setting off northward again through damp cold forest to the Offwin river where there was a break in the trees and a chance to be warmed by the sun. The trunk of a silk-cotton tree spanned the river:

> I had great misgivings about that bridge. There had been no attempt to make a flat surface to walk upon, this being unnecessary for the bare-footed natives, but to a man in heavy field-boots the round surface—giving place in one part to a high sharp ridge—looked far from inviting, and I commenced the journey with no little trepidation. When I had fairly started I found that the "monkey-rope" guide was a complete delusion, for, being fixed only at its ends, it swung completely out of reach. I was therefore compelled to rely on my powers of balancing, and an uncommonly bad five minutes I spent as I crept along, expecting every moment to topple over into the muddy river that swept swiftly along a few feet beneath me. The perilous journey was, however, completed without disaster, and when I stood once more on solid ground and looked back at the string of carriers following me across the bridge I was exasperated, remembering my own sufferings during the transit, to observe the unconcerned way in which these barefooted ragamuffins strolled across, smoking their pipes and balancing their heavy loads as easily as though they were on a turnpike road.[21]

The route was more and more waterlogged at this stage with rivers and swamps to be waded through. The last day of the year saw them struggling through such terrain for over eleven hours, after which they were too tired for a proper celebration to welcome in the New Year of 1889. The European officers drank to absent friends, "yarned" sleepily for a while and turned in.

A day later, at the forest village of Jomo, Dr. Freeman's routine medical inspection revealed an alarming number of the Hausa guard and carriers to be unfit for duty, and two days' rest was ordered. The march had indeed been wearisome, and the various ailments were no doubt the result. When the party resumed its way, the everlasting jungle at last showed signs of a slow transition to more open country. The tall straight forest trees gave way at times to smaller trees with gnarled limbs "like English fruit trees," and grassy expanses appeared, though the grass was often of enormous height.

On the morning of January 6th, the important river Tánno was reached. Readers of Freeman's *The Golden Pool*, published in 1905, will be interested to learn what really passed between Freeman and the fetish man on the banks of that river, an encounter which played an important part in the development of the plot of that book, and which, moreover, tells us something of Freeman's wit and tenacity.

> As I was about to cross the river (which was spanned by a fallen tree) the fetish man rose and accosted me. He explained that no person was permitted to carry a stick across the sacred river, as this would be regarded as an indignity to the fetish, and in confirmation of his statement he pointed to a great pile of staves that stood on the bank, to which he requested me to add my stick. Not being disposed to part with my trusty oak staff in this casual manner, I ventured to argue the point, explaining that my stick was not a common staff cut by the way-side, but a really valued piece of personal property, in fact it was one of my fetishes; moreover, I urged, being a stranger to the country I could not be expected to be fully informed in the matter of local customs, and I was sure that the fetish would have too much good sense to take umbrage at any eccentricities on the part of a white man. After some wrangling, the fetish man agreed to take this view of the matter, but stipulated that I should drop a

small quantity of gold dust into the river as I crossed, as an offering to the fetish, this being also a customary proceeding. To this I also demurred, on the grounds that I had my own particular fetish to consider, who might be inclined to view with disapproval any offerings made to other and foreign fetishes. This argument was conclusive, and the old wizard at once gave me a "free pass" and his benediction; but I observed that our men, even the Mahommedan Hausas, all left their sticks on the pile, and several of them opened little packets of gold dust and shook the contents into the river as they crossed.[22]

The expedition had now entered the vaguely defined country of Jáman, the language of whose natives was incomprehensible to the travellers from the coast. Fetish worship was a staple religion and Freeman described one of the weird dances associated with it.

At Faténta, where the country was still mainly of dense tropical forest, but with some patches of orchard-like flora, there was a stay of two days. The language of the natives might have changed but their curiosity was as insatiable as ever, and Freeman equally as imperturbable, as the following amusing passage demonstrates:

The natives of these Jáman villages took the greatest interest in our proceedings, having never seen a white man before; and I noticed, at first with some surprise, that those of our actions that interested them most, were the simple and commonplace ones. At first I expected that they would give the most attention to such of our doings as would appear to them the most strange and unlike their own; but it was not so. In any proceedings on my part which they could not understand, they displayed but a languid interest, whereas to such simple matters as eating and dressing they gave the closest and keenest attention. Every morning when I emerged from my tent I found a large audience waiting patiently for the performance to begin, and when I took my place at the washstand a crowd (consisting in the larger villages of from one hundred to three hundred persons) closed round, forming a large circle. They followed the whole process with the greatest enjoyment, discussing and explaining to one another the various details, and now and again raising shouts of applause as some peculiarly amusing feature in the performance (such as the use of the nail-brush) occurred. When I produced my toothbrush and proceeded to put it to its natural use, there was much anxious discussion, and when I brushed my hair up "the wrong way of the grain" and made it stand on end, they yelled with delight.

Being habitually almost entirely unclothed themselves they were naturally not afflicted by any severe scruples of delicacy, so that when I commenced to divest myself of my pyjamas and to take the somewhat perfunctory bath preparatory to assuming my ordinary day-clothing, there was no falling off in the crowd of spectators; in fact they seemed to regard this as the choicest part of the whole performance, and I could easily see from their excited gestures and vociferous conversation that they were settling once for all the momentous question whether I was really white all over or whether only my hands and face presented that absurd abnormality.

Their curiosity on this point was much resented by the Hausas, who, as good Mussulmans, were greatly scandalized by such an absence of modesty, and they used to surround me, some of them holding up cloths to screen me from the gaze of the vulgar, while others "shoo-ed" at the crowd of natives as though they were a pack of fowls. Their efforts, however, had little effect, for although the scared natives would scamper away for a short distance they very soon returned, curiosity getting the better of fear, and some of them lay down on the ground trying to look under the cloths, while others stood on tip-toe and peered over the screens, craning their necks to get a glimpse of the human monstrosity behind.

Our meals afforded as much satisfaction to the natives

as they did to ourselves. Our attendants, as they brought
the food from the camp fire, were surrounded by jabbering
crowds who pored over the dishes they carried, with infinite wonder, and as soon as we took our seats at the table
the crowd assembled and formed a large semi-circle in
front of us, the front rows seated on the ground, or on
wooden stools which they brought from their houses, and
the outer circle standing.

Every stage in the process was watched closely, and
freely commented on with much pointing, argument and
discussion. When the cork was drawn from the commissioner's whiskey bottle there was a general murmur of
applause and a chorus of astonished "Ow's," while the
spectacle of the white man impaling portions of his food
on the four-pointed weapon that he wielded with his left
hand, afforded boundless joy. As for the opening of a
bottle of champagne (which occurred on one occasion after
an unusually long march) it simply "brought down the
house," although the audience somewhat abruptly dispersed and viewed the remainder of the performance round
the corners of adjacent huts. The commonplace details of
our everyday life these simple folk never tired of witnessing, but, as I have already observed, when anything
was done that they did not understand, their interest was
not stimulated.

When I sat down to make a sketch I had but few spectators, not so many as I should probably have had in an
English village; when I set up my theodolite to take an
altitude of the sun little notice was taken of my proceedings; but when our attendants began to prepare the table
for a meal the spectators poured in and began to take their
seats in readiness for the spectacle.[23]

It was in this same Jáman village that Freeman observed the
most dramatic of several "route-marches" of driver ants which inun-
dated the camp for three hours and prevented anyone from approach-

ing the tents. During this period the ground was covered with a glittering black mass of insects all moving determinedly in one direction. As soon as he could, Freeman peered into his tent and observed "a densely packed mass of ants moving steadily and rapidly forward." The insects had not ascended the legs of the bed or the other furniture, but on each bed leg "a few inches above the ground, a soldier ant was stationed, and similar individuals were posted at other fixed points, apparently directing the workers."

With the forest now quite behind it, the expedition made fast progress. By the 14th of January it had passed through several neatly-tended villages, each surrounded by little plantations of tobacco, and the countryside was almost entirely open. The going was easier now that the roadway's sharp clinker fragments under-foot were giving way to a soft yellowish-grey loam. The tidy villages appeared to be prosperous, consisting of well-built thatched roofed houses, some of which were circular in design. They were quite a contrast, Freeman pointedly remarks to "the dirty and slovenly appearance of the villages in the British Protectorate."

> Even the dogs were cleaner and better cared for; one of
> them was actually decorated with an elaborately worked
> collar from which was suspended a bell, and with these
> personal adornments he trotted about the village, at his
> master's heels, with an air of bumptiousness and self-
> sufficiency very different from the abject demeanour of
> the wretched tick-bitten pariahs of the coast towns.[24]

At Soku, on the outskirts of Bontuku, the travellers waited for six days for an invitation from the King before going further. Freeman used the time to study the commercial life of the region and spent quite a proportion of his enforced leisure in the market-place, where a variety of local produce was sold, including salt from the coast (a great luxury) and Shea butter. Freeman purchased some of the latter (a white vegetable fat) from an old lady:

> I explained to the old dame that being a stranger I had no

cowries [cowry shells] and offered her two sixpences for
a calabashful of the Shea tulu, which she accepted. When
my orderly had paid her, however, she observed some shillings in his hand, two of which she picked out and returned the sixpences, remarking that "she preferred the
large ones," and we had the greatest difficulty in making
her understand the difference in their value, for a large
cowry is, of course, of no more value than a small one, and
she, not unnaturally, argued in the same way about coins.

The Shea butter turned out to be a hideous delusion.
I had read in Mungo Park's travels that this vegetable fat
when spread upon bread was a great delicacy, being equal
in flavour to the finest cow butter. I tried the experiment,
and from personal experience can recommend Shea butter
as a prompt and active emetic. I think that cows must have
greatly improved, or Shea butter greatly degenerated,
since Mungo Park's days, unless that redoubtable explorer was a person of very singular gastronomic tastes.[25]

The news from Bontúku, when it came, was bad. King Ajiman,
it seemed, had accepted a French flag from two officers who were
now visiting him and a treaty had been signed. Even more disappointing to Freeman was the report that these same French officers
had previously visited Kong, which up to that time had never been
visited by a European, since he had earlier requested permission of
the Governor of the Gold Coast Colony, Sir Brandford Griffith, and
had been turned down.

The King, who apparently had been absent from Bontúku, was
now back in his capital and willing to receive the British expedition.
Freeman's first view of the city elicited his "delighted admiration,"
so different was it from anything he had expected. Although this
opinion was later modified, it was nevertheless true that the familiar
irregular clusters of thatched houses found in the coastal and forest
regions contrasted sharply with Bontúku's "regular rows of flat-
roofed houses, their long, level walls surmounted by rows of slender
pinnacles, while out of the mass of houses rose the spires and

clustered pinnacles—all tipped with glittering ornaments—of two handsome and elaborately built mosques." The inhabitants, well dressed men and women in Moslem costume, displayed a wary attitude towards the Europeans. Already King Ajiman and Commissioner Lethbridge had exchanged sharp words by messenger, the Commissioner being unwilling to accept the King's suggestion that the palaver be postponed until the following day. The Monarch, his chiefs and people were assembled in a great semicircle, many armed with swords, knives, spears and poisoned arrows. The King himself, an amiable and dignified old man, received the party of white men in friendly fashion and, after a hand-shaking ceremony, informed Freeman and his colleagues that the ceremonies were not to commence until the next day. The Commissioner took no notice of this at all, and began a political speech, the subsequent translation of which irritated Ajiman greatly. In the ensuing exchange between the parties it became clear that the King had not himself invited the Europeans; in fact it had been the King's son, to further his own aspirations, who had sent the messenger to the Coast. The position of the visitors was now most awkward. Nevertheless, when the palaver was continued *two* days later, Freeman was relieved to find a less bellicose attitude evident among the King's subjects. There was even, behind the sovereign's chair, a man holding a Union Jack. King Ajiman explained, through his translator, the nature of the treaty he had signed with the French—described as being of a limited commercial character—and expressed his willingness to put his country under the protection of the English, whom he recognized as masters of that part of Africa. He also favoured a resumption of trade with the Gold Coast and was willing to sign the treaty the Englishmen had brought with them. This being done on the spot, the British flag was hoisted. However, Freeman's party, being unconvinced by Ajiman's claim that the Golden Stool belonged originally to the kings of Jáman, declined the royal request to recover it from King Prempeh of Ashanti, and were, thereupon, coolly asked to leave. The palaver then broke up and the English officers, after a discussion, decided that Lethbridge should return to the coast as expeditiously as possible for further instructions. In particular it was necessary to know how the new treaty would be regarded by the British authorities in the light of the earlier French treaty. The Commissioner left Bontuku on January 30 with a small number of men and Freeman and Major Ewart remained in Bontuku to await instructions. One senses Freeman's relief at the Commissioner's departure. That they didn't "hit it off" is more apparent from what Freeman does not say than from what he actually reports. Lethbridge, like Hodgson—of the foot-in-mouth tendencies at Kumasi a few years later—was a dull, unimaginative man, more conscious of his own dignity than of the natives' sensibilities. Freeman's sense of humour, his understanding of the natives and his quick intelligence and scholarly pursuits, would have quickly irritated a man like the commissioner, and the relationship could only have been antipathetic. Lethbridge's ineptitude was again in evidence on his journey back from the interior by way of Sefwi, although Freeman does not mention the incident. At Wiosu, after a carrier in the party had kidnaped one of the wives of the local King, Lethbridge, with characteristic high-handedness, ignored a demand for her return. Confronted by the King's armed detachment sent to regain the woman by force, the English officer, belatedly realizing the situation his behavior had brought about, appealed—cravenly enough—to his interpreter, Odonkwor, to extricate him. Odenkwor gallantly succeeded in doing so, explaining that the King's earlier demand had been misunderstood by Lethbridge owing to his, Odonkwor's, incompetence.[26]

With the lightening of the atmosphere after the Commissioner's departure, Freeman looked forward to a stay in Bontuku of not less than two months, which he intended to fill with explorations in and around the city, and to making friends with the inhabitants. As we shall presently see, it would have been far better for everyone concerned if Assistant-Inspector Ewart had followed the misguided Commissioner back to Accra and left Freeman in charge of things at Bontuku, for through his stupidity, Ewart, single-handedly, was destined to imperil the lives of the entire expedition, not least that of Austin Freeman.

CHAPTER II

Bontŭku and the Journey Back

Bontŭku, on closer inspection, was disappointing. The long straight walls were roughly constructed of clay; the pinnacles and spires small and ill-shaped. Nevertheless, the city was evidently the product of a more advanced people than inhabited the countries to the south: "Kumasi was the center of an art and culture that, although elaborate, was essentially barbaric. Bontŭku was a mean and squalid outlier of civilization."

The house of the two European officers consisted of several apartments arranged around two courtyards, the outer one small, the interior one of a good size. In the latter, two tents were set up because of the lack of ventilation in the permanent apartments, the tenants of which were a host of vermin.

Freeman took great delight in his walks around the town. He was prevented, as we shall see, from visiting the mosques, but there was little else going on in Bontŭku that he did not observe and

Freeman and the Limàmu in 1889 (Detail from frontispiece to
Travels and Life in Ashanti and Jaman.)

Freeman ca. 1898 (A photo found in Pitcairn's copy of *Ashanti*
(Courtesy of Mrs. T. H. Johns.)

describe.   He visited the indigo pits to study the method of fer-
menting the deep blue vat dye which was widely used throughout the
district, both on yarn and on finished cloth. He ordered a riga at a
cost of 12,000 kurdi (about $3) from Yusafu the tailor.

> A few large-eyed needles of European make, a bodkin
> fashioned in the form of a small antelope, and a beauti-
> ful little dagger-like knife (of which the steel hilt is hand-
> somely inlaid with copper and brass) formed his whole
> equipment.[1]

Then on through the "narrow, tortuous alleys and malodorous
by-streets" to the outskirts of the town to meet Mahama the glass
worker. He was famed for the manufacture of glass armlets of
marbled or agate-like appearance, fused from fragments of Dutch gin
bottles and tiny coloured beads.

Freeman was interested, as always, in *how* things were done.
It is this attention to detail which distinguishes his fiction, especially
his Thorndyke books, and makes them come alive. The prerequisite
of such writing is, of course, familiarity on the part of the author
with what he is describing. Here is Freeman's description of a Hausa
man's market stall where he was doing a roaring trade in small pan-
cakes "which he dispenses fresh from the pan to customers, who
depart with tingling fingers, whisking their purchases from one hand
to the other as one sees urchins in the streets of London when they
have just acquired a baked potato 'screeching hot' from the can."

> With a wooden scoop he accurately measures out a
> quantity of maize-flour, which he deposits in a calabash,
> and to this he adds a similar quantity of bean-meal. Water
> being added, he mixes the meal into a thin paste or batter.
> The cooking utensil is an oblong slab of earthenware
> having six hemispherical depressions, each about three
> inches in diameter. This is placed on a wood fire which

burns in a shallow earthen pot, and in each of the little
cavities a portion of Shea butter is deposited, which presently begins to fizzle and splutter with the heat. When
this occurs the cook takes a small ladle formed of a tiny
calabash lashed to a stick, and fills it with the batter,which
he pours successively into the six cavities until they are
full. In a few minutes the cooking process is completed,
and the six little hemispherical cakes are neatly fished out
of their respective cells with a wooden spoon, and laid, all
crisp and brown and smoking, in a basket tray to cool, or
deposited in the outstretched hands of some hungry
customer.[2]

As Freeman journeyed homeward he called in at the workshop
of one Braíma, a silversmith who, like Mahama the glass worker, used
a forge or furnace in the floor connected to two goatskin bellows. In
a few minutes the craftsman was able to convert one or two English
florins into a silver armlet. Without waiting for it to be engraved,
however, Freeman returned home just as the bugle was sounding
'retreat' and the Union Jack was being hauled down from the rude
flag-staff that stood in front of his house.

During his stay in Bontúku, Freeman made the acquaintance of
the inhabitants in various walks of life. The Limámu, or Imám, head
of the Mohammedans in Bontúku, was revered by all the people of
the district, both pagan and Moslem. He was a gentle, fatherly old
man whose just and benevolent disposition left a deep impression on
Freeman. In a photograph which Freeman chose as the frontispiece
of his Ashanti book, the young English physician is seen sitting on
the old gentleman's left. Here is Freeman's description of the scene:

The period intervening between afternoon tea and
dinner was devoted to social calls and expeditions round
the town, or to the market, or walks into the country. I
very frequently spent the latter part of the afternoon with

the Limámu, who was accustomed at that part of the day
to sit outside his house in company with some of the
Mohammedan elders, and pass the time in conversation, or
in reading or copying certain Arabic manuscripts.

The old man always gave me a very kindly reception
and had a large circular leather cushion placed on his rug
for me to sit on, and both he and his venerable colleagues
took an evident pleasure in conversing with me and explaining the customs and institutions of the country.
When our talk turned upon religious topics he was rather
more reserved than his sons Ali and Ibrahima, but, like
them, he appeared to regard Christianity as little more than
a variety of the religion that he himself professed: and so
far was he from feeling any antipathy to Christians that, on
one occasion, he invited me to visit the mosque during the
hours of worship, an invitation of which I was unfortunately prevented from availing myself by the collision
which afterwards occurred between us and the people of
Bontúku.

During one of my visits to him the Limámu remarked that some of his Wongára friends occasionally
visited Cape Coast, and that in the event of their doing so
at any future time he would like to have the means of
sending me a greeting. I told him my name and explained
as far as possible my position, but when he had made several rather unsuccessful attempts to repeat the words after
me he said that he thought it would be much better if I
would write my name and description on several pieces of
paper, one of which he might give to any traveller proceeding from Bontúku to the coast. So I drew out my
pocket-book and fountain pen and wrote my name and
probable whereabouts on several leaves which I tore out
and presented to him. While I was writing, the old gentleman craned over my shoulder and watched with intense

interest, exchanging whispered comments and criticisms during the performance, and when I had finished they expressed the greatest admiration at the ease and rapidity with which I wrote and the smallness of the character. They were very curious about my fountain pen, especially as they observed that the marks it made were of actual wet ink: so I explained the construction of it to them and afterwards allowed each of them to write with it, which they did with extreme delight, giggling and "chaffing" one another like a pack of schoolboys. Occasionally, when I was sitting with the Limámu and his friends, I made sketches of passers-by and I also made a couple of drawings of the mosque, of which the Limámu's house commanded a full view; but I noticed that my performance as an artist interested them much less than my exploits as a penman, in fact I think they were rather disgusted to see a man of my age and gravity wasting his time in so childish a pursuit.[3]

On other days between tea and sunset, Freeman walked in the country, sometimes with Sidichi, a Mohammedan elder, or with Mahama, the glass worker, both special friends of his. But often he would go alone, for solitary walking was a lifelong pursuit. Freeman was an extraordinarily self-sufficient man. His own thoughts, fed by a keen observation and retentive memory, were entertainment **enough** for him. Without this one wonders how **long** he could have withstood the isolation of a West African outpost.

Before considering the nature of the countryside around Bontúku, through Freeman's reflections thereon, let us observe him at work in his Bontúku quarters. Despite his philosophical outlook and mature manner, he was not yet twenty-seven years old, a rather tall muscular young man with a dark moustache and full beard, the latter being a temporary feature. Although still dressed in white drill, he wore a wide-brimmed hat and sandals in place of the sun-helmet and field-boots worn during the march. The day began with a medical inspection of the detachment. Some local invalids would also be waiting to be seen; rather a puzzlingly large number of them in fact, until upon investigation Freeman found that his native servants had been drumming up business in the neighbourhood for their own profit. The King and his Chiefs called regularly, once Freeman and the Major had made it clear that their intentions had all along been peaceful. Sidichi, the Moslem elder, "a very quiet, well behaved, amiable man," became much attached to Freeman and called frequently for long talks. One day, in fact, he came in the company of a gaunt middle-aged Wongara Negress and explained that this lady, his sister, had been brought as a gift for Dr. Freeman.

> At this, I regarded the lady with speechless dismay as she stood at Sidichi's elbow, grinning like a *memento mori* and casting on me an eye that was about as languishing as that of a defunct dog-fish. It was extremely awkward, for the gift was kindly meant by Sidichi and was a really valuable one according to local ideas. The woman was worth, I daresay, 60,000 cowries [about $15] and I feared that my refusal would be taken as a personal affront. However, I succeeded after a long explanation in making them both understand the peculiar views held by white people upon the subject of matrimony, and in proving that a previous engagement prevented me from availing myself of this exceptional opportunity.[4]

Freeman had deposited his books, instruments, sample bottles and boxes and a few bits of simple furniture in "the library." This was his name for the largest of the apartments which opened onto the large inner courtyard of the house which he shared with Major Ewart. The "furniture" consisted mainly of a table made out of four stakes driven into the earth floor and a box lid fastened across the top; his deck chair; and a sideboard or cabinet, made from an empty box set on its side with its lid propped open. Some baggage cases ranged around the walls supported his collecting boxes, theodolite, camera and traveling library. In this room he spent midday, when it was too hot to use the tents, working on his journal, sorting his specimens and plotting his survey. In spite of its welcome coolness, anyone but Freeman, I fancy, would have given this room a wide berth. In the rafters, which consisted of the untrimmed branches of trees, lived some small rats, a few snakes and lizards, and "hordes of a portly, turtle-shaped cockroach of an obese and sluggish habit, which had a most objectionable trick of dropping unexpectedly onto my head." In addition, the walls were inhabited by "a gorgeous species of wasp, the most magnificent insect, I think, that I have ever seen." The room, like the rest of the house, was infested by swarms of flies which "settled thickly all over my head and face, especially round my eyes, and wandered up my sleeves and trousers until I was driven to the verge of madness." As though this were not enough, the Major's dog had introduced a plague of fleas to the mess-hut which threatened to cover any parts of Freeman's anatomy not yet commandeered by the flies. This particular infestation was terminated by Freeman's flooding for a few days the floors of his hut and tent, where the fleas bred in the dry sandy earth.

All this sheds an interesting light on young Freeman's character. Few men could tolerate such distracting conditions, let alone work in their midst, yet it was from the journal he wrote in this room, and in other scarcely more comfortable places *en route* that he was able to publish a detailed and entertaining book nine years later. All the same, at dusk he was glad enough to leave "the library" behind him to call on his friend the Limámu, or, alternatively, to escape into the countryside via the nearby main road running east to Banda.

The absence of big game during daylight hours always puzzled him. After dark there were plenty to be heard, but while it was still light only a few monkeys and, occasionally, antelopes or tiny gazelles were visible. There were scores of birds, however, though hardly any of their songs resembled those of European song-birds. Some of the simpler tunes he heard he wrote down in musical notation. In one instance, his passion for collecting overcame his better nature.

I was walking one afternoon along the Banda road when I perceived a pair of the brilliant blue-plumaged jays flying about a tree. Filled with the collector's lust I pointed my gun and the next moment one of the jays was lying on the ground; but the other bird, instead of flying away, instantly swooped down upon the body of its mate and perched by its side, screaming in the most piteous manner. At the sight of the poor bird's distress I was so overcome with shame and disgust that I shouldered my gun and sneaked off, leaving my victim where he fell, and the bird-skin collection was never made.[5]

As we have seen before, in entomological matters he was very well informed. In one passage of his account he names, and describes, seven species of dung beetle observed in one place after the wet season had begun, and theorizes on their possible relationship to the sacred scarab beetle of the ancient Egyptians.

Late evenings, for Freeman, were set aside for making entries in his journal, writing letters, making official reports, developing photographs and sighting heavenly bodies through his telescope. Only after all this had been dispensed with did he relax by sitting in the doorway of his tent, smoking his pipe and reading from his small collection of books. Among these, we are told, were the works of Mungo Park and "quaint old Isaak Walton," but what other writers were represented is unknown.

As midnight approaches it cannot necessarily be assumed that Freeman would at last turn in. For one thing, large spiders frequented the tent; it comes as something of a relief to know that like most people even this intrepid young naturalist did have *some* dislikes. He loathed giant spiders and scorpions, and when he spotted a hairy specimen of the former he would wallop it with a sandal instead of capturing it intact for his collection. For another thing, it possibly might be necessary, at three in the morning, for him to wait in the streets for an occultation to take place in the sky. Though Freeman knew pretty accurately the *latitude* of Bontúku he was somewhat hazy about its *longitude*, having had to calculate it by

summing his compass-bearings and distance calculations since he left
Cape Coast Castle. Some independent check of his calculations
would be valuable, hence the importance of an astronomical sighting.

After a shaky start, during the first of their two months native
feelings towards Freeman and Major Ewart grew increasingly
friendly. For this Freeman claims no credit. Nevertheless, his
comportment during his calls around the town, his friendly demeanor
when the King and his chiefs visited the house, and his always willing
treatment of the sick, must have been at least partly responsible; and
with the chief irritant—Commissioner Lethbridge—gone from Bontuku, there was every hope that the improvement would be maintained. These hopes were short-lived.

Although the city of Kong was put out of bounds to Freeman
by the Governor of the Gold Coast Colony, after a month in
Bontúku Freeman became restless for an expedition to that city.
In talks with the Major he revived the idea, suggesting that the
improved political circumstances permitted use of their remaining
month's wait in that way. However, upon hearing of their plans, King
Ajiman objected to the expedition to Kong, saying only that the
journey would be a dangerous one and that their presence in that
city would be resented by his people. The two Englishmen thereupon decided to travel east, instead of north-west, and visit Banda
and Mo, but to say nothing to anybody about their intentions. The
news leaked out, however, through their bearers, and Freeman and
Ewart were visited by the King and his principal advisers just as they
were about to depart. One of these advisers, named Papi, a tall
powerful man of over eighty years, was particularly hostile to the
European officers:

> Ajiman informed us that he had heard we were pre-
> paring to set out to Banda, and he must absolutely forbid
> us to leave Bontúku. He was quite polite, but evidently
> meant what he said and, seeing this, we were prepared to
> give way without any further palaver.

Unfortunately, however, at this point Papi "put in his oar," and gave us to understand that we were not wanted at Banda nor anywhere else, and that we had better remain quietly at Bontúku until the time of our return to the coast, which latter event would, he remarked, be witnessed with great satisfaction by the Jámans in general and himself in particular.

He then made a long rambling and by no means polite speech, becoming very excited and boisterous, and talked a great deal of nonsense, being evidently strongly under the influence of the "square-face" gin with which we had presented him on our arrival.

We told the king that we would certainly give up the idea of going to Banda if he wished it, and he thereupon rose and shook hands, and the procession filed out of the compound, the king leading away the ruffled Papi, growling, muttering and showing his teeth like an aged bloodhound.

There can be no doubt that Papi's conduct on this occasion was most reprehensible, but bearing in mind his quarrelsome, excitable temperament and the quality of the gin that he had evidently been consuming, I was not disposed to attach much importance to the matter.

The Major, however, took the old warrior's rudeness very much to heart and resolved that the honour of the British flag required to be vindicated by some signal act of expiation. He considered that, as the representative of the British Government, he was entitled to punish a rebellious chief, and he determined that the punishment should take the form of a heavy fine.[6]

The Major's chance came at a palaver a few days later. The Hausas of the escort were warned to be ready for a fight and ammunition was served out. At the meeting with the King and his chiefs the atmosphere was friendly and the routine business quickly disposed of; it was evident that the King wished to make up for the bad impression Papi had made. When the King signified that the meeting was over, Major Ewart intervened and ordered Papi to come and stand before him. This, King Ajiman would not permit. When Ewart explained that he was going to fine Papi the sum of fifty pounds (in gold dust) for insulting the British Government, "the old King rose from his seat and, kneeling down, placed his hands upon the Major's feet and entreated him to forgive Papi who, he declared, was drunk at the time that he committed the offence, but who, when in his sound senses, would not think of behaving disrespectfully to a British officer. The Major, however, was deaf to the King's entreaties, although they were several times repeated, and ordered Futa with four Hausas to go and seize Papi and bring him to the place where we were sitting."

There was an immediate uproar; Papi was immediately surrounded by a crowd of would-be protectors and a contingent of Jáman natives made off for reinforcements. Soon a detachment of the regular Jáman army bearing muskets and spears came into view. The Hausas meanwhile, without being ordered to do so, had detached their bayonets and begun to load their rifles. "In a few moments more they would have opened fire, in which case," writes Freeman, "there is little doubt that our entire party, hopelessly outnumbered as we were, would have been annihilated." It was with difficulty that they were prevailed on to desist, but things still looked menacing as the Muslims advanced to within firing distance of the Europeans and their party. Luckily for the latter, the King now volunteered to pay the fine, and the Major was, at last, wise enough to accept the compromise.

Even then, Freeman and his party were in a position of some peril, surrounded as they were by hostile soldiers, but King Ajiman, walking between Freeman and the Major, escorted the party back to town, two of the Jáman chiefs forming a rearguard.

> Altogether our return through the town to our quarters was a sorry and ignominious retreat, and contrasted absurdly enough with the bumptious aggressiveness of our manner an hour previously.

As we marched through the streets under the protection of Ajiman in front and the chiefs behind, the rabble
poured out of every alley to jeer at us as we passed; the
Wongáras followed us the whole of the way challenging us
with shouts and gestures of defiance; while the housetops
were crowded with women and children who greeted us
with hoots and yells and other signs of derision.[7]

Although passions soon subsided, things were not the same as
they had been. The King and the chiefs discontinued their social
calls. "Even the old Limámu, although still kind and courteous in
his manner, had apparently rather lost confidence in us, and did not
renew his invitation to me to attend the service in the mosque."

From a practical point of view a more serious development was
a boycott which the market people began against the sale of food to
the Europeans and their followers. A severe shortage of food was
averted only by Freeman "charging" his patients an article of
food—a yam, a fowl, or some beans—when they came for medical
treatment. A little while later, though, as the number of patients
fell off, actual starvation became a real possibility for Freeman. The
doctor, his stock of yams exhausted, was reduced to making a porridge out of coarse meal which was heavily contaminated by gravel,
"but as I had no sugar or other flavoring material, it was most insipid
and unsavoury, and the gritty particles with which it was filled rendered it nauseous and disgusting." A Mohammedan friend's gift of
some wild honey was therefore gratefully received, even though dead
bees and other insects had to be removed by straining before it
could be added to his porridge.

About this time it came to light that the Hausa soldiers in
Freeman's party were misbehaving in the town. Bullocks and goats
were being stolen and killed and it was widely assumed by Bontúkians
that this was done with Freeman's consent. When it was explained to
Ali, the Wongára chief, and to the Limámu, that this was not so, and
that Freeman would be glad to deal with future miscreants himself
(reserving the right to return the favor to any Bontúku evildoers that
he encountered) the ill-feeling in the town began to subside. Shortly

after these developments, a Hausa drummer boy was brought to the Limámu and then, under the new arrangement, sent to Freeman. The soldier admitted complicity in a goat killing. Freeman arrested him and compensated the goat's owner, whereupon, after the news spread, the market boycott was relaxed, and Freeman began to eat regularly again.

Orders for the return to Accra arrived by messenger on March 22nd. This was welcome news for Freeman for, although Bontúku was more pleasant than his regular station at Accra in many ways, the rainy season was imminent and if they had to leave it were better they left at once.

The town rejoiced at the news, although many of Freeman's friends indicated regret. The Limámu sent a messenger with his blessing along with a written Arabic charm. As a farewell gift to the Limámu, Freeman sent some pens and paper and, on the evening of March 30th, with the band playing "The Girl I Left Behind Me," the party marched from Freeman's house towards Soku, where they spent the night.

The return route to Kumasi was further to the east than that of their outward path, and they found it preferable, in that they did not meet with the forest until they were within about three days' march of the Ashanti capital. However, without the overhanging branches the sun oppressed them during their long hard marches across the open parkland. The most severe problem now was the shortage of carriers, as Lethbridge had taken a large proportion of the original number back to the Coast with him, and now Freeman and the Major had to make do by hiring men at the various villages for short stints. But often the men were either not available or unwilling to come far from their homes. On one desperate occasion, when it seemed that a great deal of the party's baggage must be abandoned for want of help to carry it, the Major devised a cunning solution: the kidnapping of two dozen able-bodied men from a nearby village to act as impressed carriers as far as the next settlement. The plan boomeranged, however, when the natives escaped a short distance further on, leaving their loads behind.

Freeman never failed to marvel at the skill of the African and his adaptability to his environment, especially in contrast to more "civilized" races. Thus, when they arrived at the River Tain, a change in the weather threatened and "no sooner had we halted than the men separated into small parties and commenced building little huts to sleep in, and so adroit were they, although provided with no tools but their cutlasses, that within the space of an hour a complete little village had grown up around the tents." Each of the natives "adhered to his national style of dwelling . . . thus the Fantis raised little oblong huts with high-pitched roofs and gable ends, the Hausas little beehive-shaped dwellings with a small hole for a doorway while others built circular huts of a conical form with high pointed roofs." All of them kept their inmates quite dry and comfortable during the incessant downpour of the ensuing night.

Readers of *The Golden Pool* will recall the fictionalization of the following description of the town, Tekiman:

> While wandering about the town, picking up odd scraps of information, I came across some natives who informed me that a clear stream that rises near to Tekiman is the Tánno or Tánnor river. The place where it rises, I was informed, is called Boasi ("under the rock"), and the head waters issue as a spring from a great rock which has two objects like elephant's tusks projecting from it. The spring falls into a deep pool, the bottom of which—so my informant declared—is thickly covered with gold. This gold is the property of the Tánno fetish and no person may, on pain of death, attempt to remove it. I much regretted I was unable to visit this place, for not only would it have been interesting to compare the actual facts with the suspiciously picturesque description of the natives, but it would also have been well worth while to ascertain the exact position of the source of the river, which, next to the Volta, is the most important of the streams of the Gold Coast.[8]

In Akumádai, "a small town, extremely dirty and malodorous,"

the party arrived on the afternoon of April 7th and here the excessive
curiosity of the natives almost succeeded in unnerving Freeman at last:

> The people here displayed more than the usual interest
> in us and our doings. They crowded round us to watch
> us take our meal, and then followed us to our tents to
> inspect us while we took our baths.
>
> They not only filled up the door of the tent, but
> numbers of them pushed their heads under the fly so that
> they should not miss any detail. The front rank of the
> crowd at my tent door was formed by a row of five young
> women, and the attention with which they regarded me as
> I performed my ablutions was quite embarrassing.[9]

Freeman's relations with the carriers were particularly warm,
one or two of them "conceived so strong an affection for me that
they hung about my quarters for months after my return to the
coast." In particular, there was Kwaku Sakki who was ever mindful
of Freeman's comfort and helped to make ready his tent and prepare his food. "He fully entered into my desire to collect specimens,
and frequently while on the march he would shamble up to me with
some shell or insect that he had picked up." Then there was
Anderson, a corporal of the Fanti police who "spoke excellent English, wrote a remarkably good hand (as educated negroes generally
do), and was a most intelligent and trustworthy man." Because of
his rank and intelligence, Freeman would not allow him to perform
menial tasks, but used him as an interpreter.

But Freeman's favorite servant was a youthful Hausa called
Nyami, who became utterly devoted to the Englishman.   "On
stormy nights when the rain was roaring on my tent and hissing on
the ground outside, a black arm would insinuate itself under the
dripping fly and reach for the mallet, and then I would hear the
thoughtful Nyami hammering at the tent pegs and carefully letting
the strain off the ropes."   And he was always ready with Freeman's
deck-chair and a large native fan so that his master could rest and
cool off whenever the column was halted by a temporary obstacle.

The pace of the return journey was unrelenting, and it was an enfeebled and exhausted train that limped into Kumasi after eleven days of hard marching from Bontuku. Many of the Hausas and carriers were sick; all were worn out by the time-table ordered for the return journey. Whereas the entry into Ashanti's capital city from the south had been a grand affair, with much pomp and ceremony, the second visit passed almost unnoticed by the townspeople. Once again Freeman was struck down by malaria here, a coincidence all the more remarkable because his health in the interim appears to have been excellent. Again he shows his great strength of will. "I feared," he writes, "that I should have to leave town without completing the sketches that I was so anxious to make of the sculptured figures on the walls. However, in the morning, while preparations were being made for the start, I wrapped myself in a blanket and went round our house, with my teeth chattering and my knees trembling, and by the time the "fall in" sounded a considerable addition had been made to my notes and sketches of these curious and characteristic ornaments."

Lying ahead for the weary marchers was the desolate wilderness of Adansi, where starvation had threatened them before, but this time they packed sufficient supplies for the journey.

At Pra-su, Freeman, eager for mail, hurried across the ferry to "Government House"—a small three-roomed hut—where "a great heap of letters from home" lay on the table in the mess-room. From there on, the march was made on properly constructed roads again. On April 23rd, 1889, they ascended a final ridge and "came in sight of the sea and at the same time felt the fresh sea-breeze blowing in our faces. With this encouragement we stepped out briskly and in three hours more entered the town of Saltpond—a trading station of some importance about eleven miles to the east of Cape Coast. After staying here for a day we continued our march along the sandy beach to Accra, a distance of about sixty-five miles. On the 28th of April we entered that town and our journey was at an end."

On the coast, Freeman resumed his duties as a colonial surgeon. Sickness was rife among the Europeans, the tiny white population being further decimated largely by malaria and its *sequelae*. Freeman had found a forty-per-cent mortality rate among white men in 1887, the year of his arrival on the coast, caused almost entirely by blackwater fever.   (An even more deadly disease, hyperpyrexial pernicious malaria, was to become common there in the years following Freeman's return to England.   An 1897 report estimated the Gold Coast Colony population to be two million, with only about 150 Europeans among whom the death rate was high. In Cape Coast Castle, Freeman's starting point for his Bontuku expedition, were thirty-two white men, of whom seventeen died in the first two months of 1895.[10]) As we have seen, Freeman suffered occasional attacks of malaria but up to now had not been incapacitated by it for long.

During the days when he was on his home leave in 1890, on September 5th, he addressed the British Association (Geography Section) at Leeds. While in England, a fine outfit of instruments was constructed under his supervision (rather like a youthful Thorndyke directing a group of Nathaniel Poltons.) His navigating skill and all-round resourcefulness were meanwhile becoming known in Africa, and in 1891 he was promoted to the position of Boundary Commissioner for the disputed border between the British territories and German Togoland.   At Quittah he awaited the assembling of the Anglo-German Commission, the duties of which were to fix the boundary (presumably that part not defined by the course of the Volta river) by astronomical observation. It was here, in this small outpost of the eastern Gold Coast, that the dreaded blackwater fever struck. So debilitating was this disease that, becoming convalescent, he had to be hauled aboard a homeward-bound ship in a basket. The disease which struck him down is still not fully understood, but its diagnosis has never been difficult. *Ashanti* contains his observations of the symptoms of this and of malaria itself (of which in turn there are several forms), and he was an ideal observer, being not only a doctor with an acute sense of detail, but also someone who, as he drily put it, had "in my own person had experience of every form excepting the hyperpyrexial." Not surprisingly, he gave a great deal of thought to malarial diseases and their probable causes while in Africa and as an invalid in England, and drew some shrewd conclusions which were borne out in later years by medical research. By the time *Ashanti* was published it had become known that malaria is spread by female mosquitos of certain species, but precisely how this occurs was still a mystery. Even today, blackwater fever is less well understood than other malarial diseases. Fortunately it is rarely encountered nowadays because it attacks only those, (especially whites residing long in mosquito-plagued districts) whose systems have become saturated with malaria which has been untreated or treated only with quinine. Such victims are few in these days of improved chemotherapy and intensive insect control. The blackwater fever victim exhibits a low fever and is, from the beginning, extremely depressed; he exhibits a ghastly pallor which rapidly changes to an intense yellow caused by breakdown of hemoglobin. The degraded pigment is excreted in the urine, to which circumstance the disease owes its name. Often the kidneys cease to function, the features become pinched, the nose "thin and sharp" and the eyes sunken; delirium is the final symptom in fatal cases. Among those hardy or fortunate enough to escape a fatal outcome, prolonged ill-health is the common lot.

If we know so little of the next few years of Freeman's life it is doubtless because there is little to know. An invalid creates few records, especially if he is cared for at home. His own sketchy account, found by his son among his papers dismisses these years peremptorily: "In 1891, while acting as Anglo-German Boundary Commissioner, I contracted blackwater fever and was invalided home; and in 1896 failure of health compelled me to abandon medical practice and take to literature."

Sadly, this short statement contains three slight exaggerations. He never *acted* as a Boundary Commissioner, except in certain duties preliminary to the mission itself; his attempts at medical practice were abortive, as we shall see, and lastly, the literature he refers to was of extremely low degree.

His severe ill-health at this particular time was a multiple blow to his fortunes: his career in Africa was ruined; and, according to his son, he had served just under the mimimum term to qualify for a Government pension. Additionally he then attempted in an enfeebled

condition what he had avoided while hale: namely, to enter the
medical profession in England. Alas, this proved impossible. The
only work he could find for most of the ten long years between his
return home and his settling in Gravesend in 1902 was to act for
established general practioners during periods of illness or vacation,
that is, as *locum tenens.* In later years he was reluctant to discuss
this period of his life, but there is little doubt of his circumstances
during much of this bleak decade. They are echoed time and again
by assorted Jervises, Jardines and Berkeleys in the Thorndyke
stories. Replace "the hospital" by "West Africa" in Jervis's lament
at the opening of the first Thorndyke novel, *The Red Thumb Mark,*
and we have Freeman's condition precisely:

> My life, indeed, since I had left the hospital had been
> one of many disappointments and much privation. Un-
> fulfilled desires and ambitions unrealized had combined
> with distaste for the daily drudgery that had fallen to my
> lot to embitter my poverty and cause me to look with
> gloomy distrust upon the unpromising future.

Jervis in *The Mystery of 31, New Inn* continues the same strain of
meditation:

> The medical practitioner whose lack of means forces him
> to subsist by taking temporary charge of other men's
> practices is apt to find that the passing years bring him
> little but gray hairs and a wealth of disagreeable experience.

A passage in *The Eye of Osiris* paints the scene for much of
Freeman's day-to-day existence during this period, including "the
surgery, with its oilcloth floor and walls made hideous with gaudy
insurance show-cards in sham gilt frames."
     From time to time, literary aspirations must have crossed
Freeman's mind, but they were hardly serious at first. He had enjoyed writing his journal while in Africa, and possessed a notable
ability for observation and shrewd commentary. Probably, in

spite of his diffidence and quiet voice, his paper on West Africa had been well received at Leeds in 1890. After his illness he prepared an article on the Bontúku expedition for the Royal Geographical Society[11] and one on the city of Bontúku itself[12] the following year, but his ambitions remained fixed on a medical career for a year or two longer. In 1895 he made a final stab at starting a practice of his own, renting for the purpose premises at 129, Worple Road, a suburban thoroughfare in Wimbledon, southwest of London. All we know of this venture is its brevity; it simply ended abruptly in another physical collapse. John Freeman, a very small boy at the time, barely remembers the family's departure from London in 1896 for St. Peter's, a village one mile inland from Broadstairs on the Kentish coast. There, at 56 Church Street, the family remained for the next three or four years. When his health permitted, Freeman went up to London, where he had rooms first in Clifford's Inn, later at Danes Court, since demolished.

He spent some time writing up his West African experiences for a scholarly book on the subject. He also wrote articles and light fiction in an attempt to earn a little money. He may even have used a pseudonym or become involved either in what would now be called ghost writing or "hack" writings. Otherwise it is difficult to account for any substantial source of income in the Freeman family between 1896 and 1900, except for a moderate sum from Constable and Co., who published *Ashanti* in 1898, and the payments from *Cassell's Magazine* in which occasional articles and stories began to appear in October, 1898.[13]

At one point in my research on Freeman, I began to suspect that he had written juvenile detective stories under a pseudonym. This I now believe to have been an error, but the circumstances are unusual and worth describing briefly.

E. S. Turner, in his admirable book *Boys Will Be Boys*, described the exploits of Detective Dixon Brett, who had chambers in Lincoln's Inn. His chief antagonist was the mandarin Fan Chu Fang who had, to quote Turner, "unpleasant optical trouble."

At last he unveiled his green and evil orbs, and with

something very like a shudder of disgust Dixon Brett observed that with the uplifting of the heavily folded eyelids a filmy grey substance was likewise drawn upward over the pupils, something like the moving membrane—the *membrana nictitans*—seen in the eyes of a bird.

This last medical detail is typical of Freeman, but the matter is barely significant, until Turner continues:

Soon after the Mandarin left a young man called, 'an obvious neurotic, slender, fragile, eager.' He had wide-open blue eyes 'in which could be seen plainly the characteristic "hippus"—the incessant change of size which marks the unstable nervous equilibrium.'

This passage is remarkable when compared with the following passage from Freeman's "The Mandarin's Pearl," first published in *Pearson's* Magazine in June, 1909. The narrator, as usual, is Jervis:

. . . [Brodribb] went over to the door and admitted a tall, frail young man whom Thorndyke welcomed with quiet geniality, and settled in a chair by the fire. I looked curiously at our visitor. He was a typical neurotic—slender, fragile, eager. Wide-open blue eyes with broad pupils, in which I could **plainly** see the characteristic "hippus"—that incessant change of size that marks the unstable nervous equilibrium—parted lips, and wandering taper fingers, were as the stigmata of his disorder. He was of the stuff out of which prophets and devotees, martyrs, reformers and third-rate poets are made.

The similarity of the passages could not be mere coincidence. Mr. Turner, to whom I wrote, checked (in the British Museum Reading Room) the origin of the first of the two "hippus" passages above. He had merely taken it from No. 19 of *Aldine Detective Tales,*

incorporating *The Diamond Library*. Though the catalog date is
1893 "this story, like those accompanying it, was presumably a
reissue," since an advertisement on the back page referred to a
competition having a closing date in 1923. The Aldine story had
been titled "The Whispering Death"—A Weird Detective Story by
Jack Wylde, author of "The Case of The Mandarin's Mask," "The
Horror of Beacon Grange," etc. Some of the stories mentioned
motor cars. "Maybe they were new," Mr. Turner concluded in his
letter to me, "maybe they were old ones with motor cars inserted.
I've no way of knowing."

If the tell-tale passage first appeared in the eighteen-nineties,
then it was written by Freeman under a pseudonym. He was not
likely to have dipped into an obscure pulp magazine in 1909 to pick
out the passage unless he were the original author. More probably
the story was written in the nineteen-twenties by one of a syndicate
of writers, who was attracted by the title of Freeman's "The Mandarin's Pearl" in the collection *John Thorndyke's Cases* and was not
above plagiarism. Until a complete set of the original Aldine stories
can be found and examined, the issue must remain in doubt. The
British Museum possesses only parts of the series, which was
extensive, according to bibliographer John Carter,[14] having reached
No. 256 with its May, 1899 issue.

However Freeman struggled through these difficult years, he
was rewarded in the early summer of 1898 by the favorable reaction
to his *Travels and Life in Ashanti and Jaman,* published as a beautifully bound volume, replete with maps, photographs and sketches
(most done by the author). *The Athenaeum* praised the book in an
extensive review; Mary Kingsley, the young explorer fated to die of
fever in Africa within two years, gave it a hearty endorsement in
The Spectator; indeed there seems to have been no unfavorable
comment from any reviewer. However, the limited appeal of the
subject matter precluded a large popular sale. Modest as the
royalty payments were, they were warmly welcomed by the Freeman
family as the century drew to an uncertain close.

CHAPTER III

The Other Half of Clifford Ashdown

One book which Freeman devotees sometimes overlook is his first hard-cover volume of fiction, *The Adventures of Romney Pringle,* written under the pseudonym, "Clifford Ashdown." It has been described as "the rarest volume of detective-crime short stories published in the twentieth century."[1] Only eight copies, in various states of preservation, are known;[2] moreover, the book was never mentioned by Freeman in any list prepared by him. In view of these facts, it presumably had only a small sale on its first appearance in 1902. In the following year, a cheap sixpenny edition in wrappers was issued by the same publishers (Ward, Lock). Not even book collectors who specialize in Freeman's works seem to know a great deal about this phantom paper-back, but at least one copy, whereabouts unknown, is believed to survive.

That a pen-name was being employed was not apparent when the series first appeared in *Cassell's Magazine* in 1902.[3] The preface

John James Pitcairn in 1905
(Courtesy of Mrs. T. H. Johns.)

Freeman ca. 1902
(Courtesy of C. J. A. Freeman.)

2 Woodville Terrace, Gravesend, Freeman's home from 1902
until the end of 1921. (Courtesy of Paul R. Lorch.)

to the first adventure referred to a friendship between Romney
Pringle and "the present writer." But in the book version, published
towards the end of the year, this phrase was changed to "the present
writers," and the existence of collaboration was implicit. The
following year, *The Further Adventures of Romney Pringle* was
published in the same magazine, under the same pseudonym;
however, this time, a small notice also appeared: "Copyright by R.
Austin Freeman, 1903." Through the years the other half of the
mystery was well kept. The British Museum Catalog took the
position that "Clifford Ashdown" was the same person as R. Austin
Freeman. In the library of E. T. Guymon, Jr., of San Diego, his
copy of the book bears a personal inscription by Freeman, who
stated that he was not at liberty to divulge the identity of his
"collaborator." In a 1938 letter, Freeman told Percival Mason
Stone, of Waltham, Massachusetts, that the collaboration was
carried out with "a medical friend." This added detail, as we shall
see, was an essential clue to the mystery.

In the years following Freeman's death in 1943 Mr. Stone
worked intermittently at finding a solution. Not all the details of
his quest are clear, but we know that he corresponded with members
of the Freeman family and, later, with Miss Bertha Fowle, an artist
friend of Freeman's, to whom *Pontifex, Son and Thorndyke* had
been dedicated in 1931. It was Miss Fowle who came up with the
other essential clue. At Stone's urging, she asked Mrs. Freeman—by
this time 85 years old—and her reply, Miss Fowle thought, was
"Pitcairn," although she did not ask Mrs. Freeman to spell out the
name.[4] The rest was easy, for the medical registers of the period
definitely pointed to John James Pitcairn, M.R.C.S., L.R.C.P. The
General Medical Council were able to supply additional details,
specifically that he had been the medical officer at Holloway Prison,
London, at the turn of the century, when Freeman was already
known to have had some tenuous connection with that establishment. The G. M. C. also passed on the address at which Pitcairn
died. By writing there to Mrs. Margaret Pitcairn, Stone was able to
confirm her husband's identity with Clifford **Ashdown** and to

obtain fuller details of his association with Freeman.[5]

It was Vincent Starrett, in his column *Books Alive,*[6] who announced the literary discovery and, in his pleasant way, emphasized that the credit belonged entirely to Stone. *Queen's Quorum* gave Pitcairn's name (describing him only as "an obscure prison medical officer") but neglected to mention Stone's part in the discovery.[7]

Pitcairn was born in north London, probably in St. John's Wood, on May 19, 1860. He was, therefore, Freeman's senior by nearly two years. His father, Thomas Pitcairn, was a civil servant at the Admiralty; his mother's name before her marriage was Arabella Ashdown. As a child his health prevented regular schooling, and he was educated privately by a Canon Duckworth. Later he went on to St. Paul's School and then to the medical school at St. Bartholemew's Hospital; all of which indicates a happier financial picture and higher social standing in his family than in Freeman's. Whether the future collaborators met as students is not known; Freeman attended the medical school at Middlesex Hospital, not many miles from St. Bartholemew's and an encounter at some medical or social function is not unlikely, as they were in the same year of training, both men having qualified in 1887. Thereafter their paths diverged. By the end of 1888, Freeman was in Africa, Pitcairn, at Holloway Prison, writing to the British Medical Journal about the employment of hyoscine as a useful hypnotic.[8] (A critical doctor replied to Pitcairn's communication by reporting alarming symptoms after the administration of hyoscyamine, a related alkaloid, to "a fashionable lady in middle life." In spite of the great advance in organic chemistry since then, especially in the understanding of stereoisomerism, Pitcairn's rejoinder still reads soundly. He indicated the great difference between the two alkaloids, despite their chemical similarity, and warned of the dangers of confusing them; and he refuted his critic by claiming a reassuring outcome of hyoscine treatment in "an unfashionable lady in early life.")

Whether or not they were total strangers before 1900, they undoubtedly met about that time. Freeman, desperate for any kind of respectable job, was engaged to assist Pitcairn at Holloway Prison, which, before the opening of the Brixton establishment, was the general holding prison for the London area, to which prisoners were remanded by the magistrates to await trail for serious offences. The depressing atmosphere of the place, and Freeman's sharp observations of the treatment of prisoners there, are evident in his first Thorndyke novel, *The Red Thumb Mark* (1907). Freeman's official capacity at the prison is a matter of some doubt. He himself once described the position as "acting assistant medical officer," and this—with its overtones of impermanence—is probably more accurate than terms he used in later years: Deputy Medical Officer, Medical Adviser, Prison Visitor.[9] Indeed, it is to be suspected that Pitcairn, eager to help an impecunious colleague, created the nebulous acting-assistantship himself. Freeman's son, John, recalls that the family, who had been living at 9, Vale Square, Ramsgate, while Freeman had rooms in Danes Court, London, over seventy miles away, all moved into Dr. Pitcairn's house next to the prison. Freeman devotees must always feel grateful for the help that "J. J.," as he was called by his friends, extended to the Freemans during this somber period of their lives.

The prison post did not last long. Nor did a brief medical stint with the Port of London Authority. Freeman around this time wrote four chapters for G. R. Sims's *Living London* (1902). Meanwhile the two friends continued to meet. It was in Ramsgate, to which seaside town the Freemans returned after their short London interlude, that *The Adventures of Romney Pringle* were planned and a suitable pen-name devised. Pitcairn contributed his mother's family name, Ashdown; "Clifford" derived from Clifford's Inn, where Freeman had rooms at one time. (In another magazine, a single story was later published with Freeman's name undisguised, but Pitcairn's still hidden.)[10]

The hero of these collaborated stories, Romney Pringle, is an engaging villain, ostensibly a "literary agent" with shabby headquarters in Furnival's Inn (an obvious Freeman touch). He invariably used a bicycle in his travels from one spot of evil-doing to another (Pitcairn was an enthusiastic cyclist; Freeman, not at all). The division of plot construction and actual writing is difficult to apportion now. Freeman's hand is easily distinguished, but there are many unusual touches, for which Pitcairn was probably responsible. The stories are not brilliant, but the cool arrogant air with which Pringle mulcts his victims—usually dishonest people themselves, or else, like the Indian maharajah in the final story of the series, unpopular at the time and therefore fair game—has a dry, refreshing flavour lacking in most of Freeman's non-Thorndyke writings.

Cassell's Magazine was sufficiently impressed by the stories to ask for a second set immediately. The summer of 1902 was singularly hot and dry for England. Freeman still had rooms at No. 2, Danes Court, but he joined his family at Ramsgate whenever he could, often travelling, when time allowed, by pleasure steamer from Tower Bridge. The Pitcairns spent their summer vacation at Deal, a dozen miles to the south, and John Freeman remembers the Pitcairns and a friend, one Miss Cliff, cycling over for the day (to be quite accurate, Mrs. Pitcairn *tri*cycled). They were hot, tired and thickly covered with gray chalky dust when they arrived, (for this was in the days before asphalt-paved roads). After tea, Mrs. Pitcairn elected to return by rail, but the two bicyclists set off for Deal on their machines and were caught in a heavy storm. They managed to reach a wayside station just before Mrs. Pitcairn's train pulled in, and when they entered her carriage they were streaming with muddy water. The following day, Pitcairn cleaned both bicycles, which were thickly coated with chalky mud. "Soon after this," writes John Freeman, "a story appeared in which Pringle helps a cyclist in London and in so doing collects a sample of mud from his machine. The cyclist states that he has ridden in from Essex but the mud does not look like Essex mud. . . . Pringle learns that there has been a heavy storm in Kent but that the farmers in Essex are still praying for rain. He also learns that a wanted criminal, believed to be carrying stolen jewels, has been seen in Kent and is expected to have made for London. Pringle therefore re-contacts the cyclist and robs him." The connection between the event and the story is quite apparent.

By the time *The Further Adventures of Romney Pringle*[11] were published, Freeman had settled down in Gravesend, which was to remain his home for the remaining forty years of his life. He was already fairly familiar with the town, and its salty, sea-going atmosphere appealed to the adventurous side of his nature.

Readers of Freeman's *The Unwilling Adventurer* are treated to several views of eighteenth-century Gravesend. A more up-to-date view is presented by Richard Church, who, writing in 1948, demonstrates that, in some respects, it has not changed much.

> Gravesend is approached in the same way as Rochester, over a steep ridge of chalk that drops to the waterside. Many people consider it to be spoiled by an overlay of industrialism; but I think they are blind who cannot still see a slightly exotic, southern quality in the steep streets running up from the waterfront. Two hundred river pilots live in Gravesend, and their personality, which is that of a vocation, permeates the town. Though it stands on the closing shores of the Thames, which at this point is only a mile wide at high tide, Gravesend is a maritime, one might even say a saline, place. There is a certain robust, hornpipe character about its people. One expects to see a parrot in every front room, and a tattoist's shop round every corner. If one lands there from the Tilbury Ferry the aspect of the old High Street, with its many shop signs hanging out like those in a Chinese city, gives an impression of entering a foreign country. It is a great place for eating-houses, but rather of the forecastle than the quarterdeck kind. If you want simplicity and quantity in a meal, go to Gravesend.[12]

The town is the site of a pair of Freeman's plebeian seafaring stories for *Cassell's: Caveat Emptor: The Story of a Ship's Pram,* and *The Great Tobacco "Plant."* His first encounter with the

town seems to have been a visit to his friend Bernard Bishop who
lived there. His decision to move his family there permanently was
purely economic. Bernard and Alice Bishop had three sons and a
daughter,[13] and it was arranged that Freeman should become their
tutor in return for some kind of stipend and a house, rent free.[14]

The house at 2, Woodville Terrace, Wrotham Road was large
and old-fashioned, with a deep basement and large cellars; (the
ground-floor arrangement was that described in "Phyllis Annesley's
Peril"). Freeman's tutorial classes must have been worth attending, although decidedly eccentric as far as curriculum was concerned,
if the memory of my informant, Mrs. Moriarty, can be relied on.
"The subjects," she writes, "were biology, logic, Egyptian history,
chemistry and the evolution of the steam engine." The class consisted of the four Bishop children and the two Freeman boys,
John and Lawrence. The selection of subject-matter owed much to
the theories of the English nineteenth-century philosopher, Herbert
Spencer, whose views, greatly admired by Freeman, circulated
in magazine articles around 1855. In particular he believed that
the value of an academic subject was directly proportional to its
necessity for human life.[15]

Freeman was as mute on the history of his teaching career as
he was on some earlier somewhat bleak periods of his life, but one
indirect reference to that period can be found in a review Freeman
wrote many years later. He was discussing Bertrand Russell's
Marriage and Morals, about which he expressed strong reservations,
but also some agreement:

> His appeal, for instance, for the lifting of the taboos on sex
> knowledge and the clearing away of the cloud of decep-
> tion, mystery and prudery, amidst which a child is apt
> to gather his obscure ideas upon sex, will command the
> sympathy of most thoughtful persons; and particularly
> of those who—like the present reviewer—have had experi-
> ence of teaching children biology and human physiology
> (*without any reservations*) and have noted the frank,
> simple interest of the wholesome childish mind in the

phenomenon of sexual reproduction.[16]

At about the time that Freeman moved to Gravesend, Pitcairn left Holloway Prison to take on a post at an experimental penal institution for youthful offenders at Borstal,[17] only eight miles away, and the two friends had no difficulty in meeting and planning further short stories. Under their pseudonym "Clifford Ashdown," the men wrote another series, "From A Surgeon's Diary," which ran in Cassell's Magazine from December 1904 to May 1905. The stories are more serious in tone than the two *Pringle* series and are all the better for it. Freeman was continuing to do additional writing under his own name for *Cassell's* at this time, not only humorous short stories but also articles with a nautical flavor such as "The Royal Yacht" and "Down the River."

A more abortive literary venture by the collaborators was an unpublished novel, *The Queen's Treasure,* the story of a search for buried treasure in Kent, reputedly plunder brought to England by Sir Francis Drake. Considering Freeman's financial position during this period, we must assume attempts were made to have it accepted.

Disappointment over the book may have caused some estrangement between the collaborators. They do not seem to have met after Pitcairn's departure, in 1907, for Winson Green Prison, Birmingham. His stay there was short, as was his subsequent tour of duty at the convict establishment at Portland. In 1909 he moved back to his (and Freeman's) native city, remaining as the medical officer at Wandsworth Prison, London, until his retirement in November, 1921.

The rest of "J. J's" story is soon told. He and his wife joined their daughter, Winifred, and her husband T. H. Johns in their rambling, ivy-covered farmhouse called "Tregongon," in the remote Cornish parish of Veryan. Pitcairn, who had always been a striking and personable figure, enjoyed his retirement in this beautiful coastal area. He never went back to fiction-writing, but contributed regularly to a periodical called *The Medical World.* He was a voracious reader and did some book collecting. He also dabbled in photography. When the Johns family began to increase, the

Pitcairns moved into a small bungalow which they had built nearby. It was here, at Parc Parnall, that Dr. John James Pitcairn—alias Ashdown Piers—otherwise one-half of Clifford Ashdown—died on May 10, 1936, a few days before his seventy-sixth birthday.

It is not easy to determine just how important Pitcairn's help was to the struggling Freeman, but it was appreciable. Freeman working alone had never achieved anything more praiseworthy than anemic imitations of W. W. Jacobs. But in his association with Pitcairn, Freeman achieved his first sustained effort in fiction; twelve stories centering around one dominant character, Romney Pringle. Six of these appeared between hard covers, thereby elevating Freeman to the elite whose short stories of crime and detection have been published in book form. Ellery Queen's bibliography[18] shows the limited numbers of hard-cover collections of detective stories. The most significant of these volumes, as listed in *Queen's Quorum*, number no more than one hundred and six titles. Freeman is represented twice under his own name by *John Thorndyke's Cases* (1909) and *The Singing Bone* (1912). And *The Adventures of Romney Pringle* is also listed, not by reason of its rarity alone, but, according to Queen, for its literary significance.

More important than the *Romney Pringle* stories for Freeman's future development as a major detective novelist were the annals of medical sleuthing entitled *From a Surgeon's Diary,* published two or three years later (though never in book form). These stories are reminiscent of the two series of *Stories from the Diary of a Doctor* by the profilic authoress L. T. Meade and her pseudonymous medical collaborator "Clifford Halifax" which had appeared a decade earlier. The Ashdown stories are superior in that they are based on rational motives and eschew such pseudoscientific "explanations" as telepathy and hypnotism. The latter stories, especially the *Diary* series, require only a recognizable detective hero to raise them to the level of classics. Previously, Freeman's work gave no promise of anything more remarkable than *Flighty Phyllis* or, on a more serious plane, *The Golden Pool.*

Pitcairn's friendship, coming when Freeman's medical aspirations were at an end, and when his own efforts to replace this career by a literary one were making slow headway, must have had inestimably heartening effects. If "J. J." and Freeman drifted apart just before the curtain rose on Thorndyke's debut, it is nevertheless true that together they set the stage for the greatest scientific detective of them all.

CHAPTER IV

Thorndyke's Predecessor

So far as the British reading public was concerned, Freeman in 1905 was the author of one serious work—noted only by the handful interested in West African exploration and sociology. A few of the readers of *Cassell's Magazine* might have observed his name popping up intermittently as the author of light-hearted stories, usually with a nautical flavor, and of more serious contributions, which also had a salty taste to them, on such subjects as the Thames estuary, lighthouses and the Royal Yacht.

In 1905, Freeman's first venture into book-length fiction of a serious nature was published by Cassell and Company. *The Golden Pool*, a thick, closely-printed tome, is set in the part of the world he knew best: the Gold Coast of West Africa.

Richard Englefield, a bank clerk and amateur sailor, falls in with Captain Bithery, master of a brig engaged in trade between Hamburg and the Gold Coast. Englefield is taken on as purser to

Professor Alfred Swaine Taylor. (From a contemporary account of the Palmer trial.)

keep the books and "work the trade." A little while after landing in Africa, Englefield discovers, hidden in a secret compartment of an antique desk, a seventeenth-century account of a dying Portuguese mulatto's macabre experiences. Somewhere in the interior there was a "golden pool," so named for the accumulation of gold dust found washed down by the fast-flowing river. The gold was recovered and melted down in crucibles within a secret cavern by blinded slaves, the precious metal being cast into shapes for the treasury of a River God. The dying narrator of this story had himself been blinded and enslaved for almost two years.

Englefield is captivated by the account he has found, for he already has reason to suspect the existence of a golden hoard somewhere in the interior. Instead of returning to England with Bithery, he devises a plan for seeking the truth of the tale. He studies Arabic for a short time and then, disguising himself as a Hausa, leaves Quittah for the head waters of the Tanno and the site of the Golden Pool.

He leaves behind him his friend, the merchant Pereira, and his sympathetic, handsome daughter Isabel, first of the classic, independent-minded Freeman heroines, with whom Englefield has formed an attachment. In the company of the conniving David Annan, Englefield sets off north from Cape Coast, following closely Freeman's own route of 1888. As always, Freeman cannot resist the urge to instruct as well as to entertain, and so the adventure up to the point at which Englefield is taken prisoner and pressed into service in the legendary cavern drags somewhat.

From this juncture, the story's pace develops. The hero and a wounded slave escape bearing between them half a ton of gold, which they bury. The slave soon dies of tetanus, and Englefield is taken into bondage once more, this time in a slave caravan. He and a young Fulah woman escape, and this woman, Aminé, becomes devoted to him. Englefield, loyal to the memory of his wife-to-be, Isabel Pereira, remains unresponsive, but the brutal murder of Aminé, at the climax of the story, opens his eyes to his affection for her. He escapes from this hostile region in a boat which he builds and which bears the golden treasure and himself to safety.

Years later, back in England, his favorite memento is "a tablet of baked clay, on one side of which is scratched in rough Arabic characters, 'Praise be to God,' while the other bears the inscription, in my wife's handwriting, 'Aminé loveth thee.' "

The book is too slow-moving, too rich in native lore, to make an ideal adventure story, but it is the most significant of Freeman's non-Thorndyke works. Moreover, the publication of this lengthy story was important in promoting its author's self-confidence, despite the fact that the financial harvest was disappointing. Freeman found himself, at the age of forty-three, still largely dependent on the sale of short magazine pieces, while he spent the days as a tutor to provide his family with a roof over its head. A dramatic new approach would be needed if Freeman were ever to raise himself to the ranks of the really popular authors. Detection and medicine were intermingled in *From A Surgeon's Diary*; crime—with a dash of detection added—was the theme of the Pringle stories. For some years past and for many years to come, the archetypical sleuth was and would be Sherlock Holmes. Arthur Conan Doyle was busy with matters during the Boer War—matters which were to lead to a knighthood in 1902—but in 1901, on his return to England, he busied himself, at a hotel near Dartmoor Prison, with a new Holmes story. Holmes had apparently been killed by a fall down a sheer cliff at the Reichenbach Falls during a struggle some years earlier, but Doyle finally gave in to the intense public clamor for another Holmes adventure by recording, in *The Hound of the Baskervilles,* an earlier "case" of Holmes as recollected by the faithful Watson. The story was so well received by a loyal public that, in 1903, the *Strand* began a new series of short stories about the great detective, who had not died after all! The bookstalls were jammed that autumn when the magazine, carrying the famous first tale of the new series, "The Return of Sherlock Holmes," went on sale. All England, it seems, went wild, and Freeman, we may be sure, had cause to take note.

The second series of Romney Pringle stories was due to begin in *Cassell's, The Golden Pool* was in process. After that lengthy book was finished a decison was necessary about his future course. What could Freeman do that would be a unique contribution to the genre? Was it possible to top Sherlock Holmes?

"Dr. Thorndyke was not based on any person, real or fictitious," Freeman once wrote. "He was deliberately invented. In a professional sense, he may have been suggested to me by Dr. Alfred Swaine Taylor (the father of medical jurisprudence), whose great work on that subject I studied closely when I was a student. But his personality was designed in accordance with certain principles and what I believed to be the probabilities as to what such a man would be like. As mental and bodily characters are usually in harmony, a fine intellect tending to be associated with fine physique, I made him tall, strong, active and keen-sighted. As he was a man of acute intellect and sound judgment, I decided to keep him free from eccentricities, such are usually associated with an ill-balanced mind, and to endow him with the dignity of presence, appearance and manner appropriate to his high professional and social standing. Especially I decided to keep him perfectly sane and normal."

To be more explicit, Sherlock's little oddities—drug addiction, revolver practice in the living room, even his violin-playing—were distasteful to Freeman. His own investigator would rely on sound scientific reasoning and not at all on histrionics. All the same, Freeman's prospectus does sound more than a trifle dull, his projected hero lacked character. Light and shade being absent, one would feel that such a character could never succeed.

Herein lies Freeman's achievement, for his Thorndyke stories are far from dull. Writing to Hamish Hamilton, his English publisher, in 1949, Raymond Chandler, the hard-boiled, witty, perceptive detective-story writer, commented:

"This man Austin Freeman is a wonderful performer. He has no equal in his genre and he is also a much better writer than you might think, if you were superficially inclined, because in spite of the immense leisure of his writing he accomplishes an even suspense which is quite unexpected. The apparatus of his writing makes for dullness, but he is not dull. . ."[1]

There is something about Freeman's style and especially in his delineation of Thorndyke's character which holds the reader's attention. Instead of being a faceless wonder "the great Dr. Thorndyke is probably the handsomest detective in fiction. . . outwardly bonhomous, but spiritually detached. . . ."[2] However, in this germinal stage, Thorndyke was nothing more than a bundle of qualities, many of them negative, still to be mobilized in a novel or even a short story. Recollecting his short period of service at the Westminster Ophthalmic Hospital Freeman developed the plot of *The Mystery of 31, New Inn.* It was not published for some years; it came out first as a novella, and later, in 1912, as a full-length novel. It is actually the first Thorndyke novel and, according to Freeman, the construction of this story determined "not only the general character of my future work but of the hero around whom the plots were to be woven."

We have read. Freeman's comments on his conception of Thorndyke as a sober, distinguished scientific investigator of fine physique. He owed much to Professor Alfred Swaine Taylor, though Freeman made Taylor's acquaintance solely through the latter's famous text-books. Freeman was only fifteen when Taylor retired from teaching at the age of seventy-one and he died three years later. In spite of this, Taylor and Thorndyke resemble one another in physique and personality, as well as in professional methods, as the following obituary notice indicates:

> So strenuous and sincere was he in his character, that he abhorred all the arts of the advocate; and to have secured the assistance of Dr. Taylor on the side of either prosecution or defence in a criminal trial was in itself already a great point gained; for it was certain that he would only lend his assistance to that side which, after a conscientious examination, he had satisfied himself was apparently in the right. And, if his career be reviewed, it will be seen that in cases such as those of Palmer, Smethurst, and

Tawell, from the beginning to the end of his life, he fought always on the side of what appeared to him to be absolute justice; and that he never aimed to procure either the conviction or the defence of any prisoner because he was engaged on the one side or the other, but only consented to give assistance in a case when he had previously satisfied himself that the facts of the case demanded that he should do so. Commanding in stature, of fine expressive feature, calm, earnest and decided, but persuasive in manner, he was powerful in influencing judges and jurymen. His unrivalled experience was greatly enriched and aided by the habit which he acquired of daily noting in a systematic manner every detail, every fact, every suggestion, which he came across in his reading which could subsequently be made available for his work.[3]

Taylor incorporated his notes into successive editions of his increasingly authoritative works, especially his *Principles and Practice of Medical Jurisprudence,* which even today is periodically revised and republished. Although Taylor's great qualities brought him fame and respect in medical circles and in the law courts during his life, his reputation did undoubtedly suffer serious blows in the famous trials of Palmer and Smethurst, mentioned in the tribute above.

The third trial which is often associated with Taylor, that of John Tawell, the Quaker, is the strangest case of all. Tawell was found guilty at Aylesbury Assizes in March, 1845, of poisoning his mistress, Sarah Hart, by adding a stiff quorum of prussic acid to her glass of porter. The defense put forward was singular: that the unfortunate woman had eaten too many apples, the pips of which were known by chemists of that time to contain minute amounts of prussic acid.

Despite the obituary notice quoted earlier and the account in the *Dictionary of National Biography,* Taylor, according to contemporary accounts, was not a witness at Tawell's trial and seems to have played no part in it, though he does describe it in his textbooks.[4]

Before turning to the two most notorious trials in which Taylor actually took part, let us look briefly at the man himself. The son of a sea captain, Alfred Swaine Taylor was born at Northfleet, Kent, in 1806 and became a student at Guy's Hospital at the age of sixteen. In 1828 he attended lectures at medical schools in France. Setting sail for Naples he survived in turn an encounter with pirates and a violent storm. Taylor stayed for nine months in Naples, where the supply of fresh corpses for dissection was a decided improvement on conditions at home, where "body-snatchers" were the chief suppliers of research material. But he seems always to have been a man whose interest, like those of Freeman, spilled over into all facets of science and beyond. In France he had dabbled in geology; later in life he was to provide valuable impetus to the embryonic science of photography by recommending the use of calcium thiosulfate as a "fixer" for developed plates. Thus, it is not surprising that such a man would quickly tire of Naples and set off on foot across Europe. At Brescia, while sketching some military fortifications, he was arrested as a spy. Continuing north, he visited medical schools in Switzerland, the Tyrol and Germany before finally settling down again at Guy's Hospital; not, however, as a physician but as an "experimentalist"—or researcher—in chemistry and physics. He was all of twenty-five years old when, in 1831, he was appointed to the newly created Chair of Medical Jurisprudence, a post he was to fill with distinction for forty-six years. For most of that time he also occupied the Chair of Chemistry at the same hospital.

Although he was constantly in demand as an expert witness on matters having a medical or chemical theme, it is a puzzling fact that the court records of the two most famous of the trials at which he appeared fail to explain to the modern reader the reasons for his great reputation.

The first of them—the Rugeley poisoning case[5]—has as its pudgy central figure a one-time physician who had forsaken a medical career for the racetrack. The time was November, 1855, and William Palmer, heavily in debt to various moneylenders, had recently fallen in with John Parsons Cook, a young man of similarly horsy interests. Palmer's wife had conveniently died shortly after having been insured by her husband for a handsome sum; something of the same nature had befallen Palmer's brother. Now, Cook fell ill just after winning £2,000 at Shrewsbury races. He recovered enough to travel to Rugeley, to become sick on two successive days, each time after Palmer had brought him food and drink. While Palmer beat hasty tracks to collect Cook's winnings in London and fend off his own creditors, the sick man made a dramatic recovery. However, once back in Rugeley, Palmer bought prussic acid and strychnine. He visited Cook twice more and shortly after each visit the wretched man was taken violently ill, the second time fatally. All symptoms pointed to strychnine poisoning. Great suspicion surrounded William Palmer, the bodies of whose wife and brother were exhumed. Amazingly, in these circumstances, the suspect was allowed to be present at the post mortem examination on Cook, where he made attempts to destroy or remove the evidence. Shortly afterwards, Palmer was arrested and in due course was tried in London for Cook's murder.

Taylor described his search for vegetable and mineral poisons: all he found were traces of antimony among the organs. Experiments with rabbits fed strychnine led him to believe that Cook had died from the effects of that poison, but he claimed that no suitable color test was known which could detect the presence of that alkaloid directly. He was greatly hampered by the absence of the stomach contents (which had been spilled, under suspicious circumstances, at the autopsy).

The defense made much of this lack of direct evidence. Professors Herepath and Letheby, who were professional rivals— even enemies—of Taylor, disagreed with his statement that no tests for strychnine were available. Taylor, it was alleged, had first concluded—after the initial investigation—that antimony poisoning had caused death; now he wanted to change his mind. It was the circumstantial evidence that Palmer had bought poisons and used Cook's money to pay his own debts that led to a guilty verdict and to the gallows back in Staffordshire. Taylor, whether through carelessness or bad luck, was no great help to the prosecution.

The other famous trial in which he played a leading role was even more detrimental to his reputation. Dr. Thomas Smethurst was tried in 1859 for the murder of his bigamous "wife" Isabella Bankes.[6] The accused man was fifty-four, his alleged victim in her early forties and his real wife, Mary, as old as seventy-four. After bigamously marrying Isabella, a spinster of considerable charm, he settled down with her in Richmond, Surrey. Soon the poor lady began to feel unwell; the doctors suspected poisoning and specialists (including Taylor) were consulted. Smethurst was always in attendance and gave Miss Bankes nearly all her food and medicine. He brought in a local attorney to have the dying woman sign a will making over all her property to him. A day or two later he was arrested on a poisoning charge but was immediately released. Miss Bankes died the following day and Smethurst was taken into custody again, this time to face a murder indictment. Antimony in small amounts was found in the body, which showed considerable intestinal inflammation and ulceration; pregnancy had progressed about six weeks.

By a chemical freak, Taylor made a gross error in his findings as he reported them at the initial hearing in magistrate's court.

He employed Reinsch's test, a description of which will be found in Freeman's *The Cat's Eye* (1923),[7] in which a copper surface is blackened by the presence of arsenic. Of almost eighty tests conducted by the professor on specimens from the patient before and after death, and on various materials taken from Smethurst's medicine cabinets and elsewhere, nearly all gave negative results when examined for arsenic.

The chief sensation at the trial was concerned with a mysterious saline liquid in an ordinary medicine bottle. When Taylor tested it by Reinsch's method a strange phenomenon occurred. Instead of the copper turning gray or black, it disappeared! Evidently addition of the salty liquid caused it to dissolve in the acid. Taylor, instead of investigating the reaction (which would be recognized today as caused by the oxidizing nature of the added liquid), simply suspended a second piece of copper gauze in the liquid with the same result.

Not until several pieces of gauze had been used up in this way could the test be completed. But when it was, the result was dramatic: the gauze rapidly turned an intense black, and Turner duly reported that the bottle did indeed hold a large dose of arsenic in some soluble form. However, between the magistrate's hearing and the trial itself he began to entertain doubts. Further investigation showed the bottle to contain an aqueous solution of potassium perchlorate, and experiments with his regular copper gauze, which under the usual conditions gave no evidence of containing any arsenic, invariably gave a strongly positive result with Reinsch's test in the presence of arsenic-free perchlorate. (Pure [electrolytic] copper was not readily available in 1859.) Although Taylor claimed to have had no trouble with it previously, his regular quality of gauze, especially if a large quantity were brought into solution, contained enough arsenic to invalidate the results.

Although Taylor communicated his error to the authorities immediately, it was pressed against him vigorously by Sergeant Parry for Smethurst:

"Did you . . . tell the magistrates that you had tested all the materials you used in your tests?"

"Yes; I tested them all before I commenced making the analyses to see if they were pure. I have used the same description of copper gauze for a great many years and have never before discovered the presence of arsenic in it."

"And will you continue to use it?"

"I shall certainly continue to use it, but I shall take care not to do so with chlorate of potass."

Inevitably, Taylor's error reflected on his only other finding of arsenic, in a stool brought to him before the sick woman died. Antimony, on the other hand, was certainly present in the organs, but only in tiny amounts, and again Taylor's faulty evidence concerning the arsenic reduced the strength of his testimony here. Doctors for the defense gave the opinion (based on written reports of the autopsy) that Isobella died of dysentery aggravated by pregnancy.

The judge's charge was dead against Smethurst. It stressed such matters as the secret "marriage;" the modest but sufficient financial advantage resulting from Miss Bankes's death; her newly-discovered pregnancy, which Smethurst may have regarded as a problem; and the selfish business of the will, in which a strange attorney was brought to the death-bed while Isobella's sister was denied permission to see her. True, no poisons had been traced to Smethurst, but he was alone in the house on the last night before his final arrest and could easily have disposed of them. On the question of the medical evidence, it appeared to be irreconcilable, and the jury should therefore consider all the non-technical matters carefully in helping them to decide the case.

The guilty verdict, brought in after only forty minutes' deliberation, was at first widely approved. The London *Times,* for example, considered the medical testimony, taken as a whole, to be convincing. But soon the newspapers were printing letters, largely from physicians and chemists, doubting the conclusive nature of the evidence. The *British Medical Journal,* after averring that Miss Bankes's pregnancy was alone sufficient to account for all her symptoms, tore into Professor Taylor:

> Had Smethurst been tried on this evidence directly after his committal by the Richmond magistrates, his life would have fallen through this illusive wire gauze, and Dr. Taylor might possibly, when too late, have discovered his lamentable error. This fact should, we think, act as a terrible warning to him, and we hope that he will not persist, as he said he should, in using the impure copper gauze in future experiments when human life is at stake, otherwise the horrors which flourished in the days of witchcraft, when human life hung upon the lips of any old crone, will be but too faithfully represented by the horrors which will flow from the pseudo-scientific evidence of the present day.

And the *Dublin Medical Press* was even more severe:

> We must look now upon Professor Taylor as having ended
> his career, and hope he will immediately withdraw into
> the obscurity of private life, not forgetting to carry with
> him his favourite arsenical copper. He can never again
> be listened to in a Court of Justice, and should henceforth
> leave the witness box to the occupation of others.

Petitions were got up in Smethurst's behalf by physicians and
barristers, and the aged Mrs. Smethurst likewise begged for her
husband's life. The Home Secretary appointed a medical adjudi-
cator, the famous surgeon Sir Benjamin Brodie, to sift the facts
afresh. He reported that, while the circumstances were suspicious,
the possibility of natural death could not be quite dismissed.
Smethurst was released, to be immediately charged with bigamy and
later sent to a year's imprisonment.

Alfred Swaine Taylor's reputation seems not to have been
permanently affected by his performance at the two trials. He
went on almost to the end of his life, appearing especially in cases
involving poisons, and recording his experiences in his textbooks on
medical jurisprudence and toxicology. And it was from the books,
not the man, that Freeman built up the technical Thorndyke. As
for Thorndyke's physical exterior, this was entirely Freeman's
invention, even though, a few years after the character's inception,
a young man, who was to become the most famous pathologist in
the British courts, appeared to bear a striking resemblance to him.
The tall, handsome, dignified Sir Bernard Spilsbury (he was knighted
in 1923) first became prominent at the trial of Dr. Crippen in
1910, so it was almost impossible for Freeman to have used him as
a model, but in demeanor and outlook he had much in common with
Thorndyke. Moreover, their careers, one real, the other fictitious,
had many parallels and spanned a similar period of time. Thorndyke's first case was "Rex v. Gummer" in 1897, and he is last seen in
action around 1935. Spilsbury's first post-mortem was at Fulham in
1906, his last on the day of his death (by his own hand) in December,

1947. "The great scene," wrote Raymond Chandler, "would have been a courtroom battle between Thorndyke and Spilsbury, and for my money Thorndyke would have won, hands down."

If Taylor supplied the technique, and the physique was purely imaginary, from what source arose Thorndyke's outlook on life, his stern attitude towards evildoers, and his gentleness towards his friends? At the time of Freeman's death in 1943, the editor of the *Eugenics Review*, who had known him well, described something of his character and personal history and added: "We need not look far for the original of those qualities, above all the learning, scientific integrity and urbanity, which, for most of us, make Thorndyke the most appealing of all the successors of Dupin and Sherlock Holmes."[8]

CHAPTER V

False Impressions

It was Freeman's experiences as Deputy Medical Officer at Holloway Prison which provided the theme around which his first Thorndyke novel was constructed. As he described the circumstances ten years later on the fly leaf of his own copy of *The Red Thumb Mark*:[1]

At that time the "Thumbograph" was on sale at all the railway book-stalls and I obtained a copy by purchase or gift, I forget which. As my observations in the Finger-print Department had convinced me that finger-prints could be quite easily reproduced, I regarded the "Thumbograph" as a rather dangerous publication and I projected this story as an instance of its possible misuse. But I tested my thesis that finger-prints could be fabricated by making a set of gelatine stamps from my own finger-tips and with these I was able to produce quite good prints.

It is one thing to write a book with an important message; it is quite another, alas, to have it published in a profitable manner. *The Mystery of 31, New Inn*, probably in novella form, was already written and awaiting publication. The same delay seems to have threatened *The Red Thumb Mark*, but its author was this time determined that his latest volume, and the important message it contained, should be brought before the public. This book was perhaps the only novel ever to issue from the house of Collingwood; for, in the inscription from which we have just quoted, Freeman also remarked that his book was "a private venture, Collingwoods being publishers of a commercial directory." Evidently then, the author paid to have his book published, and selling it may not have been a straightforward matter. Those copies which *were* bought probably attracted their purchasers' attention by the vividness of their covers. Even now, a good copy of this first edition (a rare commodity for which collectors must be prepared to pay handsomely)[2] is a striking sight, with its bold white lettering stamped into the smooth black cloth and the bright red thumb-print—much larger than life—set in the center of the front cover.

But if the exterior of the book could excite only admiration, the same could not be said of the interior, which even now engenders sharp differences of opinion among those who read it. Fingerprint experts almost universally maintain that fingerprints cannot be successfully forged. They charge, in fact, that this, first of the many Thorndyke stories, is based upon a sham, and a mischievous one at that; for *The Red Thumb Mark*, famous in retrospect for its introduction of the greatest scientific investigator ever brought before the readers of detective stories, is concerned with one great central issue, the possibility that fingerprints can be successfully forged and the counterfeit impressions subsequently used to incriminate an innocent man.

The story concerns the robbery of a parcel of diamonds from the safe of old John Hornby, to whose care they had been temporarily entrusted. The parcel disappeared overnight, and in its place was found a piece of paper bearing a bloody thumb-print. Suspicion fell on Hornby's two nephews, Walter and Reuben, both of whom had access to the safe, but at first the police could make no headway with the case because the old man refused to allow his nephews to be exposed to the indignity of being fingerprinted. Later, old Mrs. Hornby showed the police a "Thumbograph" given to her by Walter some months earlier. This little book contained many thumb-prints from her friends and relatives—including one of Reuben's, identical with the bloody impression left in the safe.

Upon the inevitable arrest, Thorndyke's help was invoked and he agreed to take on the case after hearing the suspected man's solemn declaration of innocence. The subsequent story, as such, lacks a counterweight to the main narrative. Compared to the ingenuity and sheer complexity of such a subsequent novel as *The Cat's Eye* (1923), there is a simplicity and directness about the book which belongs to the turn of the century rather than to the more sophisticated 20's. There is a great deal of "action" in the story, in particular Thorndyke is assaulted twice—being injured rather badly in the first attack—and an attempt is made to poison him. There is a love interest (as usual), when Jervis meets his future wife, Juliet Gibson, who lives with John Hornby and his wife as a kind of adopted daughter. And there is much else to interest the student of "Thorndykiana," for this is the debut of the immortal trio—Thorndyke, Jervis and Polton.

But in spite of these diversions, the mystery element is too concentrated. We may not know how the incriminating thumb-print got into the safe, and forgery may not occur to us; nevertheless, Thorndyke need but clear up this one matter in order to free Reuben and to substitute an alternative suspect (well in view from the beginning) in his miserable place.

It could be said that *The Red Thumb Mark* resembles an expanded short story, just as many of Freeman's short stories are so rich in invention as to constitute condensed novels. This first Thorndyke story resembles, so far as the directness of narration and simplicity in outline is concerned, *The Shadow of the Wolf* (1925) which was originally a short story, but later expertly expanded to book length. Let us postpone the dénouement of the Hornby Case for a while until we have considered the background against which the book was written and the criticism heaped upon its central argument.

Distinctive patterns left by the fingers, and indeed by the palms of the hands and feet, were always there to be noticed by the observant, and they undoubtedly were noticed—in an idle sort of a way—by the Chinese and ancient Hindus. Sometimes fingerprints, pressed into wax seals, were used as personal signatures on important documents. But the unique nature of an individual print seems not to have been fully realised until the middle of the nineteenth century. Whether it is to Sir William Herschel, who used this method to identify Indian natives in 1858, or to Dr. Henry Faulds, who claimed some years' priority, that tribute should be paid as the first in this field,[3] certainly it was Sir Francis Galton who devised the first method of classification which could be used by the police. For many years the system used by law enforcement agencies was based on the kind of pattern left by *all* the fingers, and the thumb, of each hand, so that it was possible to obtain a simply described sequence for a whole set; thus: loop, loop, whorl, arch, loop. This served to reduce the tedium of searching. Of course, a single print was sufficient, even when *The Red Thumb Mark* was published, to pin the crime on an apprehended criminal. The difficulty came in classifying prints, especially of single digits, so that they might be reduced to easily managed codes of numbers and letters which could be filed and later retrieved when needed. Such a system of classification, devised by Harry Battley, was introduced at Scotland Yard in 1930. Freeman himself described the new system in some detail in *When Rogues Fall Out* (U. S. title: *Dr. Thorndyke's Discovery)* in 1932.

Fingerprints attracted much public attention in the last few years of the century. (Galton's book[4] was sent to Mark Twain, who read it with great interest and built his book *Pudd'nhead Wilson* on it.)[5]

At about the time Freeman was busy with his book in 1906, an interesting international case was solved by the mailing of a fingerprint from New York to Scotland Yard. The wife of "a prominent novelist" was robbed in London of £ 800; the criminal, an "old lag" named Henry Johnson, escaped to New York and was picked up for hotel robbery. Then the fingerprint was sent to London—unaccompanied, it is said, by any description—where it was promptly identified. Johnson, in due course, was separated from society for seven years.

The Red Thumb Mark seems to have had little impact on the police, or on judges and juries. In 1909, one Thomas Herbert Castleton failed in his appeal against a conviction for burglary in which only fingerprint evidence was offered. The prints, found on a candle in the burgled dwelling, had been easily identified by the police as those of Castleton, evidently a gentleman already known to them. At his trial he offered no defense, but on appeal it was suggested on his behalf that perhaps the candle, bearing the incriminating indentations, had been taken to the house in Huddersfield, Yorkshire by someone else. "He was an associate of thieves," admitted—or perhaps claimed—his counsel, and such a thing was very possible. But the Lord Chief Justice, sitting with Mr. Justice Darling and Mr. Justice Bucknill, denied the appeal, and thereby set the precedent in international jurisprudence that fingerprints could be considered conclusive evidence without corroboration. [6]

This is the kind of thing Freeman's story warned against. A few years later, in the preface to *The Exploits of Danby Croker (1916)*, he spoke more sharply:

> Those who are familiar with the practice of the Court of Criminal Appeal may find in Chapter XII something reminiscent of an actual case that was once heard in it. More than this, I suppose I had better not say; but I may be permitted to express the hope that those who are concerned in the administration of the law will subject to the most jealous and searching scrutiny all finger-print evidence that is not fully corroborated.

It is unlikely that Freeman actually believed fingerprint "forgery" had taken place in the Castleton case. The convicted man's defense did not claim it, but only suggested that a candle bearing his *genuine* prints had been taken to the scene of the crime by the real burglars. In *Croker* Freeman adopts again the more dramatic idea of fabricated fingerprints. Danby takes impressions in dental wax of Tom Naggett's fingers while that budding criminal is slumped in a drunken stupor. From these molds he prepares finger-tips in soft rubber, and attaches them to a pair of soft gloves. He then visits an old lady's home and leaves the prints on a convenient candle at the premises. Thus Naggett, Croker's enemy, is implicated in a serious crime, and it may be said that this part of a complex, uneven and immoral plot works out rather well.

Freeman used forged prints twice more. In "The Old Lag," an early short story, published in *The Singing Bone* as the only tale in that collection not of the "inverted" type, a reformed convict is "framed" by an ex-warder who had obtained his fingerprints from official prison documents. In *The Cat's Eye* (1923),[7] "Moakey" the burglar, a frequent character in the Thorndyke stories, is the object of an arch-criminal's deception. Here the prints have been developed and photographed on a piece of burgled silver plate left by "Moakey" in his flight from capture. Fortunately for him, he is in prison for a later offence by the time the false prints are planted at the scene of a murder, an alibi which baffles Superintendent Miller for much of the book despite his knowledge of this sort of thing in two of the earlier fingerprint deceptions.

However, Freeman's most important treatment of the counterfeit-fingerprints theme is his first, in *The Red Thumb Mark*, wherein Thorndyke explains in some detail the ease with which false prints can be fabricated. In his evidence at Reuben's trial he said:

> There are two principal methods that suggest themselves to me. The first, which is rather crude though easy to carry out, consists in taking an actual cast of the end of the finger. A mould would be made by pressing the

finger into some plastic material, such as fine modelling clay or hot sealing wax, and then, by pouring a warm solution of gelatine into the mould, and allowing it to cool and solidify, a cast would be produced which would yield very perfect finger-prints. But this method would, as a rule, be useless for the purpose of a forger, as it could not, ordinarily, be carried out without the knowledge of the victim; though in the case of dead bodies and people asleep or unconscious or under an anesthetic, it could be practised with success, and would offer the advantage of requiring practically no technical skill or knowledge and no special appliances. The second method, which is much more efficient, and is the one, I have no doubt, that has been used in the present instance, requires more knowledge and skill.[8]

This more efficient method, Thorndyke goes on to explain, involves the photographing, on a reversed plate, of a genuine print. The negative so obtained is exposed to light while in contact with a plate of gelatine which has previously been treated with potassium bichromate. Such gelatine is soluble in hot water until it is exposed to light. Thereafter it is insoluble. Thus, the exposed gelatine plate, after careful washing, provides a pattern of raised ridges which correspond with the parts of the negative through which light has passed; that is, with the dark parts of the original print, assuming it to have been a dark print on a light surface. Hence the forger has provided himself with quite a serviceable stamp. "If an inked roller is passed over this relief, or if the relief is pressed lightly on an inked slab, and then pressed on a sheet of paper, a finger-print will be produced which will be absolutely identical with the original, even to the little white spots which mark the orifices of the sweat glands. It will be impossible to discover any difference between the real finger-print and the counterfeit because, in fact, no difference exists." Thus Thorndyke explained the whole business in court to an attentive judge and—we may be sure—fascinated jury.

What do the fingerprint experts think of the feasibility of

such a forgery? To Galton in 1892, forgery was not even to be contemplated. At the end of a chapter concerned mainly with statistics he wrote:

> Whatever reductions a legitimate criticism may make in the numerical results arrived at in this chapter, the broad fact remains that a complete or nearly complete accordance between two prints of a single finger, and vastly more so between the prints of two or more fingers, *affords evidence requiring no corroboration* that the persons from whom they were made are the same.[9]

He was intending, no doubt, to emphasize that the digital prints of each member of the human race are, if sufficiently closely examined, found to be unique. (The chances of absolute correspondence between two people in this regard are so small as to be negligible.) But Galton's remark was too careless; he ignored the possibility of purposeful copying—that is, of forgery, and his remark emphasizing the overall infallibility of fingerprint evidence was objectionable to Freeman even before he had carried out his own experiments to disprove it. Its unsoundness must have seemed to him simply a matter of common sense. He knew commercial houses in Europe were employing fingerprints in place of signatures for purposes of identification. Yet, compared with the skill necessary to perpetrate the forgery of a signed document, involving penmanship and the use of carefully matched ink and paper, he believed fingerprint forgery to be a single matter, for "a fingerprint is a stamped impression—the finger-tip being the stamp; and it is only necessary to obtain a stamp identical in character with the finger-tip, in order to produce an impression which is an absolute facsimile, in every respect, of the original, and totally indistinguishable from it."[10]

Nevertheless the venerable Galton, who died in 1911 just short of his eighty-ninth birthday, never saw any need to amend his claim. Fingerprints to him were always quite infallible, and succeeding generations of dactylographers have echoed his sentiments.

As recently as 1954, Browne and Brock,[11] in a popularized but generally well-reasoned account of the subject, take Freeman to task thus: "In *The Red Thumb Mark* he employs his specialized knowledge to expose a conspiracy based on the fallacy that fingerprints can be successfully forged." Their remark is not occasioned by any dislike of the author or of Thorndyke, whom they characterize as "the first truly scientific detective in fiction, a medico-legal expert who in technical attainments, extreme thoroughness, lucidity of mind and speech, and even physical appearance, foreshadowed the late Sir Bernard Spilsbury." Browne and Brock nevertheless are critical of *The Red Thumb Mark* and even accuse Freeman of insincerity, charging that he "must have been better informed about the efficiency of the Fingerprint Branch [of Scotland Yard]. But he was following the tradition, established by Poe, adopted by Conan Doyle, and not yet outworn, of the brilliant amateur who must always score off the police."

Wilton, whose interesting book has been mentioned already, says simply that "a fingerprint cannot be forged, at least successfully"[12] but does not elaborate. When a man at Croydon Quarter Sessions in 1938 suggested the possibility that forged prints could be "planted" at the scene of a crime, The London *Times*[13] reported that "fingerprint experts are not disturbed by the suggestion" and that "there has never been such a case since fingerprints were used to identify criminals." Nigel Morland stated flatly a day or two later (in a letter to the editor of the *Times*) that forged fingerprints were out of the question: "A more absurd fallacy could not exist." B. C. Bridges,[14] described in his book as "an internationally recognized expert on identification," is able to provide detailed reasons why successful fingerprint forgery is an impossibility and, in effect, to destroy Freeman's theory:

> Common sense well understands that fingerprints can be copied, just as other concrete objects may be reproduced or imitated. However, the skilled technician will recognize these reproductions as imitations, no more, no less. To contend otherwise is an insult to the intelligence.

Counterfeits of any description are still counterfeits, and detectable as such by those possessing the necessary familiarity in that special field. . . . A fingerprint under the microscope is seen to be an extremely complex subject. . . . An outstanding feature of friction skin patterns, and one that defies successful imitation, is the pore openings . . . the exudation from [which] is deposited upon finger-touched surfaces. The magnified view of a normal fingerprint shows the moisture in tiny pools or droplets, the size, shape, distribution, and general appearance of which, if naturally recorded, will be unmistakable. . . . In its natural state, this moisture deposit is extremely fragile and will be certain to sustain irreparable damage from any contact whatever. A comparable situation is the surface of a dew-drenched leaf upon which the slightest touch disturbs the natural arrangement of its liquid beading. Plainly, it would be impossible to "transplant" this delicate and destructible coating of droplets without crushing them out of all semblance to their original form. The only other alternative open to the would-be forger is to produce a convincing simulation of a genuine fingerprint by artificial means. To do this, a living finger must serve as a model from which a "negative" impression might be made in wax, moulage, or other plastic medium. Then, from the "negative" mold, a "positive" casting could be made, thus furnishing an artificial finger of rubber or similar resilient substance. Its surface would be skinlike, and from it could be made fingerprints, of a sort.

As compared with the "transfer" technique's futility, the making of perfect fingerprint "simulation" is simply out of the question. An artificial "finger," no matter how carefully made to approximate the skin's true texture, certainly can not include what is most necessary to the recording of a normal fingerprint, namely, the sweat ducts. Therefore, though the false finger be

moistened with real body wax, any impression made with
it will have little resemblance to a genuine fingerprint.
Under magnification, the moisture globules, which in a
normal fingerprint appear in irregularly distributed ellip-
soids, will be seen in extremely small spheroids distributed
evenly, and in no way resembling the natural deposit of
the human skin. Nor will the rubber-stamp fingerprint's
general appearance seem genuine; it will look like a rubber
stamp.

After such a blast it would seem foolhardy to attempt any
further to vindicate .Freeman's first Thorndyke book. One   looks
a little more critically at his statement that, with Bernard E. Bishop's
help, he 'was able to produce quite good prints" of his own finger-
tips. Just how good were they; good enough to deceive Scotland
Yard?   One feels a sense of disappointment; if this, the first
Thorndyke story, is built up on a false premise, how many more of
them rest on shaky foundations?

True, neither Browne and Brock nor B. C. Bridges provides
scientific proof that experts *can* distinguish between real and false
fingerprints.   The description of moisture-globule shapes and
patterns sounds convincing enough, and a careful microscopic
examination of a fingerprint in its virgin state—on a drinking
glass, for example—should surely reveal evidence of forgery if it be
present, at any rate to an alert investigator who has the possibility of
forgery present in his mind.

Fingerprints are usually insufflated with a fine powder before
being photographed. Do the oil globules survive this treatment?
In *The Red Thumb Mark* the incriminating mark was made on
paper with defibrinated blood, and many a bloody print has sent
a—presumably—guilty man to his doom. Again, in *The Cat's Eye*
the forged impression had been made in Japanese wax on a glass
sheet. Where are the moisture globules now? The analogy of a
dew-drenched leaf, disturbed by the slightest touch, seems an incon-
gruous analogy for the robust permanence of the sanguinary (or the
waxy) impressions described by Freeman.

It would all be so much more satisfactory if Thorndyke's courtroom demonstration could be repeated with real-life experts on the stand. At Reuben Hornby's trial, two fingerprint experts were asked to withdraw from the court-room while Thorndyke, with the presiding judge's permission, conducted his experiment. A piece of paper was divided by ruled lines into twenty rectangles, and the judge directed which of the spaces should be occupied by Thorndyke's "forgeries" (made with gelatine stamps) and which by Reuben's genuine prints. All this was done in the presence of the two counsel, the judge and the jury. The two experts, Singleton and Nash, were summoned back into court and directed to classify the prints in turn, using a photograph of Reuben's genuine thumb-print for comparison. Each man decided that some of the prints were obviously genuine, some obvious forgeries and some doubtful. Although their conclusions concurred for almost the entire series of prints they were wrong in every case. As the judge phrased it: "When they are quite certain, they are quite wrong, and when they are doubtful, they incline to the wrong conclusion." This seems to be contrary to the laws of statistics. Had they simply guessed they should have performed better. But Thorndyke had a convincing explanation:

> It was quite evident to me . . . that the experts would be unable to distinguish the real from the forged thumb-prints, and, that being so, that they would look for some collateral evidence to guide them. I, therefore, supplied that collateral evidence. Now, if ten prints are taken, without special precautions, from a single finger, it will probably happen that no two of them are exactly alike; for the finger being a rounded object of which only a small part touches the paper, the impressions produced will show little variations according to the part of the finger by which the print is made. But a stamp such as I have used has a flat surface like that of a printer's type, and, like a type, it always prints the same impression. It does not reproduce the finger-tip, but a

particular print of the finger, and so, if ten prints are made with a single stamp, each print will be a mechanical repetition of the other nine. Thus, on a sheet bearing twenty finger-prints of which ten were forgeries made with a single stamp, it would be easy to pick out the ten forged prints by the fact that they would all be mechanical reproductions of one another; while the genuine prints could be distinguished by the fact of their presenting trifling variations in the position of the finger.

Anticipating this line of reasoning, I was careful to make each print with a different stamp, and each stamp was made from a different thumb-print, and I further selected thumb-prints which varied as widely as possible when I made the stamps. Moreover, when I made the real thumb-prints I was careful to put the thumb down in the same position each time so far as I was able; and so it happened that, on the sheet submitted to the experts, the real thumb-prints were nearly all alike, while the forgeries presented considerable variations. The instances in which the witnesses were quite certain were those in which I succeeded in making the genuine prints repeat one another, and the doubtful cases were those in which I partially failed.[15]

Hence the ingenious Thorndyke attained a complete success, and won an acquittal for Reuben Hornby. Of course, he first had to explain why, if forgeries could so closely resemble genuine prints as to be indistinguishable from them, he was so certain that the red thumb mark found in the safe was a fabrication. The answer was that the criminal in this case had been careless, and that the print he had copied contained a striking imperfection. Thorndyke, in fact, adduced three valid reasons why the red impression was not produced by Reuben's thumb.

If Thorndyke had not introduced misleading clues into his

test, would experts have done better? Presumably, yes, for by guess-work alone they should have averaged ten correct results out of twenty. But we do not need to leave the matter there, with the majority of fingerprint experts on one side and Freeman-Thorndyke on the other. It is possible to arrive at a conclusion on the best of all possible grounds: scientific demonstration. Twenty-one years before Browne and Brock told the world that *The Red Thumb Mark* is based on a fallacy, and eight years before internationally recognized expert B. C. Bridges averred that it would be "an insult to the intelligence" to deny that fingerprint practitioners would recognize forged prints, and four years before Nigel Morland's pontifical statement, the matter had been put to the test. Harold Cummins of the Department of Anatomy at Tulane University School of Medicine in New Orleans, a respected authority on finger-, palm-, and footprints, had posed the following question to himself: "Are the experts really justified in their insistence that a finger-print forgery would not escape detection?"[16]   To answer the question in a clear-cut way he prepared a set of counterfeit prints by "a technically crude experiment, accomplished in one evening and without any effort to perfect the results." His method was as follows: a zinc cut, made by a commercial engraver from the original print, and at exactly the original size, was pressed against dental wax and a gelatine cast made from the resulting wax mold; counterfeit prints were made from this gelatine dummy, which had a flesh-like consistency. "A card was prepared bearing a row of four prints of the same digit (a right index finger), two of them being genuine and two counterfeit, this card then being examined by the eight workers successively." These eight people, who worked independently of one another, were "finger-print experts, all having long experience and high standing." Thus, thirty-two decisions were made. If simple guessing had been resorted to, about sixteen of these would have been correct. The experts did rather better than this. They turned in twenty correct diagnoses, eleven incorrect and one doubtful. In the circumstances it is not surprising to read that of the eight experts, five refused use of their names in Dr. Cummins's report.[17]

Note that the experts were told to watch for forgeries, and that these were not fuzzy, partial or otherwise imperfect prints such as might be found at the scene of a crime. Also that Cummins's counterfeit prints could be improved by practice.

His conclusion is quoted in full:

> The results of this test point against acceptance of the common dictum that a counterfeit finger-print would be inevitably recognized as such. The conclusion is conservatively phrased, so as to leave open the possibility that *some experts* (perhaps especially those having comprehensive experience in manufacture of counterfeits and their study) may be able to make reliable judgements in at least some of the cases presented to them.

In the same journal, C. D. Lee,[18] at that time Captain of Detectives of the Police Department in Berkeley, California, wrote: "It is with considerable reluctance that finger-print experts have come to realize that finger-prints can be forged, and to have to admit as much when testifying in court," and draws a pessimistic—even horrifying—conclusion: "It is submitted that the basic idea underlying penal law is the protection of society, that the interests of society are paramount as against those of the individual, and that if an occasional individual's liberty or even his life is sacrificed in war or in peace for the welfare of his country or of society, the sacrifice is not in vain."

In the light of such a conclusion, Freeman's sober admonition of 1916 gains renewed force:

> " . . . I may be permitted to express the hope that those who are concerned in the administration of the law will subject to the most jealous and searching scrutiny all finger-print evidence that is not fully corroborated."

CHAPTER VI

Thorndyke Moves Ahead

Although *The Red Thumb Mark* did not set the Thames on fire, the book sold enough copies to warrant a paper-back edition the following year, 1908. The popularity of the Thorndyke series parallels that of Sherlock Holmes. The first Holmes story "A Study in Scarlet" was published in *Beeton's Christmas Annual* (1887) and received little attention. It required a second long story, "The Sign of Four," and several short ones, over a period of four years, to establish the great detective in public esteem. Holmes' popularity was established by the short tales which appeared in *The Strand* magazine. George Newnes was the publisher and, at his request, the original series of six was extended to twelve stories and Doyle's payments for each story were increased from ₤35 to ₤50.

In the employ of George Newnes at that time was Cyril Arthur Pearson (1866-1921) an ambitious young man who was to

Captain Freeman, R.A.M.C. (Photo
by Gill & Son, Colchester.)

A Freeman Greeting. A 1921 (?) Christmas card drawn
by Freeman. (Courtesy of C. J. A. Freeman.)

leave *The Strand* to establish a publishing house bearing his own name. Of the several magazines he was to launch, the finest, *Pearson's Magazine*, began publication in 1896, and a dozen years later was thriving with a wide, predominantly middle class, readership. It was a handsome publication, rather similar to *The Strand*, printed clearly on good paper with excellent illustrations; certainly a cut above *Cassell's Magazine*—and it paid its writers higher rates.

Freeman seems to have had little difficulty in selling *Pearson's* his first set of eight Thorndyke short stories, beginning with "The Blue Sequin" which appeared in the Christmas issue of 1908. The stories are roughly the same as the contents of *John Thorndyke's Cases,* published by Chatto & Windus in 1909, but the fortunate possessor of the magazines has several pictorial bonuses. Though the handsome portrait of the young Thorndyke was not used in the book, others of H. M. Brock's "admirable and sympathetic drawings" (the description is Freeman's) did appear. The impact of seeing in the magazine the visual clues which confronted Thorndyke when he looked down the barrel of his microscope must have given many readers their first insight into the real gifts which the scientific investigator brings to his work. The nerve ganglion in the first story, the three types of human hair in "The Anthropologist at Large" and the sand from the dead woman's pillow in "A Message from the Deep Sea" are examples of the type of illustrations which had never before appeared alongside popular fiction, and the novelty was effective. Chatto and Windus reproduced some of the photographs in the book; Hodder and Stoughton, in later reprints of *John Thorndyke's Cases* (and in *The Singing Bone* and later collections from *Pearson's*), were unable to do the same for Freeman or his readers, although he always took the trouble to have relevant illustrations prepared.

The photographs for these first stories were produced in the Gravesend home of Frank Standfield, a civil engineer and "a very keen amateur photographer with a scientific turn of mind." Standfield died in 1944 but his daughter still remembers the evenings when Freeman and her father worked on the design and construction of a miniature camera much smaller than anything then on the market. Many hours were spent bending over their combined camera and microscope photographing the strange objects which it was Freeman's responsibility to collect and prepare. Many specimens were readily available; some required a little more trouble. The clue of sea-sand from the Mediterranean in "A Message from the Deep Sea" which led Thorndyke to suspect a sponge-packer who worked in the Minories was indeed collected by Freeman from the clothing of just such a warehouseman.

In addition to such technical verisimilitude, the stories were excellent examples of orthodox detection, often with surprise endings of a wholly satisfying character. That is to say, the reader is surprised in spite of Freeman's scrupulous fairness in providing clues. He is adept at directing the readers' attention away from the vital point while yet displaying it, like a stage conjurer. An illustration of this is a key passage from the first story to be published, "The Blue Sequin." Thorndyke and Jervis are travelling by train towards the scene of a mysterious death:

> Thorndyke gazed absently at the blackened heap [of a newly burned hay-stack] until an empty cattle-truck on the middle track hid it from view. This was followed by a line of goods-wagons, and these by a passenger coach, one compartment of which—a first-class— was closed up and sealed. The train now began to slow down rather suddenly, and a couple of minutes later we brought up in Woldhurst Station.

Few readers realise, until the end of the story, that a clue has been presented here. Such craftsmanship makes much of Freeman's work worth more than a single reading.

Critics, including Miss Dorothy Sayers and Raymond Chandler, have suggested that Freeman is quite safe in presenting all the visible clues to his readers early in each story because they are not conspicuous to anyone not versed in scientific matters. This point is of doubtful validity. Even in Freeman's "inverted" presentation of stories something has to be left for telling later. In some of his early tales, moreover, no special knowledge is needed and a sharp reader should have no difficulty in solving the mystery: one example is "The Blue Sequin" mentioned above; another is "The Aluminium Dagger," about which Freeman's son John provides some amusing information:

> Mr. Standfield helped with some experiments for "The Aluminium Dagger" by lending a long-barrelled revolver which was used to fire a model of the dagger. The dagger was made at a local garage, and made very badly. The blade was made from a massive carpenter's chisel and the handle turned from a brass rod. As a result, the dagger was far too heavy and the washer too massive to expand into the rifling.
>
> The pistol was lashed to a saw bench in the long cellar of 2, Woodville Terrace and pointed at the doorway of the small cellar which opened off it. A piece of string was tied to the trigger and led out through the keyhole of the cellar door. Dr. Freeman stood well to the side of the door while pulling the string. The pistol fired the dagger through the doorway of the small cellar where it made a deep hole in the brickwork and damaged its point, but there was no damage to any other part of it, so it must have struck point first.
>
> Unfortunately, the recoil knocked the saw bench over, so we could not sight the pistol on the mark and test whether the dagger had shot straight enough to hit what it was aimed at. A point we all overlooked at the time was that the dagger struck so hard that there was real danger that it might pass right through a man's body. Which would have looked rather odd!

Another of these earliest Thorndyke short stories, "The Anthropologist at Large," in which, incidentally, Inspector Badger made his first appearance, was chosen by Alfred C. Ward in his survey of detective stories.[1] He compared it with Conan Doyle's

"The Adventure of the Blue Carbuncle" because in each story th
chief clue is a man's shabby felt hat, "and Holmes and Thorndyk
both profess to confine their attention to facts which can b
gathered indisputably from the object under consideration."

Let Sherlock Holmes begin. The hat before him is
thus described: "It was a very ordinary black hat of the
usual round shape, **hard** and much the worse for wear.
The lining had been of red silk, but was a good deal
discoloured. . . . It was pierced in the brim for a hat-
securer, but the elastic was missing. For the rest, it was
cracked, exceedingly dusty, and spotted in several places,
although there seemed to have been some attempt to
hide the discoloured patches by smearing them with
ink." From these details as to the condition of the hat,
Sherlock Holmes makes the following deductions:

(1) *That the man is intellectual.* The hat is a
large one and "a man with so large a brain must have
something in it."

(2) *That he was once well-to-do, but is so no longer.*
The hat is of a style which was in vogue three years
earlier. It is of the best quality, but is now shabby.
Therefore, Holmes argues, the owner must have been
able to buy an expensive hat three years ago, but has
since been unable to replace it.

(3) *That he was a man of foresight, but has suffered
moral retrogression, probably due to drink.* Because he
had had a safety guard fixed to his hat, but had failed to
renew the missing elastic.

(4) *That he is middle-aged, has grizzled hair which
had recently been cut, and that he used lime cream.*
Deduced from the examination of the lining.

(5) *That his wife had ceased to love him.* "This
hat has not been brushed for weeks. When I see you, my
dear Watson, with a week's accumulation of dust upon
your hat, and when your wife allows you to go out in

such a state, I shall fear that you also have been unfortunate enough to lose your wife's affection." (There
is other evidence that the owner of the hat is not a
bachelor.)

(6) *That he probably has not gas laid on in his house.*
Because there are several tallow stains upon the hat--
evidently fallen from a guttering candle.

Before Thorndyke begins to examine the hat which
had come into his hands, he remarks, pertinently, that
some misleading deductions as to the condition of the immediate owner may be made from a hat, unless very
great care is exercised. In the first place, there is a
considerable traffic in second-hand hats, and, conse-
quently, the latest owner may not be identical with the
original purchaser. (This explodes Sherlock Holmes's
second deduction!) Among the observations and reasoned
conclusions which Thorndyke then proceeds to make
are:

(1) *That the man is a Japanese.* Because (a) his
head (judged from the shape of the inside of the hat)
is nearly as broad as it is long; and (b) the small pieces of
hair behind the head-lining are circular in section and of
exceptionally large diameter (typical Japanese characteristics).

(2) *That he is employed in a mother-of-pearl factory.*
Because the dust from the hat when microscopically
examined shows a large proportion of particles of pearl
shell. (This strengthens the view that he was a Japanese,
since the pearl-shell industry is largely conducted by
Eastern races.)

(3) *That he is a decent orderly man.* Because there is
no accumulation of old dust on the outside of the hat.

Thorndyke's main deductions are fewer than those
of Sherlock Holmes, but they are sounder, less capricious,
and more practical. From the evidence provided by the
hat, Thorndyke does discover his man; but all that Holmes

sets forth goes for nothing, since he has to advertise in all
the evening papers before he can get in touch with his
wanted person.

Particularly typical of the weak irrelevances which
emanate from Holmes, is the allegation that the unknown
man's wife no longer loves him, because his headgear is
particularly dusty! Certainly it must be conceded that
Holmes had not experienced the ways of a loving wife,
nor the advantage of reading Drinkwater's *Abraham
Lincoln,* which has some illuminating dialogue concerning
loving but importunate wives and disreputable hats; but,
in any event, the point was a purposeless superfluity—
in which respect Sherlock Holmes is frequently guilty. . . .

The fact is, that Holmes was a *poseur* first and an
amateur detective afterwards. His amazing success is
rather a put-up job between him and his creator; and
his occasional failures are a confidence trick, to suggest
that there is really no deception in his triumphs. Thorndyke, on the other hand, is a straightforward scientific
investigator, with very little nonsense about him. Perhaps
he is a somewhat too-well-oiled piece of mechanism to
be a satisfactory fictional character; and he has none of
those memorable personal mannerisms which have made
Sherlock Holmes more real to the multitude than is the
whole police force.   Story for the sake of story is
more generously given by Conan Doyle than by Austin
Freeman—so far as the latter's short tales are concerned.
In the novels the position is probably reversed.

In addition, it has to be kept in mind that Conan
Doyle was the first in England to develop the few hints
thrown out by Poe; and that most later writers are in
some measure disciples—if unwilling and critical disciples—
of Conan Doyle.

Of the remaining stories in the first set published in *Pearson's,*
"The Scarred Finger" was omitted from the book *John Thorndyke's*

Cases and was included, instead, in *The Singing Bone* where it is exceptional, as we shall see, in being the only story not of the "inverted" type. In "The Stranger's Latchkey," about the kidnaping of a six-year-old boy, Freeman introduced into the book version a light-hearted passage about Thorndyke, the narrator (as usual) being Christopher Jervis:

> "What sort of man is Dr. Thorndyke?" asked Mrs. Haldean. "I feel quite curious about him. Is he at all human, for instance?"
>
> "He is entirely human," I replied; "the accepted tests of humanity being, as I understand, the habitual adoption of the erect posture in locomotion, and the relative position of the end of the thumb—" "I don't mean that," interrupted Mrs. Haldean. "I mean human in things that matter."
>
> "I think these things matter," I rejoined. "Consider, Mrs. Haldean, what would happen if my learned colleague were to be seen in wig and gown, walking towards the Law Courts in any posture other than the erect. It would be a public scandal."

"The Man with the Nailed Shoes," one of *John Thorndyke's Cases,* never appeared in *Pearson's* and has not so far been traced to any other magazine. It is about twice the length of the companion stories and may have been turned down for magazine publication on this account. "The Mandarin's Pearl," a story referred to in an earlier chapter, is about a neurotic young man with the optical "hippus." Its plot—the driving of the young man to suicide for financial gain by means of an optical illusion—is similar to that of a story written years later, "The Apparition of Burling Court," and is inferior to it. For this reason, perhaps, it was omitted along with two others of this first set from the London version of the *Dr. Thorndyke Omnibus* (1929). Incidentally, Thorndyke was to mention the affair of the Mandarin and his pearl at an inquest in *Helen Vardon's Confession* (1922).

Between the first group of stories and the second, seventeen months elapsed. We know very little about Freeman's life at that time. He was engaged in writing another Thorndyke novel—his third—which was to be titled *The Eye of Osiris,* while his first still lay around the house, unpublished.

During this period he had an inspiration, a happy thought which was to bring him fame in histories of detection. He had already made his mark—although the fact was evident to only a limited number of readers—by introducing the first real scientific investigator into the pages of detective fiction. Now he was to devise an entirely new form of story, in which he would give away the secret of the crime from the start and rely entirely on the ingenuity of his detective, and the sheer excitement of the deductive process in action, to draw the reader along to the end of the story.

It was a bold stroke for a writer with so little success behind him and such a tiny amount of money in the bank. "Would there be any story left to tell when the reader had all the facts?" wondered Freeman. "I believed that there would; and, as an experiment to test the justice of my belief, I wrote 'The Case of Oscar Brodski.' Here, the usual conditions are reversed; the reader knows everything, the detective knows nothing, and the interest focuses on the unexpected significance of trivial circumstances."[2]

In the first part of this story (and of all his other stories in the same vein) the third-person narrative style is employed. We are able to view the murder scene as detached observers and also have the advantage of entering into the thoughts of one of the principals, usually the murderer. The second part of each story is related by Jervis, and describes how Thorndyke is brought into each case and, with remarkable dispatch, soon knows more about the crime than we do.

The first and best of the stories recounts the murder of Oscar Brodski, dealer in precious stones, in the home of a small-time burglar, Silas Hickler, near a country railway station. Hickler's motive is possession of the packet of diamonds he knows his victim to be carrying, and his method of disposing of the body is to lay it across the railway track shortly before a freight train is expected, thus simulating suicide or accidental death. His mistake is forgettin Brodski's felt hat, which he leaves behind at his home when h carries the body away; however, he remembers it when he returns t the house and is able to burn it in the fireplace.

There are many explanations for the fascination the stor holds for connoisseurs of the detective story. If detection is wha the customers like, here is detection in its purest form, with mor inferences per page than in any other story up to that time or since The dramatic impact is enhanced by Freeman's skillful construction The first and second halves of the tale overlap and we see Thorndyk first through the murderer's eyes, as a stranger in the excited thron on the railway platform, and later as Jervis describes him, his antece dents nicely in place. Some of the dialogue of this scene is hear twice.[3] It is all remarkably effective. Then there is striking unit of time and place. Thorndyke is on the spot when the body i brought into the station and he has the murder solved, thanks to hi invaluable green research case, without ever leaving the scene.

Finally, there is that useful Thorndyke foil, the hostile loca official, in this case a police inspector, eager to interfere witl Thorndyke's activities at every turn, by means of sarcasm when al else fails. And against Thorndyke's imperturbable bonhomie, sar casm invariably fails too.

The story deserves its honored place in the history of detection though few of its admirers are aware that it is based on an actua case. Here is Freeman's brief account of it, written many year: later:

> The methods of even famous murderers are commonly crude and even foolish, and the gross and palpable traces that they leave can be followed by the most obvious and commonplace means. Indeed in the whole of my reading— with some experience as a prison medical officer—I have met with but a single case which seemed to be worth using for fiction: the one on which I founded my story of "The Case of Oscar Brodski." And even this case was selected less for its ingenuity of plan than for the

excellent opening that it offered for medico-legal investigation.[4]

The case was that of R. *v* Watson and wife (Nottingham
Assizes, March 15, 1867). John and Mary Watson were accused of
the murder of Henry Raynor on the evening of 17th November,
1866. Raynor was a rent collector who lived with his wife and large
family in Nottingham. He had formerly lived in half a cottage in
Carlton, a village two or three miles to the east of the city, the other
half of the modest dwelling being occupied by the Watsons and their
only child. The two families had lived, by all accounts, in an atmosphere made acrimonious by constant dispute over such matters,
for example, as who should have the use of the vegetable produce
from the garden. When Raynor left the village he kept ownership of
the Carlton property and visited the village frequently. He had
reason to suspect the Watsons of using a copper in one of his
outhouses to boil potatoes for their pigs and was determined to
put a stop to the practice.

On the fatal day, a Saturday, he travelled to Carlton with a pad-
lock in his pocket and was seen fit and well at six in the evening.
At 7:40 p.m. a railway worker observed his dead body on the line
with the neck across one of the rails, in such a position that it would
surely have been decapitated by the 8:10 train. There were blows a-
bout the head such as a poker might have caused, and some bleeding,
but no great vessels had been damaged. His watch and money had
disappeared and his hat was nowhere to be seen. Medical examination showed that death had been caused by manual strangulation.

Professor Alfred Swayne Taylor was called in, and he later
described the medico-legal aspects in his textbook, where Freeman
picked them up. "There were marks of dragging between the cottage
and the railway, and marks corresponding with Watson's boots."

On searching the house [wrote Taylor] an iron-rake
was found concealed on a shelf. This was delivered to me
for examination. A cindery substance adhered to one end
of it, looking as if it had undergone fusion. On heating

a portion of it the smell of burnt shellac was emitted, and on acting on it with alcohol a resinous solution like that of shellac was obtained. The alcohol caused the separation of some fibres which under the microscope proved to be the hair of some animal of the order rodentia. . . . On being questioned respecting the rake the male prisoner said he himself had used it . . . for cleaning out a cesspool.

A hat similar to that worn by the deceased, and purchased at the same shop, was burnt. The cindery ash was collected, and submitted to examination with precisely similar results. These hats are made of felt chiefly from rabbit's and hare's fur, and this is combined with a quantity of shellac.

. . . Where was the hat of the deceased? . . . It was suggested for the prosecution that, in dragging the body to the railway track to conceal the murder, the hat was accidentally left in the cottage. To have returned with it to the railway might have led to detection [so they burned it in the grate].[5]

The prisoners had no effective defense to offer to this. To explain blood-stained clothes found in their home they called witnesses to testify to the killing of a pig three days before the murder. Taylor, in the witness box, expressed disbelief in this explanation but could not swear that the blood stains were human. In spite of the grave suspicion attaching to the Watsons, the jury found them "not guilty," and they were forthwith acquitted. (Taylor does not make this fact clear in his account and Freeman appears to have believed that a guilty verdict was returned.)

It is not practicable to examine in such detail Freeman's other inverted stories. All are fine examples of detection, and most have convincing dramatic and human qualities. One of them, however, did not satisfy *Pearson's* and it was published instead in the *Novel Magazine,* another A. C. Pearson publication, ahead of the others. This story, "The Willowdale Mystery," better known by its

Singing Bone title, "A Wastrel's Romance," is the only one of the series which does not involve a capital crime; moreover, it is excessively sentimental.   Nevertheless, the central feature of the process of the detective has a fascination all its own. Is it possible to determine a thief's approximate place of residence solely from the dust found on a coat left behind at the scene of an attempted robbery? If he chooses his residence carefully, with a rice mill on one side, a flour mill on the other and cocoa and black-lead factories within sniffing distance, why not? Thorndyke with his microscope and Post Office directory can work wonders with such clues as that!

John Freeman remembers his father's research for this story: he left microscope slides, no doubt moistened with glycerine, on the wall of one of the factories concerned, in the Dockhead area of East London south of the Thames, to satisfy himself of the nature and quantity of dust likely to be deposited in the locality.

For another of the excellent inverted stories, "The Echo of a Mutiny," published in *Pearson's* as "Death on the Girdler," Freeman used his memories of his stay in Ramsgate, his journeys down the Thames estuary and the investigation he had made for his articles in *Cassell's Magazine* on lighthouses. While Freeman lived in Ramsgate, reports his son, two collier brigs were still using the harbour there, and the Trinity House tender "Lord Warden" was stationed in the other harbor; which would account for all the craft mentioned in the story.

The remaining tale of the inverted type to be published in *The Singing Bone* was "A Case of Premeditation" in which Freeman illustrated a point he felt was misunderstood: that bloodhounds, like fingerprints, are no use without corroboration for fixing a crime on an individual. As Thorndyke put it: "The hound possesses a special sense—the olfactory—which in man is quite rudimentary. He thinks, so to speak, in terms of smell, and his thoughts are untranslatable to beings in whom the sense of smell is undeveloped. We have presented to the hound a knife, and he discovers in it certain odorous properties; he discovers similar or related odorous properties in a tract of land and a human individual—Ellis. We cannot verify his discoveries or ascertain their nature. What remains? All that we can say is that there appears to exist some odorous relation between the knife and the man Ellis. But until we can ascertain the nature of that relation, we cannot estimate its evidential value or bearing."

Pearson's published one more inverted story, "The Dead Hand," in October and November, 1912, but by that time *The Singing Bone* had been issued as a collection of five stories, comprising the first four inverted stories from *Pearson's* together with an as yet uncollected tale from the earlier series, "The Scarred Finger," which for *Singing Bone* purposes was retitled "The Old Lag" and rather awkwardly divided into two parts so that it took on the semblance, though not the substance, of the inverted stories which appeared with it.

Freeman wrote two more inverted stories during 1913 and 1914, "Percival Bland's Proxy" and "The Missing Mortgagee," both of which appeared in *The Great Portrait Mystery* (1918) which we shall consider in a later chapter.

"The Dead Hand" was much longer than the previous inverted stories published in *Pearson's,* but it was accepted by the magazine eagerly enough, for they recognized its high quality, and it appeared in the two parts into which it naturally falls. Freeman thought so highly of the story that, when his next volume of short tales was brought out in 1918, he withheld it, put it aside for several years, and then greatly increased its length to produce the full-scale Thorndyke novel, *The Shadow of the Wolf.*

Critical interest in *The Singing Bone* at the time of publication was moderate. It has taken many years for critics to appreciate Freeman's masterstroke and he has continued to appeal to a rather small but discriminating minority. As John Adams said in a contemporary article on Freeman:

> The objection to this duplicate method, which Mr. Freeman claims to have been justified by its success, is that it emphasises the purely logical aspects of the different cases. It is not so much a series of stories as

a set of exercises. A teacher might be tempted to **use** them as problems in applied logic. This logical interest is no doubt prominent in other books, notably in the summing up at the symposium at the end of *The Eye of Osiris,* but in the short stories it is deliberately brought forward as the chief matter. Nothing but the author's remarkable skill in character delineation and graphic narrative could save the stories from being regarded as technical studies, such as find a suitable place in a course on forensic medicine.

Indeed, the whole position of Mr. Freeman depends upon the class of readers to whom he appeals. His work is certainly beyond the range of the ordinary devourer of "sleuth" novels. He makes very great demands on the attention of his readers. To read these books intelligently implies a definite exercise in the use of Mill's Canons of Inductive Logic and the books might form a very practical means of testing the student's mastery of these canons. A very obvious and natural criticism of the stories is that they are too clever: they ask too much of the reader. But, unlike some clever writers, Mr. Freeman is clever enough to carry off his cleverness. His exposition is so clear, his arrangement of events so methodical, that the reader is led along with the minimum amount of effort consistent with a very definite exercise of the reason. Stupid and lazy readers may be warned off, but the ordinary intelligent reader may rely upon having from Mr. Freeman a course in mental gymnastics conducted under the pleasantest conditions. [6]

It may be added that the class of readers to whom Freeman's books appeal has steadily increased in proportion since these words were written so that in recent years, with a new emphasis on the scientific method as opposed to the romantic or intuitive— in detection as in most other matters—Freeman can be said to be well suited to those modern readers who stumble upon his books.

At least one reader can testify to his capacity for teaching a young mind, in a most fascinating way, the validity of the scientific approach, not only to criminal problems but, by extension, to the affairs of life.

Dorothy Sayers also praised the inverted stories: "Mr. Freeman has had few followers, and appears to have himself abandoned the formula, which is rather a pity."[7] Actually, although Freeman wrote no more inverted *short* stories, the full-length Thorndyke novels *The Shadow of the Wolf* and *Mr. Pottermack's Oversight* are of this form. On the same subject it should be pointed out that *When Rogues Fall Out* (*Dr. Thorndyke's Discovery*, 1932) is partly of the inverted type and that in many other stories Freeman subordinated the surprise element to matters, such as scientific accuracy, plausibility and fairness to the reader, which he considered more important.

Between publication of the inverted stories in *Pearson's* and *The Singing Bone, The Eye of Osiris* appeared. It is an excellent early Thorndyke novel and the first to employ a narrator other than Jervis, although he is awkwardly present, for he has no active role to play. The new story-teller, Paul Berkeley, is yet another young physician, and he is introduced to supply the story with a suitor for the heroine when the detection has been brought to a satisfactory conclusion by Thorndyke, Freeman having thoughtlessly removed Jervis from the matrimonial stakes by betrothing him to Juliet Gibson in *The Red Thumb Mark*.

There is a subtle nostalgic charm about *The Eye of Osiris*. Much of the action of the story takes place in the Egyptology department of the British Museum, where Berkeley and the heroine, Ruth Bellingham, are engaged on a literary project, but spend a great deal of time observing the mummies instead. The mystery concerns the sudden disappearance of Ruth's uncle, John Bellingham, and, two years later, the sporadic appearance, in assorted fish ponds and water-cress beds, of bits and pieces of a human skeleton. There is space here only to touch on one or two high spots of what is undoubtedly a major detective story of the century.

In one fascinating chapter Thorndyke pits himself against

the crusty old lawyer, Jellicoe, in a battle of wits and finds he has met his match. In another chapter, following the discovery in the water-cress bed Freeman waxes eloquent on the life-cycle of the liver-fluke which afflicts sheep. Additionally, *Osiris* contains one of Freeman's best jokes. An action for presumption of death is underway in Probate Court, and counsel has just explained that " 'the application is based upon the circumstances of the disappearance [of John Bellingham] which were, in many respects, very singular, the most remarkable feature of that disappearance being, perhaps, its suddenness and completeness.' Here the judge remarked in a still small voice that 'It would, perhaps have been even more remarkable if the testator had disappeared gradually and incompletely'." But what is most surprising of all for a detective novel of that time is Thorndyke's advice when Berkeley's love affair appears headed for disaster:

> "We should be bad biologists and worse physicians if we should underestimate the importance of that which is nature's chiefest care. The one salient biological truth is the paramount importance of sex; and we are deaf and blind if we do not hear and see it in everything that lives when we look abroad upon the world; when we listen to the spring song of the birds, or when we consider the lilies of the field. And as is man to the lower organisms, so is human love to their merely reflex manifestations of sex. I will maintain, and I am sure you will agree with me, I know, that the love of a serious and honourable man for a woman who is worthy of him is the most momentous of all human affairs. It is the foundation of social life, and its failure is a serious calamity, not only to those whose lives may be thereby spoilt, but to society at large."

Hodder and Stoughton, the publishing house, began their long association with Freeman with their acceptance of *The Eye of Osiris* for their autumn list in 1911. Undaunted by a lack of

popular acclaims and quite convinced of the superiority of his
detective over much of the competition, Freeman persuaded Hodder
to take the manuscript of *The Mystery of 31, New Inn*. This was
the story, mentioned earlier, which was born of Freeman's ophthalmic experiences at the Westminster Hospital. It was probably first
written like *The Shadow of the Wolf* in novella form and lengthened
for publication. The Ridgway Company of New York, which was
about to launch a new magazine concerned largely with action stories
from the distant, exotic parts of the world, had bought the story in
its original novella form. It duly appeared with the shortened title
31, New Inn in *Adventure*, Volume 1, No. 3 dated January, 1911.
One interesting variant concerns the symptoms of a patient examined
under mysterious circumstances by Jervis, acting as *locum tenens*
to a general practitioner. In the novella version, Jervis and Thorndyke
had no difficulty in deciding on a diagnosis of morphine poisoning.
In going over the story, Freeman brought the facts more completely
into line with current medical thought by introducing at least the
possibility of sleeping sickness.

More than one critic of detective fiction has been annoyed by
Freeman's preface to *The Mystery of 31, New Inn*, in which he
observed:

> Commenting upon [*The Red Thumb Mark*] in respect
> of which I had claimed to have been careful to adhere
> to common probabilities and to have made use only of
> really practicable methods of investigation, a critic re-
> marked that this was of no consequence whatever so
> long as the story was amusing.
>
> Few people, I imagine, will agree with him. To
> most readers, and certainly to the kind of reader for whom
> an author is willing to take trouble, complete realism in
> respect of incidents and methods is an essential factor in
> maintaining the interest of a detective story. Hence it
> may be worth while to mention that Thorndyke's method
> of producing a track chart, described in Chapters II
> and III, has been actually used in practice.

Freeman then explained that it was a modification of one devised by him in Ashanti, and that "the resulting route-map was surprisingly accurate."

The anonymous critic referred to by Freeman was joined by others in later years. "The trouble with Dr. Freeman," wrote H. Douglas Thomson,[8] "is just this: he takes too much pains. . . . As regards the practicability of the experiments, the general public would just as soon have him confess in a monthly magazine the impossibility of them. One and all would acclaim him as the perpetrator of a capital hoax." One and all in the meantime can probably agree that H. Douglas Thomson and Dr. Thorndyke would be unlikely to see eye to eye on any subject. Readers can discover for themselves the reasons for Jervis's need of a track chart through the streets of London. The story is not one of Freeman's best, lacking the romance of *The Eye of Osiris* and depending too much on the reader's failure to discern a fairly obvious connection between two sets of ostensibly separate events.

Freeman's personal life at this time was quiet. His years of ill-health undoubtedly taxed what had been an abundant store of natural energy, and he was no longer a young man. His first Thorndyke book was published as he turned forty-five, and he led thereafter a reflective life, restricting his exercise to daily walks which lasted for hours, during which he would arrange a chapter in his mind, to be later set down on paper with his favorite fountain pen in his small neat hand, with only an occasional correction made before he sent it to be typed.

James S. Warrack tells me that Freeman called in the evenings quite frequently to talk to Warrack senior, a Gravesend barrister and physician, about the medical and legal details of the books he was planning. In the summer the Freemans and the Warracks sometimes went off to the seaside together, Mrs. Freeman being accustomed to take the children off on rambles to give her husband "peace and quiet."

During such periods of reflection, Freeman pondered the question of his literary future. He was building up a small reputation among thoughtful people by his carefully constructed detective stories, but the financial returns were modest.   His novel *The Queen's Treasure,* written with Pitcairn, was an adventure story set in England, and for some reason it had not been sold.   Still, he was satisfied that his only published adventure story up to this time, *The Golden Pool,* was sound.   It had given him great satisfaction to write it and to do the small amount of historical research it demanded, and now it occurred to him to attempt something of a similar nature again.   Freeman, at some period prior to 1905, had taken a course of nautical astronomy at the Royal Geographical Society, and he had picked up a great many details of seamanship in the course of his various journeys to and from West Africa "and in conversation with such ship-masters and shellbacks as I met from time to time."   Freeman loved the sea, and enjoyed visiting boat-building sheds around Gravesend to watch the men at work and engage them in conversation.   "I may say that my son and I built a sixteen-foot boat in the back garden (he did most of the work) having fitted a steam trunk to the scullery boiler; which was necessary as the midship section was broad and there was conse-quently a sharp twist in the garboard strake at each end.   We made quite a workmanlike job of it."[9]

When *The Unwilling Adventurer* was published by Hodder and Stoughton in September, 1913, many readers must have been disappointed to find it was not another detective mystery.   Instead it is the story of young Robert Hawke of Shorne, a real village near Gravesend, in 1791.   His troubles begin when he is wrongly accused of the murder of a neighbour, but this little misunder-standing is on the point of being cleared up when he is suddenly impressed into the Navy with the connivance of his rascally cousin, Percival, commander of the frigate "Asphodel," outward bound for the South Atlantic.   From this point on, Freeman's prose is awash with references to flying jibbooms, topgallant-masts, studding-sails and orlop decks.   They encounter more than once the pirate schooner "Autolycus," which ironic name was given to it by its remarkable and erudite captain.   After being briefly marooned on a South Atlantic island Hawke finds himself a guest on the "Autolycus."

The pirate captain, Ishmael Parradine, ranks as one of Freeman's most striking characterisations. With the possible exception of Jules Verne's Captain Nemo, he is also the most lettered brigand the seven seas have witnessed. Here he is in his cabin as Hawke first meets him:

> Seated in an elbow chair, with a book on his knee and several others open on the table, as if for reference, was a grave-looking, middle-aged man, primly dressed in a suit of black and wearing a neat, grey wig. His neck-cloth and ruffled shirt were white as snow, his hands daintily clean and well-kept, and his appearance generally marked by the precise care of externals that one might look for in a fashionable attorney or physician.

Parradine and Hawke, despite their disparity in outlook, get along well together. The crew of cutthroats is hostile to both, resentful of Hawke as an outsider, and suspicious that their captain desires to decamp, "in which surmise," Parradine tells Hawke, "they have been entirely correct, for it has always, since I entered the trade, been my fixed purpose to retire, in due course, with a modest competency, and spend the remainder of my life in the society of persons of cultivation amidst the delights of gentle and rural surroundings. My worthy company propose to acquire, by summary measures, the reversion of my small property, but with your esteemed support, I have little doubt of disappointing them."

Note that Parradine's conversation has more than a hint of Brodribb and Penfield in it. In the captain's diabolical "alarum," described a little later, Freeman's mechanical ingenuity is evident. Parradine has just been warned, by one of his officers, of the ugly mood of the crew:

> "Ha!" exclaimed the captain, looking up quickly from the chart over which he was poring, "think ye so, my dear Starbuck. Well, we must be prepared; we must set the alarum. Tell Crump that we are setting the

alarum in case he should wish to speak to me in his
watch.   And if you let the fact leak out, 'twould be no
harm.   An accident would be such an unspeakably
shocking thing."

"I'll tell Crump, and let someone overhear me,"
replied Starbuck with a chuckle. "They won't want no
badger-drorin', I'll answer for it," and he departed,
gurgling with inward mirth.

Shortly afterwards the captain proceeded to set
the alarum, and a very curious process it was. Taking
from a drawer in the cabinet a very large and powerful
blunderbuss, he cleaned out its vent with great care,
oiled the lock and examined the flint. Then he poured
into it an enormous charge of powder, and, having
secured this with several wads, filled up the barrel with
about three-quarters of a pound of buck-shot, mixed
with slugs and pistol balls, and crammed another wad
on top of it all; and when he had primed it liberally
with fine, mealed powder, he lashed this formidable engine
of destruction to a large cleat—apparently fixed for the
purpose—on the side of the cabin about two feet from
the deck, in such a position that its muzzle pointed at
the opening of the door . . .

"Do you often set your alarum?" I enquired, as
my host stepped back [after attaching the triggers to a
booby trap on the door] and viewed his invention with
a satisfied smile.

"Not often," he replied, "On occasions when little
misunderstandings arise, such as the   present, I am led
to take this precaution; but they are rare. On one of these
occasions, not long since, a most regrettable accident
occurred; for the silly fellows, in their high-spirited,
frolicsome way, must needs burst into the cabin at
midnight.   A dreadful explosion followed, and it pains
me to recall that many suffered injury—some, indeed,

were cut off from among us—at which I was the more
afflicted from being, as one might say, the innocent
cause of the mishap."

How Hawke and Parradine escape from the "Autolycus"
and thereafter separate; how Hawke becomes an unwilling passenger
on a slave-trader and later is taken to England as a deserter; and
how he defeats the charge while at the same time getting even with
the villainous Percival; these matters make up the remainder of
The Unwilling Adventurer.

As the reader closes the book, he is likely to reflect that this,
the author's only historical romance, is well wrought. His technical
mastery of sailing ships and natural history are sound and no less
than we expect of him.   His hero is never in mortal danger and
suspense is as absent here as in most Thorndyke novels.   On the
other hand, *The Unwilling Adventurer* lacks also the frivolity
which gravely mars *Danby Croker, Flighty Phyllis* and *Shuttlebury
Cobb,* and comes close to duplicating the steady, informed pace of
The Golden Pool.

I have found no corroboration of a statement, in a local
obituary notice, that Freeman regarded *The Unwilling Adventurer*
as his best book.   It could be true.   Conan Doyle rather despised
Sherlock Holmes; Tschaikowsky hated his "Casse Noissette;" Sullivan
resented the popularity of the Savoy operas, which he felt put his
oratorios in the shade.   "It is true, as Andrew Lang pointed out
years ago, that of all people authors appear to be their own
worst critics."[10]

On the other hand, what was undoubtedly Freeman's worst
book had been appearing in serial form in *Pearson's* during the
summer of 1913 as Freeman completed writing his sea story.
Originally called *A Hunter of Criminals,* it was to have two other
titles in its book editions.   It took time to find a publisher for the
series, however.   Hodder and Stoughton rejected it, saying it was
"a horrible book."   The John C. Winston Company of Philadelphia,
who had earlier published *The Mystery of 31, New Inn* in a handsome
edition, were willing to buy the American rights to the new book.

It was retitled *The Uttermost Farthing,* Freeman's only book to be published first in America. When it did appear in England six years later, it was as a small undistinguished book; Freeman described it as "a scrubby little volume," its almost undiscernable title, *A Savant's Vendetta,* on the front cover. Its most striking feature was an advertisement for Fry's Breakfast Cocoa stamped in black on the back. Even the publisher C. Arthur Pearson, proprietor of the magazine in which the six installments had appeared, was apparently embarrassed by the unfortunate format and described it as the "first cheap edition."

The story is made up of a series of episodes. Professor Humphrey Challoner's wife has been killed by an unknown burglar. He thereafter devotes his life to enticing members of that nefarious profession to his home and therewith disposing of them. His wife's slayer, he knows, possesses ringed hair (an unusual condition, except in Freeman stories) and he examines the hair of each victim under the microscope before adding the skeleton and the shrunken head respectively to his two collections. Each chapter recounts a new killing, with remorseless monotony. The Professor, who dies a natural death as the story opens, leaves his private museum and diary to his physician, Wharton, who only then discovers the macabre story of his patient's last years. Wharton and, to some extent, Freeman seem to sympathize with Challoner's ends, if not with his means, and it is this which makes the book so chilling. A little-known pendant to this series of adventures appeared a few years later. In "The Mystery of Hoo Marsh,"[11] Challoner was brought back to life in an episode involving fifteen anarchists. The Professor, disguised as a barber in the East End, blows them all up in a ramshackle shed to which he has lured them. The tale is, incredibly, even more tasteless than those in the main series in which, after all, the bereaved Professor had something approaching a reasonable motive for his overkill philosophy. The Challoner series, in short, is vastly inferior to Freeman's other work.

Before Freeman's routine was disrupted by the First World War he wrote one more Thorndyke novel, *A Silent Witness,* and it is one of his best. The opening became a favorite one with Freeman, who was to use variants of it in *The D'Arblay Mystery* (1926) and *The Stoneware Monkey* (1938). In *A Silent Witness*, published in the autumn of 1914, young Dr. Jardine stumbles on the dead body of a priest in a Hampstead lane one rainy midnight. While the police are being summoned the body vanishes and from there on the plot, as they say, thickens. There are, for example, two attempts on Jardine's life (by carbon dioxide suffocation in a mineral water factory and then by drowning in the Thames); and complicated romantic situations between Jardine and two women, each very different from the other: a landscape artist, Sylvia Vyne, and the enigmatic Letitia Samway who ultimately saves Jardine's life at the cost of her own. It is Letitia, the married woman, not Sylvia, the conventional heroine, who fills Jardine's mind as the book comes to an end. The nature of his concurrent emotional involvements with the two women deserves a separate study, and alone would raise *A Silent Witness* to a level decisively above most detective stories. Add to this the most convincing laboratory-workshop scene ever described and a superb summing-up by Thorndyke, and a remarkable book results.

Freeman's point of departure in constructing the story was consideration of which causes of death could still be detected after cremation. To sustain a lengthy story on this topic, the time factors would have to be confused sufficiently to lead readers astray. Freeman achieves this brilliantly, and in the final experiment depicts a little world astir in Thorndyke's laboratory, with the furnace glow lighting up a strange and busy scene. A certain Professor Woodfield assists Thorndyke in powdering a casket-full of cremated bones and turning them into slag. The indispensible Polton is in attendance of course, as well as the utterly dispensible (in this book especially) Jervis, and several onlookers, one of whom is a scandalized priest, Father Humperdinck. " 'Ashes to ashes' was an intelligible formula, but 'ashes to slag' was quite another matter, for which no provision had been made in any known ritual." To another historian of the detective novel, this book is a classic portrayal of a criminal fighting to the end. "Such a war," he wrote, "is better than a tame pursuit."[12]

From Thorndyke's first appearance in *The Red Thumb Mark* (1907) until *A Silent Witness*, published in 1914, the stories in which the great detective appear show steady improvement. (This is more evident if they are placed in order of *composition*.)

Freeman's non-Thorndyke tales exhibit no parallel progression during the same period. *The Golden Pool* (1905) is a good, hearty adventure story, as is *The Unwilling Adventurer* (1913). Neither story is superior to the other, although this writer prefers the earlier book, which is based on a sounder sentiment. *The Uttermost Farthing* is a lamentable falling off, being not only technically poor but lacking Freeman's customary detachment and irony.

In June, 1914, the events leading to the first World War were set in motion. It was at this inopportune time that *A Silent Witness* was offered to an inattentive public, and, not long after, its author was to be called away, leaving Dr. Thorndyke in limbo for several years.

CHAPTER VII

Arms and Superman

When Freeman joined the Royal Army Medical Corps in February, 1915, he was almost fifty-three. Although his health had improved over the years it was out of the question that he could be sent abroad, especially to a malarial country—as even France was then classified. It is interesting to glance through his Army records and find under languages: "Latin (elementary), French, German and Hausa." His qualifications are recorded as "Member of the Royal College of Surgeons and Licentiate of the Society of Apothecaries;" a Royal Geographic Society certificate in surveying is also noted.

Freeman began his four years of service at Maidstone, as a Lieutenant in the 3/1st Home Counties Field Ambulance, but Mr. S. Lewis Stevenson, writing from Gravesend in 1964, recalls him as "Captain Freeman" (as do most of his acquaintances of those days) because he was promoted after six months and retained that

116

rank for the remainder of his active service:

I knew him quite well. It was in May 1915 that I went
down to Maidstone to enlist in the 3/1st Home Counties
Field Ambulance, and Captain Freeman gave me a medical
examination. He was very thorough, pointing out that
I had a small varicose vein at the back of my knee.
This, he said, would not interfere with my military
service, but might become more serious in later years.
(How right he was!)   I was accepted and was posted
to C Section, and found that Captain Freeman was in
charge. He was always extremely kind and thoughtful,
too much of a kindly gentleman to be a really good
soldier. He did well, however. I remember how he used
to take us in "Squad and Company" drill and marched
us up hill and down for hours until we were all thoroughly
tired out.   Then, having stood us "at ease" he would
say very quietly and with a smile, "Now, if you will all   sit
down on the grass, I will proceed to give you a lecture."
And he could do that!

On his promotion to Captain, Freeman moved briefly in turn
to Smith's Lawn, Windsor; Heston Park, Tring; and Tonbridge,
Kent.   Perhaps some or all of these postings related to training
programs.   At any rate, he was back in Maidstone at the end of
March, 1916, and put in charge of the newly formed 4/1st and
4/2nd Home Counties Field Ambulances. The unit soon moved
to Halton Camp, near Wendover in Buckinghamshire. Let us hear
again from Mr. Stevenson, who met Freeman's younger son
Lawrence (Leo) at Halton.

In August, 1916, I was on a draft for Salonica and so
was Leo. I shall never forget that 12th August (my
21st birthday). We left Wendover at 6 am and Captain
Freeman, as our C. O., marched at our head from the
Camp to the station. Arriving at Baker Street, Captain

Freeman marched us all through London to Waterloo Station (a distance of about three miles), where we entrained for Southampton.

Captain Freeman chatted with us all on the quayside until we went aboard the "Gloucester Castle," and at 3:30 pm the gangways were down and we began to move. I shall never forget that as we moved we hung over the rail and waved to our C. O. whom we really loved as a father, and he—as a father—stood there on the quay waving his stick and then his hand. As I looked I could see that his eyes were filled with tears, for he was waving farewell to "his boys" and to his own son. As long as I could see that quay I saw that solitary figure waving a long farewell, a sight that is indelibly printed upon my memory.

Mr. H. C. Bryan is able to tell us something of Freeman's service at Halton Camp. He writes:

I myself was wounded in May, 1915, shortly after the Germans launched the first gas attack, and was invalided home. It was in November or December, 1916, after being in hospital for a further operation, that I went to a reserve medical unit at Halton Camp, Buckinghamshire, of which Captain Freeman was the officer commanding. The unit was composed of men who were convalescing after service overseas. . . . I was put into the Section office with the rank of Corporal, and this is how I came into touch with Captain Freeman, and learned that he was a writer of detective stories with a medical issue in the plot. In the evening when I took letters, etc., for him to sign he would be busy writing in his study and occasionally would ask my opinion as to whether certain points were feasible. . . .

Captain Freeman was a most unassuming man with a quiet sense of humour. His *bête noire* was the Senior

Medical Officer of the camp, a bumptious, cocky Welsh-man—a Colonel. Captain Freeman was fond of modelling and his clay model of the Colonel was a good likeness although definitely not very flattering.

I myself was an unwilling victim of Captain Free-man's humour. There was to be a general inspection of the Camp by the Red Hats [senior officers] from London. As a preliminary the Colonel had an inspection of the medical unit. Everyone was roped in—cooks, clerks, orderlies, etc. Owing to a disabled leg I was excused wearing puttees, and so appeared on parade without them. When the Colonel saw that I was "im-properly dressed" he asked Captain Freeman the reason, and was told. "There is no reason why he can't wear one puttee," said the Colonel.

When the general parade came, in spite of protests on my part Captain Freeman insisted that I should go on parade with one puttee. I remember now his smile and chuckle as he said that he must obey orders. His plan was, of course, to show up the Colonel for his stupidity, but unfortunately it did not work as the Generals failed to notice my queer attire.

In 1917 the Brigade was split up, as the Camp was to become the Head quarters of the newly formed RAF. Captain Freeman went with his unit to Blackpool, whereas I was transferred to the Colonel's office and went to Crowborough. Later the Colonel told me that he knew all about Captain Freeman's model caricature and also the trick he tried to play at the general pa-rade. . . .

At the time of Freeman's death the following reminiscence appeared:

One who served under Freeman in this period recalls his quiet dignity and that constant consideration for the men's welfare which inspired in them feelings of genuine devotion. "His lectures on human anatomy, delivered without any notes, were a never-failing delight; they were graphically illustrated on the blackboard and punctuated with a dry whimsical humour. On route marches he always walked with us, leading us along the more interesting by-paths; occasionally he would play the organ in a village church during the fall-out. For he was musician as well as artist, author and naturalist. I never heard him raise his voice in anger; yet no one commanded greater authority."[1]

The writing which Mr. Bryan reported Freeman to be engaged in during his leisure hours in barracks did not relate to Thorndyke, but were of a considerably lighter nature. Perhaps Freeman was unable, in the circumstances, to undertake the discipline of a detective novel. At any rate he busied himself, at Halton, with *The Exploits of Danby Croker,* a series of inconsequential adventures fittingly subtitled "Extracts from a somewhat disreputable autobiography" and published, not by Hodder—who may have been out of Freeman's good graces after *The Uttermost Farthing*—but by Duckworth, in October 1916.

The preface of this book was discussed in an earlier chapter when fingerprint forgery was under review. Freeman considered such forgery to be a real danger and therefore deplored the use of unsubstantiated fingerprint evidence to send men to prison or the gallows, even though the Court of Criminal Appeal in a 1909 decision had left the door open to such a possibility. However, *The Exploits of Danby Croker,* unlike *The Red Thumb Mark,* is not a serious treatment of the subject. It is, in fact, disturbingly flippant. The issue cannot be avoided: Freeman throughout most of his career assessed his literary worth at a low level. Most of us now accept Howard Haycraft's valuation of Freeman (in his *Murder for Pleasure* (1941)) as the "living dean" of scientific—and perhaps of all—detective story writers. We are pained therefore when we come across his slighter efforts. He is the creator of the immortal Thorndyke and, even in those of Freeman's books where the Great

Fathomer is absent, his readers expect to find vestiges of the familiar magic.   Alas, Thorndyke's presence, it seems, was as necessary to Freeman's proficiency as it is to his readers' delectation.   He had attempted two serious adventure stories in *The Golden Pool* and *The Unwilling Adventurer* with considerable success, but in later years it almost seems that without "the Doctor" in the plot, Freeman didn't really try.

Danby Croker is an unmitigated rascal; Tom Nagget, an acquaintance of his, is an even greater one.   By one of Freeman's too-numerous coincidences, the young men are perfect doubles except that Croker is blond while Nagget has black hair.   Hair dye changes Croker into Nagget, while peroxide works the reverse transformation for Nagget.   Croker, for no reason the reader can see, impersonates Nagget and is clapped into jail for a burglary he did not commit.   He somehow escapes before his fingerprints have been recorded and changes back to his original appearance.   But he cannot remain honest for long.   He takes over a curio dealer's business and is soon, like a disreputable Polton, forging a Cellini medallion by the electrotype process.[2]   The Castleton case, discussed earlier, is re-enacted, with variations, in a chapter entitled "The Votive Candle."   While Nagget is in a drunken stupor, Croker takes impressions of his finger-tips in warm wax.   From these molds he fabricates soft rubber casts which he affixes to rubber gloves.   Croker breaks into an old lady's house, taking with him a candle bearing Nagget's prints and leaving behind, with the aid of the gloves forged prints in various places where they are likely to be found.   In later chapters Freeman exhibits some knowledge of church organs and old violins, but we must also tolerate an extended masquerade of Croker in women's clothing.   In the denouement, Croker and Nagget appear together at the Old Bailey, Nagget being at that moment a blonde.   Following a confused scene it is Croker who is freed and the innocent Nagget who is incarcerated on the evidence of the "planted" candle.

The book has an outlook almost as immoral as *The Uttermost Farthing.*   It has the advantage over the latter work of not involving murder, and its facetious tone allows one to take some of the more outrageous passages with a pinch of salt. The most striking character in the book, in spite of her small role, is undoubtedly Judith Lyon, the Jewish girl who helps Croker to run the antique shop, and who would, one feels, have made a better mate for him than the insipid creature whom he does marry. Despite its weaknesses, most Thorndyke enthusiasts will want to read *The Exploits of Danby Croker*—once!

In 1918, two Thorndyke short stories written just before the war were published—on atrocious paper of wartime quality—by Hodder in a strange pot-pourri entitled *The Great Portrait Mystery*. Because this volume never appeared in the United States, the two Thorndyke stories included in it—"Percival Bland's Proxy" and "The Missing Mortgagee"—are almost unknown here.[3]

Neither story is to be found in the collection of thirty-eight Thorndyke tales in *The Dr. Thorndyke Omnibus* (New York: Dodd, Mead, 1932) though they are included in the similar British omnibus (*The Famous Cases of Dr. Thorndyke: Thirty-seven of his criminal investigations. . . .* (London: Hodder & Stoughton, 1927)). This is all the more unfortunate in that they are inverted short stories, of which Freeman wrote only six altogether.

Percival Bland is an ingenious young man who desires to disappear; after insuring his life for a tidy sum, he sets fire to his lodgings. He buys a human skeleton and leaves it in the blaze after arranging the bones before the fireplace to suggest a drunken torpor. Thorndyke expresses himself strongly on the subject of non-medical coroners, and the technical aspects are. masterly, as usual. As Bland has selected a proxy of the wrong gender, the story contains a rather humorous exchange in the mortuary. After Jervis takes a long hard look at the remains he exclaims, "But my dear Thorndyke, what on earth does it mean? Are we to suppose that a woman can have palmed herself off as a man on the examining medical officer of a London **Life** Assurance Society?"

"Thorndyke shook his head. 'I think not,' said he. 'Our friend, Mr. Bland, may conceivably have been a woman in disguise, but he certainly was not a Negress.' "

In "The Missing Mortgagee," Elton, an artist of small talent and less success, is in heavy debt to Solomon Gordon, a money-lender. They meet on the esplanade at Margate and shortly afterwards Gordon, wringing wet after a fall into a rock pool on the shore, is offered a change of clothes by Elton. So it comes about that, when Gordon falls from a cliff during a scuffle with his mortgagee, his body is mistaken for Elton's. Gordon's over-exaggerated "Jewishness" is constantly emphasized and is associated with a variety of unpleasant physical and moral characteristics. "Elton looked askance at the vampire by his side, at the plump blue-shaven cheeks, the thick black eyebrows, the drooping nose, and the full, red lips that embraced the cigar, and though he was a mild-tempered man he felt that he could have battered that sensual, complacent face out of all human likeness with something uncommonly like enjoyment." Gordon's tastes are predictably in accordance with his appearance. "Money first, for its own sake, and then those coarser and more primitive gratifications that it was capable of purchasing." Hyams, Gordon's clerk, is "a small gentleman, of sallow and greasy aspect with heavy eyebrows and a still heavier nose." It is almost an anticlimax to learn he is also dishonest.

If Freeman's racial prejudices surprise us, it is not because they differed from those of other British writers of the period, but because they betray an outlook which we would not expect of a man of broad tastes and enlightened scientific leanings. We have had evidence of Freeman's detached but friendly sentiments towards the West Africans with whom he came in contact years before, and Negroes in his stories[4] fare well at his hands. His hostility towards Jews most likely stemmed from his childhood associations. Though little is known of his impressionable years in the West End of London, nevertheless we know that he was a tailor's son, and was expected to enter his father's trade when he became old enough. The table talk no doubt was largely about "the competition" which was almost synonymous with the Jews of East London. The slums of Whitechapel and neighbouring districts were filled with sweatshops run almost exclusively by Jews, many of them recent immigrants from Eastern Europe. Their employees were largely English girls working at machines in non-unionized, overcrowded workrooms, turning out racks of men's suits and coats at low prices. These garments, while similar in appearance to the West End product, lacked the latter's superior hand-stitching and careful lining and so soon lost their shape. Nevertheless, "the competition's" prices were much more attractive than those of the adequately lighted, well-regulated establishments further west. The rivalry caused so much fiction that it was the subject of a Royal Commission in the eighties.

Freeman seems never to have discerned the basis for his dislike of Jews. Indeed, his avoidance of the tailoring trade as a whole, despite the frequency of scenes in the East End in half a dozen of his books and stories, is in itself eloquent. He found the Jews' "foreignness," their mannerisms, customs and appearance, a lamentably convenient target. His prejudice finally contaminated his objectivity in the book to be discussed later in this chapter, which dealt most directly with social and racial matters, and with which he made his final claim as a serious writer.

It is for the reader of the novels and stories to decide whether Thorndyke's remarkable immunity from Freeman's prejudice throughout the entire series was a sustained effort on the author's part to endow his hero with an excess of benevolence, or whether Thorndyke is Freeman undefiled, Freeman as he would have preferred to view himself.

"The Great Portrait Mystery" itself is a novella which occupies the first half of Freeman's book of the same title. It is a light story about the theft of a portrait of James the Second from the National Gallery. The painting is returned, apparently intact, the next day; but young Joseph Fittleworth, a member of the Gallery staff, and his fiancee decide to investigate the motive for the robbery. They find the secret, which involves a hidden treasure, in Samuel Pepys' papers at Cambridge University.

The book contains four other stories. "The Bronze Parrot" is a humorous tale about the effect that possession of a small effigy of a parrot from Ashanti has on a meek and unassuming curate in a small village. The bronze bird, like the portrait, really exists—in the British Museum, West African section. "Powder Blue and Hawthorn" derives its title from fine Chinese porcelain which is stolen and hidden in an empty coffin until the hue and cry has died down. "The Attorney's Conscience" is a ghost story, of mediocre quality, about an old lawyer who is visited by the specter of an eighteenth-century man of the law. The visitor wishes to set right a wrong he committed two centuries earlier. The final story is "The Luck of Barnabas Mudge" which concerns the discovery of gold coins hidden in the wall of an old cottage by a jobbing bricklayer. Mudge, contemplating how to spend the money without raising suspicion, decides in the end, not to take the chance; but the coins indirectly make him rich anyway.

Freeman had always possessed a sharp social eye, as readers of his Ashanti book are aware. His philosophy of education, derived from the works of Herbert Spencer, has already been touched upon. His war service brought him into contact with physical and mental types of all kinds, as had his prison service earlier, and during his leisure hours he must have wondered whether he could not write a serious work on some subject related to these experiences.

Social Decay and Regeneration, which engaged Freeman's full energies for nearly two years, came out in March 1921. While working on it, Freeman was a contributing book critic for the *Eugenics Review,* a scholarly quarterly for which he was to continue to write sporadically until his final illness.

The renowned Havelock Ellis provided Freeman's book with an Introduction in which he wrote:

> Some twenty years ago I chanced to come across a volume of *Travels and Life in Ashanti and Jaman,* presenting a fresh and vivid picture of a strong and primitive people just then being "civilized" off the earth. The author was evidently a man of penetrating judgment, capable of outspoken criticism when it was required, so that his name and his book remained in my memory. Therewith he passed out of my ken. But in the meanwhile, as I learn, and as indeed one might expect in a writer of so

vigorous a mind, he has been active in another field, and now, with the present volume, he has again by chance come into my line of vision. It is incomparably a more mature book than the *Travels*. I realize how profitably the author must have spent the intervening years. . . . Moreover . . . he gives the impression of having learnt to approach his task, not in the study, but by a large contact with human life and affairs and by a sensitive intellectual receptivity to that contact.

Freeman's thesis was twofold: first, that machines were ruinous to human physique, culture and environment and their use should be avoided, whenever possible. Second, that eugenic reform was essential if human life were to be preserved and enabled to evolve upwards. With regard to this latter objective, Freeman recognized that segregation of unfit members of the community was impracticable in a democratic society, and rejected compulsory sterilization and restrictions on marriage as being undesirable in the one case and ineffectual in the other.

His solution was the voluntary segregation of the fit. His aim was not the setting up of a small group of supermen, for such beings are rare. His "League," to use his own term, would simply exclude the obviously unfit, both physical and mental. Defectives born within the League would, after adolescence was reached and the subnormal condition verified, have the choice of undergoing sterilization or leaving the community. The adult members of the League would live utopian lives of farmers and skilled craftsmen.

Professor F. C. S. Schiller[5] and others who reviewed Freeman's book pointed out that the League would need heavy protection from industrialized competitors and even then would fail because of political difficulties with its neighbours. *The Saturday Review* drew attention to the inherent conflict between Freeman's blanket condemnation of "inferior" immigrants from Eastern Europe who lowered the standard of life in England, and the undoubted fact that Eastern Europeans in their native lands used fewer machines than the English and on that account, on the basis of

Freeman's own philosophy, should have been superior. The same reviewer suggested that "eugenics, as propounded by some of its advocates, would prove a grinding tyranny far more drastic and soul-destroying than any possible penalties from the rule of the machine."

Professor Schiller took Freeman to task for his loose thinking in racial matters; for example, he refers to an "English race," when there is no such thing. In wishing to exclude from his League all who are not descended from "the indigenous population of the British Islands" he argues for the ideal of racial purity "as practised by the Jews for thousands of years with the greatest success." But, Schiller rebutted, the Jews, like most of mankind, are quite a mixed bunch, exhibiting "a considerable proportion of Nordic types, derived perhaps from the Pelasgian Philistines, and appear to have adopted their Armenoid and unsemitic noses from the Hittites."

One of Freeman's colleagues on the Eugenics Council between the wars was Dr. C. P. Blacker who is now Chairman of the Simon Population Trust. At the present writer's request he took the time to reappraise *Social Decay and Regeneration* in the light of all that has happened since it was published. He summarizes Freeman's chief recommendations and continues:

> These ideas were easier to advocate in 1921 than in 1961. Hitler and his policies intervened. Yet the project has potential merits which, though scouted today, might be rediscovered in a few decades. By this time the pendulum might have swung away from the doctrinal egalitarianism which is now almost *de rigueur.*
>
> I think, however, that there are grave difficulties in the way of selecting, as members of a planned community, individuals and families on the sole ground of "fitness." More feasible, I think, would be to use as one's selective criterion some quality other than "fitness" with which fitness might be associated. . . .
>
> I believe that it would be easier today to graft [Freeman's] eugenic ideals on to any existing system or

creed with firm principles and loyal followers than to establish an independent "League" whose sole objective and recruiting appeal was the voluntary segregation of the "fit."

Had he succeeded in his endeavor to strike out a new path, and had the resulting book been taken seriously by the scientific world, Thorndyke, most likely, would have been no more. Luckily for us, if unluckily for Freeman, his book engendered respect rather than enthusiasm, and so Thorndyke survived to delight his readers for many more years.

Although Freeman had perforce to return to fiction writing, he continued to busy himself with eugenics and kindred subjects throughout his remaining years. In "Sub-Man"[6] he recalls the inferior physical and mental specimens he had seen in his prison and R.A.M.C. days and compares them with the natives of West Africa. The native is vivacious, polite, and dexterous to the point of economic independence. On the other hand, the Negro, according to Freeman, is inferior to the average "European" on the basis of U. S. Army intelligence tests and the absence of an indigenous African civilization. (Recently, of course, the validity of both these arguments has been seriously questioned.)

In "Some Ethical Considerations of the Industrial Revolution,"[7] Freeman again harks back to his experiences in West Africa. "There were no totally unskilled individuals. Even the children could take their part in the simple industrial life of the community. . . . The more developed industries, however, had already specialized into trades. While everyone was a spinner, or a spinster, the weaver was a tradesman. . . . On his simple loom he could weave excellent cloth . . . so much superior to European cloth that the natives— even on the coast—readily paid three or four times the price for it, while in the interior I had to give away my stock of Manchester cottons since no one would buy them at any price."

His final article on eugenics appeared several years later.[8] It consisted of a further and more urgent plea for a beginning in eugenic reform: "Nothing hinders. No money need be collected; no statutory powers need be obtained. A dozen resulute persons could make a beginning—and it is the beginning that matters. . . . All that is necessary is a small body of convinced eugenists, ready to make an effort, at the eleventh hour, to save at least a remnant of a people whose great qualities once commanded the respect of the whole world."

What had begun as an intellectual commitment to the eugenics movement had gradually become an emotional involvement. Never did Freeman sound less detached than in this article. But it was the last he wrote on this or any other subject. He continued to attend meetings of the Eugenics Society Council, however, and on the outbreak of the Second World War, although by now seventy-seven years old, he was elected to serve on the Emergency Com - mittee. (Earlier he had served on various subcommittees.) As Dr. Blacker recalls him:

> He was often silent at these meetings but when he spoke everyone listened. I recall an occasion when another member of the Council took exception to the praise which Freeman had accorded in a review to a certain book. The controversy was unduly prolonged and became heated. Freeman, though the leading actor, sat silent and was the most unperturbed person sitting round the table. When the matter was settled in his favour, he thanked the meeting for showing an under- standing of why he had written as he had, and then he apologized to his critic for having given him offence. He showed a rare detachment and magnanimity. . . .

Freeman's most public work for the Eugenics Soceity was in his eminently readable book reviews for its official organ, the *Eugenics Review*. He began this work in 1920 and, except when interrupted by an occasional period of poor health, kept it up until his final illness. He was able equally to review works on biology, sociology, childbirth and other subjects of interest to eugenicists, and he brought to each of them an attitude of tolerant detachment and understanding of the author's point of view. Often it is apparent, he found the subject of his review distasteful, but was able to reach a point of balance by prefacing his remarks with a phrase such as: "If we assume, as the present author does, that such-and-such is the case, then one can understand his arguing that. . . ."   It is in fact almost impossible to find a totally un-favorable notice by Freeman,[9] and many of them, especially those about books by J. B. S. Haldane, Bertrand Russell and Havelock Ellis, still make good reading.

All the same, his own bid in 1921 to become a leading figure in the eugenics field did not quite succeed. His book achieved a temporary importance in the minds of a few specialized readers, but after a few years even they had largely forgotten it. Meanwhile, with a family to support, Freeman, approaching the age of sixty, had little alternative but to turn back to fiction and to Thorndyke.

109 Darnley Road, Gravesend; Free-
man's home from the late 1921 until
September 1926. (Courtesy of Paul
R. Lorch.)

Freeman in the early 1928s.
(Photo by Wm. T. Munns.)

2 Portland Villas, Gravesend. Actually a part of Windmill St., Freeman moved here
in the fall of 1926 and moved across the road in 1930. (Courtesy of Paul R. Lorch.)

CHAPTER VIII

The Prolific Twenties

Money must have been an everlasting worry to Freeman. He was invalided out of the Colonial Service without a pension, his health never recovered sufficiently to allow him to take on a full-time practice (though we may suspect that his heart was not in it anyway), and his fiction-writing career was severely interrupted by his war service of four years in the R. A. M. C. Financially, then, Freeman's career had been less than satisfactory. Yet his thoughts on being demobilised in the spring of 1919 turned not to the creation of a fictional best-seller, but to the forbidding subjects of eugenics and sociological phenomena from which he could hardly expect to gain monetary reward. His sons John and Lawrence, away during the war, were now making their own way in the world, John as a draughtsman and Lawrence as a dentist. But a steady income for Freeman and his wife was necessary, and it was for this reason that a book every year or so was to become his permanent preoccupation.

131

We are fortunate in having access to a correspondence, begun at this period and continued intermittently for several years, between Freeman and Vincent Starrett, then a handsome young newspaperman and editor in Chicago. A lifelong detective-story enthusiast, Starrett had long been especially fond of Sherlock Holmes, whose first and best biographer he was to become. In the 'thirties he was to play an important part in the affairs of The Baker Street Irregulars, both the original society, begun by Christopher Morley in New York, and the Chicago chapter. But in 1920 he was an impoverished writer of short pieces whose major claims to literary attention were biographies of Arthur Machen and Ambrose Bierce. He was then, as he still is, a perennial enthusiast, his sound judgment paired with a sanguine temperament. He was corresponding with a number of British and American writers and had been successful in promoting the works of some of them in the United States.

In answer to Starrett's first letter, Freeman wrote as follows:

> 2 Woodville Terrace
> Gravesend
> 8th December, 1920

Dear Mr. Starrett,

I was very pleased to get your letter of the 11th November and proud to learn that you like my principal puppet, John Thorndyke. I rather like him myself, and I have introduced him into a good many of my books. . . . [He here lists his Thorndyke books and promises to send some cheap reprints.]

I enclose with this a letter from Dodd, Mead, & Co. sent here by mistake and opened by me with deliberate malice. You will observe some spots of paraffin wax on it and will perhaps infer that John Thorndyke has allowed his chemico-physical researches to invade his writing table.

I am sorry there are not more books to offer you,

but the war was a great interruption. I was away for over four years and got to work immediately on my return. I was demobilized in March 1919 and have since then written the large sociological book and the greater part of a rather long novel, as well as a few short stories. So I have not been slacking.

I shall be glad to hear how you like the stories when you have read them, and I should like once more to thank you for writing to me about my works.

Yours sincerely,

R. Austin Freeman.

The "rather long novel" on which he was then engaged was *Helen Vardon's Confession,* probably the most difficult Thorndyke novel to find nowadays, and the only one never to appear in the United States. It has a gothic quality, not so much in its narrative style as in the circumstances of the plot. It is the longest (about 130,000 words) book to feature the great medical jurist, and yet makes use of him to only a minor extent. All the same, as the London *Times* critic indicated in his review, Thorndyke's appearances, though brief, are to the point, and the book as a whole—a kind of regular novel with Thorndykian episodes—is "not a page too long, and the somewhat abrupt termination leaves the reader wishing there were more of it."

Helen Vardon, an independent young lady of **twenty-four,** overhears the large and ungainly Lewis Otway threaten her father with criminal prosecution for an indiscretion connected with a trust fund. He offers to stay his hand if Helen will marry him, but Vardon refuses even to have his daughter approached about the matter. Helen, fearing her father's certain ruin and possible suicide, secretly meets Otway and agrees to his demands, though he is twice her age and repellent to her. Thus far, Helen's actions are barely credible, but thereafter the plot unravels in an orderly and fascinating manner.   The shabby ceremony is barely over when Vardon, apprised of the affair, accosts Otway in an angry scene which ends in Vardon's death. Helen leaves her husband forthwith and, being of slender means, determines to eke out a livelihood by making small articles of precious metal.   Dr. Thorndyke, an acquaintance of her dead father, counsels her to take up residence in the house of Nathaniel Polton's sister in Wellclose Square. This establishment in London's dockland is the home of a guild of young women artists, bound by a common purpose and a common philosophy.

It must be remembered that Freeman wrote *Helen Vardon's Confession* while his mind was still full of his previous work. Indeed, the novel had been completed by the time *Social Decay* was published and, not surprisingly, the Thorndyke book introduces many of the themes with which the author had so recently been preoccupied.   Here is Thorndyke conversing with Helen:

"I think we often appreciate insufficiently the wisdom of the artist's choice of his profession.   In choosing a means of livelihood we are choosing the way in which we shall spend the greater part of our lives. We have some-thing to sell—the bulk of our waking lives: and we are apt to think too much of its selling price—its value to the purchaser—and not enough of its value to ourselves. A man, such as a navvy [unskilled laborer], a miner, a bank-clerk or a factory hand, barters for the means of subsistence so many hours a day spent in doing something that he does not want to do. He sells the best part of his life.   But the artist or craftsman makes a much better bargain, for he contrives to make a subsistence by doing what he enjoys doing and what he would elect to do for his own satisfaction. He sells only the by-products of his life; the whole of that life he retains for his own use, to be spent as he would, in any case, wish to spend it.   But there is an inevitable proviso; his acceptable occupation must really yield a subsistence. His wares must be of value to the purchaser, and he must be able to find a market. Do you think you could satisfy these conditions?"

One of Helen's companions at Miss Polton's establishment is Winifred Blake, destined to appear in subsequent Thorndyke novels and to become the wife of Thorndyke's friend, Robert Anstery, K. C. It would be unfair to reveal all of the plot in detail. Helen meets Jasper Davenant and they fall in love; marriage for Helen is impossible while Otway lives, and the idea of an illicit union does not attract her. In a characteristic Freeman touch, her lover plans a ceremony before witnesses with declarations of intent by both parties that they regard themselves as man and wife. But suddenly Otway is found dead and Helen is suspected of murder. At the inquest, Thorndyke intervenes to save her from certain arrest.

Freeman found the book tiring to write and, for once, errors crept in. Helen's father's name, William Henry, changes unaccountably into John; Nathaniel Polton is described by Thorndyke in evidence as *Francis* Polton; and Thorndyke confuses a hundred-weight (112 pounds) with a one-hundred-pound weight. Such slips are worth mentioning only because they are rare in Freeman's work. They certainly do not detract significantly from an unusual and successful novel. The Thorndyke enthusiast may deplore not being served a larger portion of his hero, but the great man's triumph is so satisfying and convincing that few will cavil.

A minor point is the absence of Jervis, who is missing also from the next Thorndyke novel. Thus, he is absent from Freeman's novels from 1914, in *A Silent Witness,* until 1924, when he reappears in *The Mystery of Angelina Frood.*

Helen's publication was delayed for over a year, apparently, as the following letter implies, because of printing difficulties. It did not appear in the bookshops until April or May 1922.

2 Woodville Terrace
Gravesend
9th March 1921

Dear Mr. Starrett,

I must apologize most humbly for leaving your letter so long unanswered. Your delightful little book "The Unique Hamlet" I read as soon as it arrived and was highly entertained. There is great satisfaction in seeing somebody else's leg pulled. I must congratulate you on the skill with which you have simulated the Sherlockian manner both of speech and thought and on the fine anti-climax. And the little volume itself is charming in appearance. I am very pleased indeed to have it and most appreciative of your kindness in sending it to me.

I have just finished a very long novel (which the present state of the printing trade may render impracticable) and begun another, which I shall keep down to economic dimensions. A more serious book "Social Decay and Regeneration" is just now in course of publication here and in the U. S. A. where it is being issued by Houghton Mifflin. It has been announced and may be out any day. But perhaps you are not keen on sociology.

Once more thanking you for sending me your book.

I am
Yours sincerely

R. Austin Freeman

Starrett's "The Unique Hamlet," which is included in his *Private Life of Sherlock Holmes,* has been described as the finest of all the many Sherlockian pastiches. Freeman's newly started book, which he promised to keep to "economic dimensions," was *The*

Cat's Eye, but it was some time before he could complete it, for *Pearson's Magazine* requested more Thorndyke short stories, and *Helen* had yet to go through the press.

109, Darnley Road
Gravesend
England

7th January, 1922

Dear Mr. Starrett,

As I am now enjoying a brief interval between the job I have just finished and the one that I am about to begin, I take the opportunity to reply to your letter, which has been laid down to mature and is now getting quite fruity and crusted. And first as to my forthcoming work.

I am now correcting proofs of a long book called "Helen Vardon's Confession." It is a Thorndyke story, but as the plot is rather complex the detective interest is rather slow in coming to the surface. The climax required a good deal of preparation. It is to be published by Hodder & Stoughton, and, as far as I know, no arrangements have been made with any American publisher.

I have finished a second series of "John Thorndyke's Cases" for Pearson's Magazine. They also have not yet been placed in the U. S. A. but my American agent (Harold Paget of New York) has a copy. I am rather puzzled by the very slight vogue that my work has in the States. There seems to be a good demand for detective stories and the supply seems to be, as you remark, of very poor quality. I cannot help thinking that editors must be somewhat lacking in critical judgement, or else they take no trouble in looking for good-class work. And an English author is at a great disadvantage, as, if his work is not placed in America as soon as it is written he loses it altogether; for the iniquitous copyright law of the U. S. A. then allows anyone who pleases to take possession of it without payment.

In addition to the works I have mentioned, I have in hand a Thorndyke novel of the orthodox type—a detective story pure and simple. I shall probably go on with this as soon as I have finished· with the proofs and the technical illustrations for the series (six) of short stories, and I believe it will turn out fairly well. Possibly your friend Mr. O'Donnell might like to have it; or he might like the series.

Please let me thank you for the interest you have taken in me and my work. I assure you I appreciate it very much, and I have no doubt that it will be the means of making my work better known in America.

With kindest regards,
Yours sincerely,

R. Austin Freeman.

The year 1922 was a busy one for Freeman as he turned sixty. The short stories were a success in Britain and more were asked for. But *Helen Vardon's Confession* was never given U. S. publication and the stories were not to American magazine-readers' tastes, in the opinion of those who saw them.

12th August, 1922

Dear Mr. Starrett,

In reply to your questions, my last novel, "Helen Vardon's Confession," introduces Dr. Thorndyke, but not on the usual scale. He comes in at intervals and finally appears to solve the mystery and extricate the heroine from an alarming set of complications. I doubt if you will like the book as well as the others.

The series of short Thorndyke stories is running in the English "Pearson's Magazine." It began in April and I am asked to continue with a second six. Munseys have taken two and may take one or two more; but my work does not seem to hit with the American taste. O'Donnell saw the stories and did not like them.

I am very appreciative of your enthusiasm, and wish there were more like you in your continent. The American taste seems to favour a more crude type of detective story.

What sort of publication is "The Wave"? If you have a spare copy, I should be interested to see it. The title seems to suggest something of the comprehensively literary type.

To return to my own productions: I have a novel three quarters finished—one of the regular Thorndyke class—which I had to put down to do this series. When I have finished the latter I shall go back to the novel and complete it, and I think it will turn out to be of the kind that interests you.

Yours sincerely,

R. Austin Freeman.

(*The Wave* was an enterprising literary magazine begun by a group of young Danish artists on Chicago's North Side and edited by Starrett. The little magazine, "copies of which," wrote their editor recently, "I understand are now rare and even desirable" thrived, if that is the word, only from January, 1921, until about three years later, eight issues in all.)

16th May, 1923

Dear Mr. Starrett,

These presents are to inform you that I am sending you a copy of my new volume of short stories and trusting in the Lord that I have addressed it correctly (709 N. Mayfield Avenue), there being a slight ambiguity about your 7. I won't make any comments on it excepting that I didn't print it or bind it; I should like to be quite clear on that point.

I received the copy of *The Wave* that you kindly sent, and hereby offer thanks. It is a pleasant-looking production, and one appreciates the relief from the horrors of glazed paper and half-tone reproductions. Perhaps the illustrators have swung the pendulum rather far on the opposite side; the woodcutters seem a little inclined to hit below the belt. But it is better to be archaic than mechanical. I like Frank Pape's drawings immensely (the Christmas numbers). They are admirable in spacing and construction and the drawing is very fine. . . . I also liked your somewhat Chestertonian "Princess Antimacassar," in fact I must congratulate you on the get-up and the matter of your venture and I wish you luck with it.

I shall be interested to see your detective stories (or story) and rather expect to find a fantastic and ironical element in it (or them). We shall see.

To return to my own productions. I have finished a novel, "The Cat's Eye," which is now being serialized by the "Westminster Gazette" and I am a quarter through yet another—both Thorndyke stories.

With best wishes,
Yours sincerely,
R. Austin Freeman

During 1922 and at intervals during later years, Freeman wrote groups of stories for *Pearson's Magazine* which together made up the three collections entitled *Dr. Thorndyke's Case Book* (1923), *The Puzzle Lock* (1925) and *The Magic Casket* (1927). The first of these, which in the United States was called *The Blue Scarab*, used some of the twelve stories published in the magazine as an unbroken series between April, 1922, and the following March. The remainder were put into the other collections in a haphazard order and were sometimes renamed. In this chapter we shall examine only the more interesting of the stories with just a mention of the others. As Alfred C. Ward once observed, while the short Sherlock Holmes stories are superior to the longer ones, the opposite is probably true of the Thorndyke tales. Nevertheless, all of Freeman's short detective stories hold one kind of fascination or another, and the omnibus volumes (the Hodder and Stoughton version is still in print) offer unrivalled entertainment.

Looking first at the stories in *Dr. Thorndyke's Case Book,* one finds the quality fairly uniform. Perhaps the most painstaking detection is set out in "The Funeral Pyre" which is one of the few concentrating on Thorndyke's great speciality, medical jurisprudence. Each story is built up from one particular clue: "The Blue Scarab" concerns a code based on Egyptian hieroglyphics; "The White Footprints" show that the little toes are missing from *both* feet of the criminal. ("To lose *both* looks like carelessness," as Lady Bracknell might have said.) "The New Jersey Sphinx," like a story discussed in an earlier chapter, features the clue of a man's hat, an example of Freeman's versatility in treating similar subjects in different ways. Thorndyke uses wax rather than the more usual plaster to preserve footprints in "The Touchstone," but rabbit hairs provide the vital clue. "A Fisher of Men"—surely a more thought-provoking title than the original "The Blue Diamond Mystery"—revolves around the choosy little land-snail *Clausilia biplicata*, which is found in a highly restricted habitat. It was, according to Thorndyke, indigenous only to a certain area of Wiltshire and in a small area along one bank of the Thames near Hammersmith, just west of London. Because such a shell was discovered in grass pulled up by a thief and used as temporary packing material, Thorndyke deduces where the loot is buried. A. E. Boycott commented on this story in a scientific article.[1] In "The Stolen Ingots" the clue concerns the specific gravity of metals.

It is convenient to consider the remaining short stories at this point, although the fortieth and last of them was not published in *Pearson's Magazine* until early in 1927.

The Puzzle Lock consists of nine short tales, the title story being the one most often anthologized and an excellent example of a lock and cipher riddle. A comparison of "The Apparition of Burling Court" with the earlier and inferior story, "The Mandarin's Pearl," is of interest. In both a rather frail young man is being frightened into suicide by an apparition engineered by unscrupulous conspirators; in the later story the plan is foiled.

In "The Green Check Jacket" Thorndyke refers to a monograph on the foraminifera of chalk by one "Warnford," an author unknown to both the British Museum files and the Library of Congress. This bit of unnecessary invention is not Freeman's style. It may have been a slip caused by his writing under pressure for the magazine. Mr. Ronald F. Jessup, of whom we shall hear more later, tells me the Geological Society records in London are likewise lacking in traces of the mysterious Warnford. On the other hand, a dene hole not far from Gravesend which is the scene of a murder is not fictitious. "The topographical details," writes Mr. Jessup, "are quite exact and from them the reader could easily have found the dene hole, which was well known to me in my boyhood days. It could be recognised clearly for many years after Freeman wrote his story, though it may by now have been filled in as there has been much housing development in that neighbourhood. When we knew it, it was completely isolated and the footpath close to it used very infrequently. It had no name. . . . The other dene hole in the story, Clapper Napper Hole, was filled in and covered over when the old Roman Watling Street was converted into an arterial road in 1921-22. Nothing now remains of the site."

My friend Mrs. Paul Lorch of Gravesend likewise was familiar with the unnamed dene hole as a child. She kindly visited the site on my behalf very recently—it is located between Perry Street and the Spring Head Road—and found it, and the pit which gave access to it, to have been filled in.

A further point of interest is that Freeman, in bringing Thorndyke, Polton, Brodribb and Jervis down to Gravesend in search of the dene hole, actually had them pass very close to his own doorstep, for he had moved, in late 1921, to 109, Darnley Road, "a prosperous, suburban-looking thoroughfare," which lay on the route of the investigators.

Of the remaining stories in *The Puzzle Lock*, one seems to have been inspired by cases, reported in the newspapers and medical press from time to time, of belladonna poisoning caused by eating rabbit meat from animals which had browsed on deadly-nightshade foliage shortly before being killed.[1a] The villain in "Rex v. Burnaby" improved on this scenario by having nightshade plants in profusion in the enclosure where his young rabbits were reared, and his intended victim, to whom gifts of rabbit-for-supper were being offered, was known to be particularly susceptible to atropine alkaloids. Thorndyke is alerted by Jardine (whom we first met in *A Silent Witness*); he, rather than Jervis, is the narrator in this story, and in "The Mysterious Visitor." Jervis is absent again in "The Seal of Nebuchadnezzar" when Robert Anstey, K. C. takes over the narration of a story otherwise unremarkable except, perhaps, for an exchange between Thorndyke and Brodribb *à propos* a small cylindrical gold seal, which the investigator is measuring with his caliper gauge. There was, it seems, a discrepancy of almost two millimeters between the actual and the expected diameter, but "precise measurements don't seem to matter much" said the old lawyer. "On the other hand," retorted Thorndyke, "inexact measurements are of no use at all."

"A Mystery of the Sandhills" hinges on different varieties of sand. "Phyllis Annesley's Peril" by contrast explores the subtleties of parallax, while "A Sower of Pestilence" hinges on fleas.

The nine remaining Thorndyke short stories were collected in

The Magic Casket (1927) which included tales that had first appeared as early as 1922. It was Professor Silvanus P. Thompson—(better known to present-day students for his delightful *Calculus Made Easy*)—whose writings interested Freeman in Japanese "magic" mirrors.[2] Thompson explained that the Japanese themselves were unaware of the special properties of their mirrors, which were caused by an accident in the manufacturing process. Application of force during the grinding of the mirror face caused it to "give" slightly where it was thinnest, while any embossed design on the back, by strengthening the mirror, caused these parts to resist the grinding process and to be imperceptibly raised above the (apparently) smooth surface. It was this which caused the disturbance in the path of the reflected light which rendered the pattern on the back visible in the reflection. Freeman's mirror, which he probably actually constructed, was an improvement on those described by Thompson. The latter were not satisfactory for hiding secret messages, which could, after all, be easily exposed by turning the mirrors over. Nor did he use a refinement introduced by Thompson, who etched—for three seconds only—the *face* of the mirror with acid and then polished it apparently smooth; this reveals the etched message quite clearly. Freeman's "magic casket" had a polished metal base of which the inside had been *chased* with a message, ground smooth and, to render detection even less likely, *etched* by an ornamental design. The ostensibly plain base reflected the message, which told of the hiding place of a stolen necklace.

One other of the stories is of interest because of its association with Freeman's own experiences. Both as a physician and as a victim of blackwater fever he had studied malarial and other animal parasites found in various human diseases. One of these, *Filaria nocturna*, is, like the malarial organism, spread by mosquitoes, and the discovery of its unique habits is an interesting story in itself. Laboratory workers at first had difficulty in finding filarial specimens in the blood of sufferers of elephantiasis but one particular technician began to produce slides showing a profusion of the tiny worm-like creatures. The secret of his success was that he worked only at night, and that the parasites emerge from the tissues and enter the bloodstream only after dark, thereby suiting their habits in a remarkable way to those of their secondary host, the mosquito, which forages for mammalian blood nocturnally. On this discovery Freeman built his story "The Pathologist to the Rescue."

The tale entitled "The Contents of a Mare's Nest" permits us to look over Thorndyke's shoulder into a cremation casket, the contents of which are highly perplexing. "The Stalking Horse" supplies details of a novel means of transmitting invisible messages by a simple chemical method. "The Naturalist at Law" is a lesson in the fauna and flora of British ditches. (Jervis was never more in error than when he said, "Duckweed is just duckweed, and there's an end of it.")

"Mr. Ponting's Alibi" may have had the saving grace of novelty when it was written, but it now seems one of Freeman's feeblest Thorndyke tales, depending as it does on an alibi effected by a phonograph record. It should be remembered, incidentally, that Freeman never wrote in an automatic or colorless fashion. The characters in his stories are far from being puppets. So it is that, though a particular scientific basis may be weak, the story on which it hinges may succeed for reasons of incident and character. Only when both fail, as they do in the present case, does an inferior tale result.

"Pandora's Box" allows Thorndyke to dilate on post-mortem tattoo marks, while in "The Trail of Behemoth" he finds an elephant hair and does some house-breaking into the chambers of a barrister in the Temple. The final story, "Gleanings from the Wreckage," deals, like "Percival Bland's Proxy" earlier, with false identification by means of arson, this time in a factory rather than a private dwelling.

Towards the end of the series of forty Thorndyke short stories, Freeman was showing signs of weariness and repetition. None of the three collections published in the twenties can compete in quality with *The Singing Bone* stories written between 1909 and 1911. But on the whole the tales maintained a surprisingly high standard and often achieved an outstanding level of detection and dramatic invention, especially considering the speed with which each was written.

All the same, Freeman's working habits were better suited to the turning out of one novel a year, a rate which he almost maintained during the last two decades of his life, producing in that period eighteen novels—not all of them Thorndyke books—beginning with *The Cat's Eye* in 1923 and ending with his last work, *The Jacob Street Mystery,* in 1942. Add to this the various collections and the total reaches twenty-four, a surprising figure for a man who was past sixty when the period began.

Let us go back to our point of departure in the spring of 1923 when Freeman had finished *The Cat's Eye* and had immediately begun work on another Thorndyke novel. Publication of *The Cat's Eye* posed an embarrassing problem for its author. As Freeman explains in his preface, an incident in his story had "found an almost exact duplicate in an actual case which had been reported in the Press;" he continues:

> The real case was concerned with a most alarming misadventure which befell a distinguished police official of high rank. The fictitious incident occurs in Chapter X of this book; and the reading of that chapter will inevitably convey the impression that I have appropriated the real case and incorporated it in my story; a proceeding that the reader might properly consider to be in questionable taste.
>
> It seems, therefore, desirable to explain that Chapter X was written some months before the real tragedy occurred. Indeed, by that time, the book was so nearly completed that it was impracticable to eliminate the incident, which was an integral part of the plot.

Chapter X of *The Cat's Eye,* written in the summer of 1922, tells the story of an attempt on the life of the heroine, Winifred Blake, and her young brother Percy. Thorndyke happens to be present at their studio home when a box of chocolates arrives from an unknown donor. Luckily, Thorndyke is able to dissuade them from sampling the contents, for, upon examination, each candy was found to have been impregnated with about two grains of white arsenic.

On November 9th, 1922, Brigadier-General Sir William Horwood, formerly of the 5th Lancers, who had been appointed Commissioner of the Metropolitan Police two years earlier, was sitting at his desk in New Scotland Yard. Miss Drysdale, his secretary, brought in to him a package which had just been delivered, and opened it while he looked on. The cardboard box contained large filled confections known as "whipped-cream walnuts." Sir William sampled one of them immediately. This exceptional lack of caution was due to his expectation of the arrival of a **birthday** gift from a relative. This gift, which was indeed also a box of chocolates, did arrive a few hours after the arsenical whipped-cream walnuts had begun their work, but by that time Sir William was in St. Thomas's Hospital and not expected to survive the night. Sir William was ill for many weeks but, though the effects of the poison were long-lasting, he lived another twenty years to enjoy a lengthy retirement. Investigations were immediately set in motion, of course. It was not until the end of January that Walter F. Tatam, a horticulturist of suburban Balham and a former mental patient, was arrested and charged with attempted murder. He had made similar attempts on other high officials of Scotland Yard. At his trial at the Old Bailey he was found unfit to plead and was sent to Broadmoor Criminal Lunatic Asylum.[3]

The actual incident was sufficiently similar to the one in his latest Thorndyke novel to prompt Freeman's explanation, but the coincidence was hardly remarkable. Arsenic is a common enough instrument of murder and chocolates by mail perhaps the most suitable method of administration to a stranger. Indeed the early months of 1922 had witnessed several other cases. In a notorious case Major Armstrong of Hay, a village on the Welsh borders, not only was convicted of murdering his wife with arsenic, but was suspected of sending doctored chocolates to a fellow lawyer in the same little town. It was the height of wit at Oxford University in those days to hail fellow undergraduates with the phrase, "Have a chocolate," and the unpopular Vice Chancellor, Dr. Lewis Farnell, did indeed receive a box of the sweetmeats containing, according to which report you heard, powdered glass, a mysterious Indian poison or just tooth-powder. (The perpetrator, an undergraduate, owned up and was forgiven.) A young married career woman, Edith Thompson, read of the Oxford prank in the newspapers and sent clippings to her lover, a waiter aboard a P. & O. liner. Her motive was, according to the prosecution at their trial, to suggest ways in which Percy Thompson, the unwanted husband, might be eliminated. (The unfortunate man was stabbed to death by the lover, Frederick Bywaters, in a London street some months later in the presence of Edith. The two conspirators were hanged.)

As a matter of fact, the poisoned chocolates play only a small role in *The Cat's Eye,* which is crammed with more ideas and incidents than any other Thorndyke novel, perhaps because it first appeared in serial form. Briefly, it has two interlinked mysteries. The first pertains to the murder of a collector of "inscribed objects," Andrew Drayton of Hampstead. Present at the scene of the murder is Winifred Blake, whose young brother, Percy, is claimant to a large estate. The claim is dependent on the discovery of certain ancient deeds, and this constitutes the second mystery. Robert Anstey, the narrator, acts as protector to Winifred when her life is threatened (subsequent to the poisoned candy attempt) by a direct physical attack. The labyrinthine plot also brings in dubious fingerprints (again), scriptural messages in a locket, blue hair in the same location, a porcupine anteater's third cervical vertebra, and a nearly fatal search for secret chambers by Thorndyke and Anstey. The way in which Freeman is able to juggle these disparate elements and keep them all "in the air," as it were, until the end of the story, wins our admiration.

Freeman made use of his wartime knowledge of the Aylesbury district in his description of Thorndyke's excursions to Beauchamp Blake. The details of his walk from the town in Anstey's company through the village of Stoke Mandeville and along the Lower Icknield Way were obviously culled from Freeman's remembrance of strolls around Halton Camp during the period a few years earlier when he commanded the ambulance unit there. As for the inn, "The King's Head," where the two investigators enjoyed a cold repast, Freeman evidently transported it from another locality. It occupies a site very close to the (actual) manor house at Weston Turville.

By this time, 1923, Freeman's daily routine was well established. Ronald Jessup recalls some of the details in a recent letter to me:

He rose in midmorning and always took a long walk. His tweed-clad figure with brown boots—never have I seen him wear anything else, except at the livery dinners of the Apothecaries' Company (of which he was a staunch member)—was a familiar sight on the country roads around Gravesend. He used a walking-stick always, and to leave his hands otherwise free had made himself a light strap harness by which his rainproof was carried rolled up on his back. He lunched about four in the afternoon and then worked for as long as he wished, often into the small hours of the morning. Once he was at work he would allow no disturbance whatever, and even Mrs. Freeman was not allowed into his study. He wrote directly in manuscript with an old but efficient fountain-pen, and his scripts, although most carefully revised before and after typing, required very few alterations. His facts he checked carefully, and only once so far as I know—in *The Mystery of Angelina Frood*—did he invent an important non-existent physical surrounding; he used a small lane [in Rochester] which did not, in fact, exist, and to Freeman's joy, no one ever noticed it. He took the greatest possible care in replying to his many correspondents, especially to those who did not realise that his extensive topographical knowledge of Hampstead, Soho and north-west London was acquired largely in his student days at the Middlesex Hospital. He would often walk to and from his lodgings in Chalk Farm to the hospital, and whilst walking in the London streets he was never, even at that time, without his notebook.

Mrs. Paul Lorch writes:

> When my sister and I were children, in the 1920's, on
> Sunday mornings we used to go for country walks with
> our parents.   There was only one country route left
> leading out of Gravesend . . . and here frequently as we
> were coming home to our Sunday dinner about 12:30
> or one o'clock we would meet Dr. Freeman starting out
> on his walk.   He often stopped and spoke to my father.
> I can see him quite clearly.   He was of medium height,
> stocky and wore country clothes, not very well-fitting.
> He spoke quietly and in a scholarly way, and gave the
> impression of gentleness and kindness, but was always
> reserved and withdrawn.   I am almost sure he used a
> walking stick.

During his daily walks Freeman, of course, was settling in his
mind the details of the story he was currently working on.   "To a
man whose mind is working actively, walking is a more acceptable
mode of progression than riding in a vehicle.   There is a sort of
reciprocity between the muscles and the brain—possibly due to the
close association of the motor and psychical centres—whereby
the activity of the one appears to act as a stimulus to the other.   A
sharp walk sets the mind working; and conversely a state of lively
reflection begets an impulse to bodily movement."[4]
The book Freeman's "psychical center" was working on during
his daily walks in 1923 was another Thorndyke novel, *The Mystery
of Angelina Frood*, a commentary of sorts on incidents in Charles
Dickens's unfinished novel, *The Mystery of Edwin Drood*.   The
great Victorian novelist was about half-way through the book,
which was being published in periodical parts, when he was
suddenly taken ill.   He died, on June 9th, 1870, at age fifty-eight,
twenty-four hours after writing the last words of Chapter 23.
Vincent Starrett, in his introduction to the handsome Heritage
Press edition (1941) justly describes the incomplete story as
"one of the most famous fragments in the seven arts" and one

which has proved over the years a powerful magnet to scores of literary detectives eager to penetrate Dickens's secret and complete his story.

Freeman himself was one of several mystery-story writers at Central Hall, Westminster, on April 11, 1928, when a "Drood" night was held by Dickens enthusiasts. Surprisingly, he seems not to have mentioned his own novel, published three and a half years earlier, based on related themes. Perhaps he felt it was not entirely relevant. At any rate his own view of the unfinished mystery, as expressed that evening, was that there was no mystery to be solved. In his opinion, as reported by W. Lawrence Gadd,[5] "the story was simply one of a murder and its subsequent discovery; and he (Freeman) showed how every salient fact bearing upon the crime had been honestly and clearly put before the reader in the fragment left by Dickens. The transfer of the ring by Grewgious to Edwin Drood he considered of primary importance in the construction of the plot; and we had to assume, with Dickens, that quicklime would completely consume a human body, even to the bones. . . .

> "As to the disposal of the body, Dr. Freeman thought that Dickens would have avoided a tomb of any sort, on account of the formalities necessary before such a vault could be opened and investigated, but in this [Mr. Gadd observes] he ignored the significance of Jasper's efforts to identify and obtain possession of the key of the Sapsea vault."

Quite so. But though we can disagree with Freeman's view of Dickens, his remarks tell us a good deal about the different attitudes of the two writers. The great Victorian novelist was a more emotional writer than Freeman; a man of infinitely deeper feelings, possessing, like Freeman, considerable legal knowledge but, unlike him, lacking any profound respect for legal niceties.

In constructing his own novel, though, Freeman *did* avoid tombs of all sorts, and now we know why! The scene of gruesome discovery in *Frood* is, in fact, a newly repaired city wall on the edge of Rochester. As to the quicklime, which Dickens apparently believed would destroy a human body completely, it was Freeman's main thesis that this was a fallacy well-known as such to modern medical jurists.[6] Freeman carried out investigations on the bodies of freshly-killed rabbits from which the fur had been removed by shaving. A rabbit buried in quicklime during the six summer months did not decompose but simply underwent some shrivelling— or mummificaton—because of abstraction of moisture from the body by the lime. Rabbits buried respectively in dry earth, slaked lime and chlorinated lime were all in a more objectionable condition.

In *Drood* it is Durdles who draws attention to the lime:

" 'Ware that there mound by the yard-gate, Mister Jasper."
"I see it. What is it?"
"Lime."
Mr. Jasper stops, and waits for him to come up, for he lags behind. "What you call quick-lime?"
"Ay!" says Durdles; "quick enough to eat your boots. With a little handy stirring, quick enough to eat your bones."

In *Frood* it is an unnamed old man engaged in repairing the city wall who detains the narrator, young Dr. Strangeways, and his companion, Bundy, with a frightful story of a seaman who fell headfirst into the hold of a barge loaded with quicklime, to be utterly consumed in a matter of weeks.

Freeman's story is not an explanation of Dickens's story but is a fresh narrative using some of the earlier writer's materials as a starting point. The quicklime fallacy of the earlier work is transformed into the chief clue of the later one. Edwin Drood, the doomed young man, becomes Angelina Frood who, it may be said, is much the more attractive personality of the two. On this issue, many modern readers overlook the parallelism of the two names.

Mr. E. T. Guymon, Jr., has kindly sent to me a copy of Freeman's inscription from a presentation copy of the novel in his possession. It reads, in full, as follows:

> This book was written as a playful commentary on Dickens's great story, *The Mystery of Edwin Drood;* but, as few people are now familiar with Goldsmith's *Edwin & Angelina,* the mild joke fell flat.

Oliver Goldsmith's poem is better known by its later title, *The Hermit,* especially for the famous couplet:

> Man wants but little here below,
> Nor wants that little long.

Readers may find Dorothy Sayers' commentary[7] on *Drood* and *Frood* of interest; there have been many excellent speculations[8] about Dickens' novel.

It was around the time of *Frood's* publication that Vincent Starrett visited Freeman. The young American bookman had turned thirty-eight years old a day or two earlier; Freeman was sixty-two. As Starrett recounts it in his memoirs[9] he set sail from America and journeyed first to Paris, where he was disappointed in his hope of meeting Anatole France and instead found himself attending the impressive public funeral of the great French author. Crossing to England he visited the Haldane Macfalls and Arthur Machen; with the latter there had been some unpleasantness a few months earlier over Machen's American publication rights, but the two men patched up their differences in a London pub. By contrast, Starrett also called on William Murray Graydon, writer of juvenile fiction and at that time one of the stable of writers who manufactured "Sexton Blake" detective stories for Harmsworth publications. He met also Gordon Browne, son of Dicken's "Phiz" (Hablôt K. Browne) and himself an illustrator.

It was around October 27th, 1924, that Starrett took the short train ride from London to Gravesend, twenty-four miles away. "I took him by surprise, I am afraid, and interrupted an afternoon of work; but for an hour we chatted over coffee and ultimately I was permitted to see, nay, to explore, the famous top floor laboratory.

Yes, there I was, if you will believe me, in Thorndyke's very rooms, quite as if I were Marchmont or Brodribb dropping in for a conference with the Doctor. It was like participating for a moment in a chapter of *The Red Thumb Mark* or *The Eye of Osiris*."[10]

Starrett wrote of his visit to Freeman in two other books, *Bookman's Holiday* and *Books and Bipeds*. In the latter, which is a selection of his pieces from the *Chicago Tribune* book section, may be found a contribution entitled "Good Bye, Dr. Thorndyke," written on the occasion of Freeman's death, from which the following is taken:[11]

John Evelyn Thorndyke, M. D., F.R.C.P., was the first authentic scientific fathomer in detective fiction. Whatever the perils and excitements that beset his way to solution, his triumphs ultimately were won in the laboratory, and his science was sound. For Freeman was his own Thorndyke (and his own Polton); he checked his problems in his own workshop. This was on the top floor of his home in Gravesend, England, when I visited him in 1924—a little world of test tubes, cameras, microscopes, and all manner of medico-legal apparatus that would have caused a pseudo-scientific pretender like Craig Kennedy to stammer and retreat. Even the great Sherlock himself, I think, might have been a little dazed.

This was the doctor's playground, although in the stories it is located at No. 5A King's Bench Walk and boasts an outer doorway designed by Christopher Wren. We sat together and drank tea or some other beverage in the famous living-room, while Dr. Freeman—envy me—talked of Thorndyke and his cases for all the world as if I had been Dr. Jervis or the lawyer Brodribb come to visit his old friend Thorndyke. I felt, of course, that I was participating in the saga, that I was now, indeed, one of the "figures of the tale," an innocent reflection that still gives me pleasure. When, in the following year, the doctor dedicated *The Puzzle Lock* to me, I acquired delusions of importance that must have been very trying to my friends.

I had the great pleasure of meeting Mr. Starrett in his Chicago home in 1964. His visit to Freeman remained in his recollection after forty years as a warm and stimulating experience.

Freeman wrote to Starrett upon the latter's return home:

1st January, 1925

Dear Mr. Starrett,

At last I send you a copy of *Angelina Frood* with apologies for the delay. . . .

I am very glad to have met you and to be able to call up an actual visual memory of you; but I had the feeling that our meeting was a little inadequate, seeing that we are quite old friends. I should have liked to have a longer talk with you on the many topics in which we have a common interest. But I suppose that when a cultured American visits Europe he has a pretty full programme.

Your suggestion that the next volume of short stories should be dedicated to you seems a very appropriate one seeing how much you have done to god-father them in the States. I always remember gratefully what I owe you in this respect.

With best wishes for the New Year,

Yours sincerely,

R. Austin Freeman

Freeman had just completed a series of six stories for *Pearson's* and three of them were already in print. "The Puzzle Lock" was due to appear in the March, 1925, issue and duly gave its name to the collection put out a month or two later by Hodder & Stoughton. As usual, a novel had been interrupted by his work on the short tales; this time it was *The Shadow of the Wolf,* in which Freeman, with considerable skill, took an old *Pearson's Magazine* story of his and neatly spliced into the center of it a large quantity of new matter. So skillfully was this done that most readers must have been unaware of the story's original form, and Freeman did not draw attention to it. In the earlier version, entitled "The Dead Hand,"[12] the story is of the inverted type with the crime described in the first instalment and the detective process in the second, the complete tale being too long for inclusion in one issue of the magazine. No doubt it was this latter consideration which prompted the author to husband the tale for so many years and try his hand at lengthening it into a novel. The first chapter of the novel is an almost verbatim copy of the first magazine instalment. In this, two men set out from a point just north-west of Land's End to sail around the promontory to Penzance. Varney, who is being blackmailed by his present companion, Purcell, into forging bank notes, kills his tormentor during the trip and dumps his weighted body over the side near the Wolf Rock, eight miles south-south-west of Land's End. A thick sea-mist hides his actions from the light-house keepers on the rock and he is able to complete the sail alone and make some false tracks for Purcell in Penzance. (This journey, or one very like it, was, according to Jessup, once undertaken by Freeman and some friends.)

In the second part of the original version, Jervis and Thorndyke are present at a biology lecture when the lecturing professor produces, as a curiosity, a waxed cork disk on which a marine worm, *Terebella rufescens,* has attached itself. The disk is recognized by the Rodney brothers, two men affected by Purcell's unexplained disappearance, as having been used as a makeshift fastener on the missing man's oilskin. Thorndyke, of course, is drawn into the problem and uses the marine specimen as virtually his sole clue in determining where Purcell's body is.

All this is present in the final account; nothing is lost. But, on the other hand, much is added. Jervis, the original narrator of the second part, is dropped and the third-person method adopted, the action being seen largely through the eyes of Thorndyke. The Thorndyke student who reads both versions is afforded a deep insight into Freeman's methods of story construction. Observe the following new episodes. The widow, Margaret Purcell, unconscious of her new status, had been unhappily married and becomes increasingly eager to be free of her missing husband. She has received a mysterious letter from a lawyer in London, Mr. Penfield. Margaret consults him and then visits Thorndyke; Thorndyke interviews Penfield in what must be a high-water mark of Freeman's dramatic talents. The verbal duel of the two men, so evenly matched, so determined to give nothing away, is a fine thing to read. Penfield will be met again in Thorndyke novels, but he is at his best, and driest, in this first appearance. Thorndyke also calls on Purcell's business assistant, and is introduced by Superintendent Miller to a "flash-note factory." Meanwhile Varney lays more false clues in the shape of forged letters and Thorndyke cunningly feigns acceptance of the new leads. Another passage which is exceedingly effective is the face-to-face meeting of the detective and the murderer, already under suspicion, at Margaret Purcell's home.

The clue in *The Shadow of the Wolf* depends on the habits of *Terebella* and the restricted occurrence of phonolite, the mineral of which the Wolf Rock is composed. Mr. P. A. Sabine, the chief petrographer of the Geological Survey and Museum in South Kensington, was most helpful in recent discussions on these matters. He had cited *The Shadow of the Wolf* in the introduction to a recent paper[13] of his own in which he discusses such detecting matters as the origin of a sample of concrete substituted for the genuine contents in a package of gold watches sent by air from Switzerland to Accra via London, Rome and Tripoli. (Marine shells in the material, including one stained with Tyrian purple, pointed to the substitution having occurred at Tripoli, as was later established.)

Mr. Sabine, in a footnote, tells me that a jingle current among students in the elementary geology class at Birmingham University in the early thirties ran something like this:

The Greek tycoon who came by night,
His body disappeared from sight.
They found him off the Wolf Rock Light
His boots were full of phonolite.

Freeman wrote twice to Starrett around the time his new novel was due out:

2nd September, 1925

Dear Mr. Starrett,

I meant to write to you when I posted off my new volume of short stories a week or two ago but the good intention has been in abeyance since then.

I hope the book reached you safely and that the contents have given satisfaction. The dedication looked rather bald, but after all it sets forth the relevant fact that you are a friend sufficiently valued to be associated with one of the milestones on the literary pilgrimage, and the most verbose dedication couldn't say more.

Your approval of "Angelina" is most satisfactory. I was a little doubtful how the book would appear to a critical reader, but the general verdict has been in agreement with yours. The next book, "The Shadow of the Wolf," comes out this month, I understand, here and in the U. S. A. (Dodd, Mead). It is a rather queer book and I am curious to hear what the verdict on it will be. It is a Thorndyke story on the lines of "The Singing Bone.". . .

Yours sincerely,

R. Austin Freeman.

25th October, 1925

My dear Vincent Starrett,

Your book "Coffins for Two,"—a remarkably ar-
resting title, by the way—reached me some time ago and
was immediately consumed with that sort of surprised
admiration which one feels for work that is quite outside
one's own powers. It reminded me a good deal of Stevenson's "New Arabian Nights." All the stories seemed to be
admirable in their grim, fantastic way, but the one I
enjoyed most was "The Elixir of Death." There is a fine
gruesome, body-snatching atmosphere about it, and I
found myself half regretting that you had expended such
a good plot on a short story. There was really the material
for a novel in it. But perhaps you have a better market at
present for short than for long stories. Many thanks for
the gift and for the very kind inscription, which I assure
you is very much appreciated.

I am sending you a copy of my new book "The
Shadow of the Wolf," which is a long story in the manner
of "The Singing Bone" stories—with the plot inside out.
It is all told in the third person and the machinery both
of the crime and the detection is exposed to view. Your
desire to purchase the volume has got to be ignored
this time; but I quite understand your point of view and
will give it consideration in the future.

By this time, I hope the climate of Chicago has settled
down and that you are none the worse for last month's
roasting, only a little brown and crisp on the surface.
Here we are having the usual assorted samples of climate
at which Americans jeer; but the one on tap at the
moment is a very pleasant one—a sort of St. Luke's
summer. But I understand that bedevilments are on their
way across the Atlantic.

I remain,
With warmest regards,
Yours sincerely,

R. Austin Freeman

About this time, Freeman was getting under way with his latest novel, *The D'Arblay Mystery,* a good sound Thorndyke investigation possessing, in Marion D'Arblay, a typical Freeman heroine. Julius D'Arblay was a wax modeller and thus, as Freeman remarks, almost unique in England, for members of his craft were, and perhaps still are, almost exclusively French, hence Freeman's choice of the name. The story begins with the discovery of Julius' body in a woodland pond by young Dr. Stephen Gray. The murder—for such it is—has been carried out by means of an aconitine injection in the back, and no motive can be discovered by Thorndyke, who is quickly consulted by his old pupil. An apparently separate mystery develops when Gray is narrowly missed by a falling derrick on a London towpath on his way home after certifying (for purposes of cremation) the death of old Mr. Bendelow. Marion is Julius' daughter, independent, good-looking and sufficiently proficient in her father's craft to make her own way if need be. A murderous assault by an unknown assailant disables her sufficiently to make physical protection, as well as some help in her workshop, necessary for a time; with the result that both Gray and Polton are pressed into service. The descriptions of the workshop practices are, as usual, authentic, and humor creeps into the tale in exchanges between Thorndyke and a local Medical Officer of Health at the scene of an exhumation. The funniest remark, albeit unconscious, is Polton's in an exchange with Gray. Polton bears a verbal message from Thorndyke: Would Dr. Gray please be present the following day at King's Bench Walk when Superintendent Miller is expected to call; and would he please refrain from comment on anything that might be said?

"This is very mysterious, Polton," [Gray] remarked.

"Why, not particularly, sir," he replied. "You see, the officer is coming to give certain information, but he will try to get some for himself if he can. But he won't get anything out of the Doctor; and the only way for you to prevent his pumping you is to say nothing and appear to know nothing."

[Gray] laughed at his ingenious wiliness. "Why," [he] exclaimed, "you are as bad as the doctor, Polton. A regular Machiavelli." "I never heard of him," said Polton, "but most Scotchmen are pretty close."

For the rest, Thorndyke commands admiration for his adroit handling of the case and for his masterly exposition, after the affair has been neatly concluded, to Gray and Marion (newly affianced) at 5A, King's Bench Walk, where the young doctor is recovering from a leg wound sustained during the arrest of the criminals. Jervis does not appear in the story at all, but Polton plays a prominent part throughout, even sacrificing his eyelashes in the interests of justice.

As he so often did, Freeman wrote to Starrett before settling down to his next major project. He usually began his novels in the autumn and completed them by spring, and therefore wrote most of his letters on returning from a short summer vacation. In 1926, as he explains, he did not journey from home:

Future address: 1 Portland Villas
                  West Hill
                  Gravesend
                  Kent.
                              109 Darnley Road,
                                  Gravesend,
                                      21st September, 1926

My dear Vincent Starrett,

I am sending you by this post my new book,

"The D'Arblay Mystery" and I had better take the opportunity to send you also a few lines in reply to your letter of the 25th May, which is by now getting a little over-ripe.

I am glad you liked "The Shadow of the Wolf" and that you approved of the character study in it. Detection pure and simple becomes rather monotonous after a time and I am disposed to make some further experiments in this direction—the emotional interest. But the present book is a reversion to the original type.

I have only two books of yours: "Coffins for Two" and "The Unique Hamlet." Your other book "Banners in the Dawn" would be very welcome indeed.

Your question with regard to my MSS will have to be considered. I have written all my works in longhand, and I do not, as a rule, send the MS to the printer, but have it typed—three or four copies. At present I have the MSS of everything I have written, having kept them carefully filed to refer to in case a reprint should have to be made. I have occasionally considered how the collection should be disposed of, but have not yet come to any decision. If I decide to break up the set, I should like some of the MSS to go to my friends. But I must also hear what my family wish.

I have been better in health this year, but the hot weather put me off work almost completely and I did not feel up to going away for a change. Perhaps I shall take a fortnight by the sea before settling down for the winter's work.

Next month I am going to move into a new house, and it will probably be my last move—but one. The new house will be much more suitable than this, and I hope I may have a chance of showing it to you. Meanwhile I hope *you* have not moved again. I always write to you with an anxious feeling that the letter is addressed to the wrong place. But perhaps your post-office is accustomed to your nomadic habits.

With all good wishes,
Yours sincerely,

R. Austin Freeman

The move referred to was *not* Freeman's "last-but-one." He
was to change addresses once more, simply from one side of the
street to the other, Portland Villas 'being the name given to a
section of Windmill Street.   Starrett answered Freeman's letter
almost immediately and, evoked a prompt reply:

1 Portland Villas,
West Hill,
Gravesend.
11th October, 1926

My dear Vincent Starrett,

I shall be delighted to have one of my stories
included in your anthology—or more, if you want them.
So you can tell Messrs. Dodd, Mead that you have my
sanction.

I am afraid I can't help you in the matter of
unknown or neglected detective stories. I very seldom
read fiction and have extremely little knowledge of contemporary detective work.

E. M. Wrong's little book seems to be having
deserved success; but I agree with you that the non-
detective stories in it were not much to the point. I
read the book with great interest, especially the admirable
introduction, and was surprised to find how little I know
about my fellow writers in this field.

Many thanks for your interesting letter—received
today. I visualize you in your cottage by Long Island

Sound and am reminded of Knickerbocker's description of the early settlers—though some of it, I am sure, does not apply to you.

With thanks for your good wishes and cordial greetings,

Yours sincerely,

R. Austin Freeman

The well of Freeman's inspiration was running dry. He had felt his age during the hot weather of 1926 and was without ideas for a new Thorndyke novel. *Pearson's* had asked him for a set of short stories, and he responded as best as he could. But although some of the stories, like "The Naturalist at Law" and "The Magic Casket" were among his most superior efforts, others, like "Mr. Ponting's Alibi" with its obvious phonograph clue, were hardly worthy of their author. Ultimately only five stories were published in the series, raising the possibility that one was turned down by the editor.[14] By midwinter, Freeman was at low ebb. For light relief he turned to *The Surprising Experiences of Mr. Shuttlebury Cobb,* one of his shortest works, though bearing the longest title of them all. It is a light romance in the form of a series of connected episodes, containing a dollop of mystery and a modicum of treasure-hunting in the Canterbury district. In a letter to Starrett, which we shall read in a few moments, Freeman described the book as a "resuscitated pot-boiler" which suggests that the story dates from some years earlier and may originally have appeared in some magazine.

He shortly afterwards did get down to work on another Thorndyke story, which may have begun life in Freeman's mind in the form of a straight adventure story. It ended as a hybrid; over half of *A Certain Dr. Thorndyke* is set in the Gold Coast area and deals with the adventures of John Osmond, a fugitive from English justice. The book is unique in opening in a foreign land and reverting to Thorndyke and the Temple only for the investigation of the mystery. There is some discrepancy in dates, for the West African scenes occur in 1897, while back in London the scene corresponds closely to London in the 1920's. The old lawyer, Penfield, first introduced in *The Shadow of the Wolf,* appears again, by this time quite won over to Thorndyke's methods. Jervis appears briefly to provide an audience for Thorndyke, but the third-person narrative method is used throughout the book, the action being sometimes seen through Thorndyke's eyes.

The most important scientific clue here is a collection of spindle-shaped castings left by a wood-boring insect. Freeman had earlier observed such characteristic particles lying on his own workbench near a wooden object placed there for a special purpose. What that purpose was, the reader can discover for himself from *A Certain Dr. Thorndyke,* for the origin of the castings is precisely the same there.

On the whole, this is not one of the better Thorndyke mysteries. Unless the reader is a devotee of light-hearted adventure he will probably feel cheated at being given so little of Thorndyke. Moreover there is no capital crime to be cleared up, only a jewel robbery, and the hero's initial reason for flight can only be regarded as pretty unconvincing. The Thorndyke devotee, on the other hand, will be glad to read another episode in his champion's career, even though confined to half a book.

After finishing work on this novel, Freeman took a breather and caught up with his correspondence, including an overdue answer to a Starrett letter:

> 1, Portland Villas,
> West Hill,
> Gravesend,
> 24th August, 1927

My dear Vincent Starrett,

There is a certain stage of moral turpitude at which it seems idle to offer excuses or extenuations. I have reached that stage. Your letter is nearly three months old and contained a postal order which I never even acknowledged. Those are the bald facts. There is nothing to be said—or if there is, I expect you have said it.

I send by this post "The Magic Casket" and also "Mr. Shuttlebury Cobb," which is not a Thorndyke story but a resuscitated pot-boiler. My publishers are now re-issuing a number of my older books including "The Golden Pool"—my first novel—and "The Unwilling Adventurer," which followed it. Both are simple romances of adventure, not detective stories, and the "Adventurer" is a cheap (and rather shoddy) reprint. I suspect they would not interest you, but, if they would, you might let me know next time you write to me. I like you to have my books, and the only reason you don't get them more promptly is that I am a fearful shirker in the matter of making up parcels and taking them down to the post office.

With many apologies, and wishing you the very best of health,

Yours sincerely,

R. Austin Freeman

P. S. I am sending you the English edition of "The Magic Casket," but should like to know, for future guidance, whether you have any preference. I think the American editions are rather better turned out than the English.

RAF

Freeman's next book was, like *Shuttlebury Cobb,* very light-weight and very short. Back in 1868, Dickens **had** been pleased by *The Moonstone,* written by his friend Wilkie Collins for serial publication in Dickens's weekly magazine, *All the Year Round.*

"It is a very curious story" wrote Dickens to his assistant editor, "wild and yet domestic with excellent character in it, great mystery, and nothing belonging to disguised women or the like." From which we may infer that women in men's clothing, and *vice versa,* were anathema to the great Victorian novelist, and that he would therefore have disliked several of Freeman's novels. The device is used in *Pontifex, Son and Thorndyke* (1931) and two other Thorndyke novels. In a more light-hearted manner, but not less objectionably because of that, Danby Croker had impersonated a suffragette for a period spread over weeks. And now Freeman compounded his offense by building an entire book around a young lady who became a young-man-about-town. Originally named *The Flights of Phyllis,* the episodes appeared in *The Grand Magazine* before being issued in January, 1928, by Hodder and Stoughton as *Flighty Phyllis.*

Phyllis Dudley, in Munich for vocal training, was a lady with a deep contralto voice; as the story opens she has just recovered from an illness, not described, during which her head has been shaved. She therefore has need of a wig, but when that is removed and she is garbed in male attire, she passes quite adequately as a man. Moreover, she closely resembles her cousin, Charlie, a fashionable young man of dishonest character. Why she should choose, on returning to London, to play a male role and thereby inherit Charlie's various debts and embarrassments is never explained. Those who choose to read this type of novel must leave their scepticism out of account. In any event, Phyllis's adventures lead her into innumerable predicaments, including a kidnaping in the East End, from which she is rescued by Charlie, who kills two of her captors with his pistol. Justifiably, no doubt, but with the bantering tone of the narrative chillingly maintained throughout, and, of course, with no notification of the authorities at any time.

Freeman did not think enough of the book to mention it when he next wrote to Starrett in April. (The letter deals almost entirely with Starrett's books and is therefore not reproduced here.)

Freeman made up for his preoccupation with trivial fiction in his next work, *As a Thief in the Night,* one of the finest in the

Thorndyke saga. The great man is seen from a distance by the narrator, a young lawyer called Rupert Mayfield. (Freeman's non-use of Jervis in the novels is explained, of course, by his need to produce a fresh bachelor on each occasion as a mate for the heroine, whereas in the short stories there is not time for the development of love interest, and the faithful Jervis is therefore employed in almost every case.) As it happens, Mayfield's unhappy romance is over long before the story begins, for his Stella had died after a lingering illness years earlier when she was little more than a child. Now, in the present, he becomes part of a household in which Harold Monkhouse, the elderly husband, dies of arsenic poisoning, and he rather hesitantly calls in Thorndyke, who warns him ominously of what his investigations may uncover.

It is a fascinating story, in which Mayfield's diary and a wax medallion play a part, as does also a muzzle-loading pocket pistol, sent to Thorndyke as part of an infernal machine. (The author's son John remembers the weapon as it existed in fact: "When Dr. Freeman returned from Africa he brought home a small mahogany box containing a cap lock pistol and powder flask—a beautiful little toy, but the most inefficient fire-arm I have ever handled.")

As a narrator, Mayfield views Thorndyke in the same detached, almost unfriendly fashion as that adopted by his fellow attorney, Anstey, in *The Cat's Eye.* Thus, after a search through the vacated Monkhouse residence, Mayfield reflects: "In spite of my great confidence in Thorndyke, I was sensible of a chill of disappointment in respect alike of his words and his deeds. In this rather farcical grubbing about in the dismantled house there was a faint suggestion of charlatanism; of the vulgar, melodramatic sleuth, nosing out a trail. . . ." So that, having commissioned Thorndyke to investigate, Mayfield becomes something like an adversary. But worse is to come, and the climax is reached in a nightmarish chase across London in the middle of the night after which an appalled Mayfield spies on Thorndyke's shocking activities in Highgate cemetery. A current of horror passes between narrator and reader. It is one of the few occasions when Freeman successfully appealed to his reader's emotions rather than their reason. If only he had chosen to do it more often!

Freeman's life, as we have seen, had now settled down to an uneventful routine, the years marked by a steady progression of books and by little else. The year 1928 saw Freeman's name entered in *Who's Who* for the first time; he had achieved this recognition just before turning sixty-six. The same year apparently saw the end of his correspondence with Starrett. Here, in full, is Freeman's last letter:

> 1, Portland Villas,
> West Hill,
> Gravesend.
> 25th September, 1928,

My dear Vincent Starrett,

I am just back from my holidays and clearing off arrears of letters, so I will begin with yours, which is a little over-ripe.

I haven't got a recent photograph, but I am going one day shortly to have some new ones done and will then send you a signed copy.

I am wondering how your mystery novel is faring and hoping that it is by now in the hands of the printers and that I may have a chance of reading it before long.

My last book is now nearly due for publication and has already been announced. Now that I am back home, I am regretfully putting away the painting materials with which I have had such a pleasant time and settling down to perpetrate the next shocker.

Wishing you the best of luck with your new novel.

> Yours sincerely,
>
> R. Austin Freeman

"Perpetration of the next shocker" was interrupted by ill-health. Freeman was stricken by a painful attack of neuritis at the close of 1928, and he was slow to regain his usual tempo. In fact, his new book did not appear until the autumn of 1930. Meanwhile, Hodder and Stoughton issued the collected Thorndyke short stories in September, 1929, as an attractive volume in blue cloth, an all-time bargain at seven shillings and sixpence. The two detective stories from *The Great Portrait Mystery* are included, together with all those from the five collections with three exceptions: "The Man with the Nailed Shoes," "The Mandarin's Pearl" and "A Message from the Deep Sea," all of which originally appeared in the first collection, *John Thorndyke's Cases* (1909). The latter was published in the U. S. as *Dr. Thorndyke's Cases* in 1931 by Dodd, Mead and is fairly easy to obtain. In this way the reader may readily become possessed of all forty of the short Thorndyke adventures, for the Hodder omnibus is still in print at this writing.

Freeman never wrote another short story of any kind, but he still had several more years of writing ahead of him, and some of his finest Thorndyke novels were yet to come.

Freeman in the early 1930's.
(Courtesy of C. J. A. Freeman.)

THE PENROSE MYSTERY

To my friend, Mr Elmhurst (who has
been known to masquerade under the
name of R. F. Jessup) with all good
wishes & happy memories of the late
Inkleberry.

R Austin Freeman

Nov. 1940.

A Freeman Inscription. In replacement
of Jessup's inscribed first edition, lost in
the London Blitz. (Courtesy of R. F.
Jessup.)

94 Windmill St., Gravesend. Freeman died here 28 Sept. 1943,
his widow 22 April 1948. (Courtesy of Paul R. Lorch.)

CHAPTER IX

The Last Decade

Freeman remarked that he seldom read detective stories by other authors; in much the same vein Sibelius told a visitor that he never listened to the music by other composers. "If I did," he explained, "I could not continue to compose like Sibelius." Probably Freeman's motives were different. Very likely he was not greatly interested in detective stories as such, but preferred to read about medical and sociological matters. He had to do a good deal of reading in these areas anyway, for the editor of the *Eugenics Review* regularly sent him volumes and articles for review, many of them with formidable titles like *Notes on a Case of Linkage in Paratettix* by J. B. S. Haldane, and further "duty reading" was probably distasteful. Nevertheless, Freeman's isolation from the developing patterns in detective fiction served to keep his style rather old-fashioned.

It is startling to realize, for example, that E. C. Bentley's masterpiece, *Trent's Last Case,* appeared as long ago as 1913, the year before *The Silent Witness* was published. Many of the writers of the twenties surpassed Freeman in important aspects of technique and presentation. Thus, 1920 saw the first appearance of Mr. Fortune, H. C. Bailey's rather affected but highly effective physician-investigator, and the same year brought forth Agatha Christie's Hercule Poirot in *The Mysterious Affair at Styles* as well as Freeman Wills Crofts' first effort, *The Cask.* Lord Peter Wimsey made his entrance in 1923 in Dorothy Sayers' *Whose Body?* and Anthony Berkeley's *The Layton Court Mystery* (1925) marked the beginning for another notable writer in the genre. All these authors made important contributions to the modern detective story; some, notably Miss Sayers, were better writers than Freeman, and many of them told a more thrilling story than he did. Yet, on rereading even the best books of these masters, one cannot fairly say that their styles are more interesting than Freeman's. Crofts is frequently dull; Christie manipulates cardboard characters to enable the least expected—and often the least credible—solution to emerge. Bailey and Sayers created detectives whose manufactured affectations are difficult to tolerate nowadays, except in small doses. Thus, Lord Peter refers to indigestion as "the indijaggers" and much of his conversation is in the same embarrassing strain, while Reggie Fortune groans peevishly through his cases. By contrast, Thorndyke and his friends converse in a straightforward manner; in fact most of the time their conversational level is an echo of Freeman's own. Some critics have suggested that they sound too much like a textbook. Thus H. Douglas Thomson[1] ridicules Thorndyke's remarks to Jervis in "The Case of the White Foot-Prints":

> "Assuming the little toes to be absent, we account for
> their absence by considering known cases in the order of
> their probability. Excluding—quite properly I think—
> Raynaud's disease, we arrive at frostbite and ergotism."

But after all, Thorndyke and his friends talk precisely as *scholarly* men talked during the early years of the century, and not so differently from the way they talk still. For this reason the style of the Thorndyke books and stories fails to jar where Sayers, Bailey and others—and, for that matter, Freeman himself in his lighter fiction—jar badly, for they use slang and transient forms of sub-standard English which have long since passed out of fashion.

So Freeman, ignoring other detective-story writers of the period, went on plowing his lonely furrow, assured of a steady but not massive audience in Britain and a small select one in the United States.

The Thorndyke book which engaged his labors throughout 1929 was one of his best. It is also something of a rarity in being a full length inverted story. Since inventing the form in *The Singing Bone* stories he had used it twice more in short tales published in *The Great Portrait Mystery* (1918) but only once in a full-length novel, *The Shadow of the Wolf* (1925), which, as we have seen, was an inverted short story in its original form. Now he tried it for the first time in a story conceived and constructed directly as a novel. The result was *Mr. Pottermack's Oversight*, published in October 1930, and a steady favorite ever since. The prologue depicts Jeffrey Brandon's escape from jail, where he was unjustly serving time for embezzlement. He makes a new life for himself in America and in due course returns to a pleasant seclusion in a provincial English town. The man who engineered the false evidence against him turns blackmailer, and Brandon—now renamed Pottermack—not only disposes of him down the well in his garden but ingeniously fabricates his footprints to lead investigators away from the scene of the crime.

The introduction of Thorndyke into this orderly affair is a matter of some difficulty for the author, for in the "perfect" crime no investigator should ever had become suspicious. Only Pottermack's oversight enables Thorndyke to solve the case, and what that oversight is becomes evident to most readers only in the final chapter. Freeman is eminently fair however, and it is possible to spot the flaw early in the book.

Although the *quantity* of Thorndyke offered in *Pottermack* is somewhat less than the average, the *quality* leaves nothing to be desired. When he does appear he is at his most perceptive and most benign. He is never officially engaged in the case at all, his role being that of a detached observer. For all that, he leaves a thoroughly satisfying impression in the reader's mind.

John Freeman believes the original of the unfenced chalk pit in the novel to be one in the Gravesend area near the cart track leading from Ifield Court to the Wrotham road. It was surrounded by a small coppice and contained at the end opposite the entrance a deep cave, its roof and sides blackened by wood smoke and its floor littered with old tins and cooking pots. This was the setting Freeman used for the nerve-shattering scene in which Pottermack parted company, with a marked lack of reluctance, from Khama-Heru.

The periscope, disguised as a rather clumsy-looking walking stick, with which Thorndyke was able to peer over Mr. Pottermack's high garden wall, was constructed in actual fact by Freeman for his own edification. He did not pretend that it was perfectly disguised. "It had the stark mechanical regularity of an elbow joint on a gaspipe, and to make matters worse, its end was finished by a sort of terminal cap. . . . A sharp-eyed rural constable would have 'spotted' it at a glance as a walking-stick gun; and he would have been wrong." But it served its purpose.

In the late twenties, Freeman had met Ronald F. Jessup, a young bank employee in Gravesend with lifelong archaeological interests. It was Jessup who supplied the banking details for *Pottermack* and some years later, as we shall see, was the prime mover in the creation of another Thorndyke novel. He wrote, at a remarkably early age, the contribution on Kent in the *County Archaeologies* series, and thereby became acquainted with Freeman around the time we are reviewing. He writes:

> As a very young man I was greatly honoured to become a founder-member of the Pudden Club at Gravesend. This was a re-founding of a very old dining club, but the new foundation was restricted to authors who had written

about Kent or who lived in or near Gravesend. Freeman
was a much-loved member and never missed a dinner. We
ate always steak, kidney and oyster pudding, larded with
a mutton chop, at *The Three Daws* tavern by the river-
side at Gravesend. The chairman of the evening had the
duty of providing a guest, choosing the subject for discussion after dinner if he wished, and writing the minutes.
Freeman's guest was often the welcome Rupert Gould, to
whom *Mr. Polton Explains* is dedicated. It was during
these years that I came to know Freeman so well, and the
Pudden Club dinners were often followed by an invitation the next week to port and cigars at Freeman's
house. He himself rarely smoked cigars, however, and the
Trichinopoly cheroots never existed in fact. He had never
smoked one, though he was much touched when we gave
him a bundle at a Pudden, a bundle which I regret to say
had not seen the Customs Officer, and which we had been
able to import through the kind offices of a friend
specially for Freeman.

One other direct link, apart from the personal
inscriptions in my copies of his books, I still have. On
my desk lie a pair of outside callipers, beautifully made
of mahogany and finished with Victorian farthings as
fulcra. These were a gift from Freeman and he made
them especially for me at a time when I was much
concerned with making scale drawings of globular Roman
urns and finding some practical difficulty in measuring
external girths.

Pottermack was dedicated to Lady Lynden-Bell who lived with
her husband Major General Sir Arthur Lynden-Bell (1867-1943)
near Sevenoaks. She was the daughter of the first Viscount
Chilston of Maidstone, and the origin and nature of her acquaintance
with Freeman is a mystery. Her Christian name was Bertha, as
was that of Miss Fowle, whose home, "The Studio," was located in
Campbell Road, two-thirds of a mile across town from Freeman's

new home at Portland Villas. Bertha Fowle was something of a protegée of Freeman's. She was a fellow-member of the Nomen Ignotum Art Club, being better known in this connection than Freeman himself. Both exhibited their water colors at the annual collections, which Jessup recalls as being "remarkably fine." She appears to have shared Freeman's love of arts and crafts generally and, indeed, is locally reputed to have woven on her own hand-loom the cloth from which Freeman's not particularly well-fitting outer garments were tailored. In his will, dated March 1933, Miss Fowle was bequeathed "all my drawing painting and modelling materials instruments and appliances including my lay figure complete with its accessories and turntable all my books on art and handicraft (excepting those of which she already possesses copies) and the bookcase in which they are at present contained."

Freeman moved house for the last time in 1930, a transfer of only a few yards across the road to "Rosemount" at No. 94, Windmill Street. A young curate at Gravesend Parish Church, newly arrived in town with his wife, rented the vacated house at No. 1, Portland Villas. The Reverend Edward L. Howland recalled his memories of Freeman at that period. "It is difficult to convey," he wrote, "the charm and courteousness of Dr. Freeman and, indeed of Mrs. Freeman too. He was quite brilliant and most versatile, but with these qualities went a deep humility and modesty. . . . I found his wide knowledge of medicine, the law and the arts a little frightening at first, but his charm and modesty soon put me at my ease." Altogether Freeman seems to have left a deep impression on young Mr. Howland. They never discussed religion, he writes, but "I still remember some of the things he told me about the habits of frogs; natural history seems to have fascinated him."

By this time, the next Thorndyke novel had been begun. *Pontifex, Son and Thorndyke* is a strange mixture. Although the book is a favorite of many Thorndyke devotees it is difficult to understand why. Absent from *Pottermack*, Jervis "returns" (an inappropriate word, as we shall see) as narrator of part of the tale. The other part is provided—in the first person—by seventeen-year-old Jasper Gray, who is involved in a ludicrous adventure right at the start when he is bribed to be nailed up in an egg chest and—to his surprise—is delivered to a nest of crooks in the East End. Later he finds himself forced to exchange clothes with an escaped convict and, quite unnecessarily, leads the police a chase across north London to the "Angel" at Islington where he takes refuge in the "duds" of an artist's model (feminine). If all this sounds too preposterous a situation in which to involve the benign but austere Thorndyke, it can only be reported that the great man *is* relatively ill at ease in these surroundings, even at second-hand, and performs less satisfactorily than is his wont. The mystery proper concerns the disappearance of Sir Edward Hardcastle and his apparent suicide (by hanging) in an empty house in a remote corner of Stratford. Thorndyke, of course, analyses the situation in masterly fashion, and concludes that this is a case of murder by a gang. The murderers are again (as in *Helen Vardon's Confession*) East London Jews with unpronounceable names. Even Freeman seems confused about them, and eager to bring the story to a conclusion as best he can. Jervis, more astute than usual (he almost takes the lead in drawing deductions from the evidence at the scene of the "suicide") is dissatisfied by his senior's summing up of the affair: "Well, . . . you have a better case than I thought, though it isn't up to your usual standard."

"No," he admitted, "but it is the best that we can do . . ."

Usually the lack of denouement, in the sense of exposure of the criminal, does not trouble the Freeman reader. He receives his satisfaction from learning *how* the crime was committed; *what* the essential clue was; *why* things happened as they did. In this story, though, there is a grave deficiency in almost every field. The intended climax—revelation of Jasper Gray's true identity—has been guessed early by even the dullest reader, and nothing is left with which to ring down the curtain with an appropriate flourish. Altogether it is disappointing.

We said earlier that Jervis "returned." To be more precise he had not yet left Thorndyke's employ, for Freeman set the story back in 1903, thereby not only avoiding an explanation of Jervis's presence but also acquiring the nostalgic flavor of hansom cabs and the scent of the London he remembered so well.

A few months after *Pontifex* appeared in London, a *Dr. Thorndyke Omnibus* was put out by Dodd, Mead in New York. Like the London version of 1929 it is an attractive volume, printed on good paper, but it differs from it in content, containing thirty-eight rather than thirty-seven of the forty Thorndyke short stories. Whereas the London contents were entirely reset, Dodd, Mead simply used the plates of the five separate Thorndyke collections with the original paginations. The two inverted stories which appeared in *The Great Portrait Mystery*, a book never published in the U.S., were absent.

By this time (January, 1932) Freeman was hard at work, and had come to a difficult decision. His new plot called for a shocking murder. An old friend—or at least an old familiar—of Thorndyke readers needed, he felt, to be sacrificed. Looking back at Freeman's decision from this distance in time one wonders whether, perhaps, Superintendent Miller should not have been the victim. This would have increased the impact of the crime in a highly satisfactory way. But perhaps Freeman considered him too valuable to lose. At any rate it was foxy Inspector Badger who was found dead in the railway tunnel near Greenhithe, and his murder automatically wiped out much of Thorndyke's and Jervis's ill-feeling toward him. It was Badger, one remembers, who played a practical joke on Thorndyke in "A Sower of Pestilence," although the investigator more than returned the favor by sending Badger on an unnecessary sea voyage in "The Stolen Ingots."

Freeman also resorted to his earlier stories in search of a criminal. Walter Hornby, at the end of *The Red Thumb Mark*, was not entirely disposed of. He was last seen leaving the court room with Miller in hot pursuit. For a quarter of a century readers were free to imagine him as having been sent to prison for grand larceny. But not so: it appears that Miller lost sight of him on Ludgate Hill and that he was never put under lock and key, so all along he was available for use in another story as a fingerprint faker and all-'round bad 'un.

In complexity this book, *When Rogues Fall Out* (U. S. title:

Dr. Thorndyke's Discovery), approaches *The Cat's Eye*. It is more adult and less facetious than *Pontifex;* on the other hand, it lacks the suspense of *As a Thief in the Night* or even of *Pottermack,* although it is engrossing. It is partly an inverted story, for we observe the criminal in action in the first part of the book, although his identity is not quite evident. Mr. Didbury Toke, an antique dealer, finds a valuable necklace hidden in an old clock he has just bought at a country cottage. The "owner," a burglar, tries to recover it, employing as his agent Arthur Hughes—actually, Hornby in disguise. Later Hornby and Toke enter into a nefarious partnership which ends with Toke's death.[2]

Jervis returns as narrator in the second part of the book, which begins with Miller's announcement of Badger's apparent murder and Thorndyke's "discovery," presumably that of a half-smoked cigar found in the Greenhithe tunnel. The latter provides evidence both of the murder method and of the possible identity of the murderer. Incidentally, the "single-print" method of coding, developed at Scotland Yard by Inspector Harry Battley just before this novel was written, is described rather fully by Freeman, who provides a facsimile of Hornby's thumb-print so that Thorndyke's discourse might be more intelligible.

The later incidents mesh with customary ingenuity. The third (and final) part of the book, also narrated by Jervis, describes an interesting appliance for taking photographs through a keyhole, a gadget which, according to Ronald Jessup, in fact existed. The remainder of the story, replete with secret passages, family vaults and suspenseful night vigils, rounds out this vintage Thorndyke novel satisfactorily.

Though some eminent critics have claimed that Freeman's books resemble one another too closely, it is not truer of Freeman's than of the works of other authors. The flavor of *Pottermack* is quite different from that of *Frood,* while *The Shadow of the Wolf* and *Helen Vardon's Confession* are completely distinct again. On the other hand, the stories and novels fall into groups, with in which the resemblances are close, as Freeman would return to a type of plot he had used before. Moreover the rigid format to which Freeman, by 1932, had perforce resigned himself made the conception of markedly novel plots difficult. At seventy his writing powers were not yet on the wane, but the launching of each new venture was a greater labor than it once had been. The years 1930 through 1932 had been heavy in book-reviewing for the *Eugenics Review*, since Freeman was loath to turn down any request from the Society's editor. Now, in the fall of 1932, another book had to be planned.

In 1927, Freeman had observed that only once (in "The Case of Oscar Brodski") had he made use of a real case in his fiction; most true crime was unsatisfactory as a basis for plot-building. In particular, the forensic medical deductions, he felt, were too obvious to present to the detective-story reader.

But *Dr. Thorndyke Intervenes,* for the only time in a Thorndyke *novel*, does introduce a real case, and a famous one at that. The Druce-Portland case concerned a claim made by George Hollamby Druce that he was the true Duke of Portland and heir to the Portland estates; a claim founded on the assertion that Thomas Charles Druce, proprietor of the Baker Street Bazaar in London, was in reality the fifth Duke of Portland, who led a double life. Furthermore, he also claimed T. C. Druce's funeral in 1864 was bogus, the coffin containing no body but only lead. All sides agreed that the Duke died at his ancestral home, Welbeck Abbey, fifteen years later.

Lengthy civil actions having produced no result, the claimant attempted to force the issue by bringing a perjury action against T. C. Druce's son, Herbert, who had sworn to having seen his father in his coffin. The action turned into something of carnival, and one prosecution witness quit the country to avoid, in turn, being arrested for perjury. Meanwhile a faculty was obtained at last to open the Druce grave. December 30, 1907 was a bitterly cold day with a touch of snow, but people began to gather at an early hour opposite the entrance to Highgate cemetery, made famous as the last resting place of, among other notables, Karl Marx, and endeared to Thorndyke disciples as the scene of the harrowing climax in *As a Thief in the Night*. Inside, hoisting equipment had

already been installed in readiness; a heavy monument had first to
be lifted clear and flagstones laboriously removed. At last the coffin
was reached, and the dirt was wiped away to reveal the inscription:

Thomas Charles Druce,
Esqre.,
Died 28th Decr.
1864,
In his 71st year

Photographs were taken under the electric lighting which had
been specially installed, and the famous Dr. Pepper, (who at the
Crippen trial was to say things about quicklime with which Thorndyke would find fault in *Frood*), and Sir Thomas Stevenson
were awaited. Powerful pliers, said the *Times* account, were employed to remove the screws, which had remained undisturbed for
over forty years, and the inner lead coffin was cut open to reveal
the shrouded remains of a bearded, elderly man.

The claimant, who was forbidden to be present at the grave-
side, put on a bold front, insisting that the body was not properly
identified, but the steam was effectively removed from his case and
it came to nothing.[3]

In Freeman's novel the putative double life of the Earl of
Winsborough as Josiah Pippet, landlord of "The Fox and Grapes"
in the City, closely parallels the claims made in the Portland case.
The claimant is Christopher Pippet, a courteous American of
impeccable manners, whose case is handled by a shady lawyer called
Gimbler. He engages in a little forgery with an old diary which
Pippet puts in as evidence of his claim and is not even above a
touch of sleight-of-hand with a coffin in the Pippet family vault.
Then there are the matters of a human head found in a railway
cloakroom, as well as the robbery of half a hundredweight of
platinum during shipment from a Baltic port.[4] All these elements
are presented independently, but Freeman's devoted readers are
not deceived. Everything must be connected. Thorndyke, of course,
finds out how, though he never does explain his early apparent lack

of interest in the gruesome cloakroom discovery. The properties of platinum-lead alloys are an important ingredient of the mystery. Apparently Freeman was prompted to this theme by an accident he once experienced with a pair of platinum-nosed crucible tongs which suffered grievously from being dipped into molten lead.[5]   Mr. Elmhurst, the archaeologist and dene-hole specialist, makes his debut in this work. He was inspired by young Ronald F. Jessup, already mentioned, whose home in Gravesend was called "Elmhurst." The newspaper account of *his* adventure is fictional but the setting is not:

> ". . . A local archaeologist, a Mr. Elmhurst of Gravesend, happened to be making a sketch-map of the features of the wood [beside the arterial road three or four miles on the Rochester side of Dartford] when his wanderings took him to the edge of the cutting. Looking down the cliff-like descent, he was horrified to observe, lying on the shelf immediately below him, the headless and perfectly nude body of a man. . . .
>
> "Mr. Elmhurst did not stay to make any further observations, but taking the shortest way to the road, hailed an approaching motorist, who very obligingly conveyed him to Gravesend, where he notified the police of his discovery."[6]

"The ledge from which I looked down," Jessup told me, "is still there, and the local story was that these great concrete ledges contained the bones of Romans found when the road, the Roman road of Watling Street, was made into an arterial road in 1922."

The latter fact makes nonsense of Freeman's dates, for he chose to place the events in 1921 with the intention of having Jervis's services available. A little later, it will be recalled, the honest fellow more or less left Thorndyke's employ, a fact which caused Freeman difficulty in some later books, until he finally decided to forget Jervis's defection entirely and to use him or not as necessity dictated.

Finally, it may be mentioned that the frontispiece of the novel provides a Freeman drawing of a tombstone with what is presumably his own epitaph for Innkeeper Pippet, and a perfect one it is:

> He that buys Land buys Stones
> He that buys Meate buys Bones
> He that buys Eggs buys Many Shelles
> But he that buys good Beer buys Nothing Elles

If *Dr. Thorndyke Intervenes* can be rated a good mystifying example of the Great Fathomer at work, the next volume in the saga, *For the Defence: Dr. Thorndyke*, must be considered somewhat inferior. (It is dedicated to Lady Adams, wife of the Professor John Adams who was the first, in 1913, to analyze—and praise—the quality of Freeman's detective stories.) When Andrew Barton is interrupted in the task of clipping his privet hedge by the arrival of a begging letter from his "look-alike" cousin, Ronald, we fear the worst. For weren't Croker and Nagget strikingly similar? Likewise Flighty Phyllis and her cousin? There is one new factor: Andrew has suffered a severe disfigurement which results in his having virtually no nose. The plot becomes even shakier when Andrew, after an improbable mix-up with two armed bandits, fails to report the matter to the police and becomes a fugitive from justice. The details of how Ronald is killed and Andrew, after a strange back-street operation, takes his place detract still further from the plausibility of the story. There are interesting scenes, as when Andrew goes to visit his wife in his new identity and is not recognized. Finally, he is accused of the murder of Andrew Barton, that is, of himself, and it is at this point that Thorndyke enters the picture. The trouble is, the task of demolishing the charge against Barton is hardly much of a challenge; almost any ordinary detective could do it. It has to be reported, on the other hand, that the court-room scenes are, as usual, extremely satisfying, with Thorndyke producing an overwhelmingly convincing effect by a series of parallel chains of evidence.

So far as we know, Freeman was never the equal of Sir Arthur Conan Doyle when it came to true-life detection. Perhaps this was less a lack of investigative skill than of his quite different personality.   Doyle, to a much greater degree than his younger rival, was interested in people, and, as in the cases of Oscar Slater and George Edalji, fought for their legal rights regardless of his personal feelings towards them.   Freeman, on the other hand, showed a more aloof attitude towards his fellow men; abstract issues, such as eugenics, attracted him more than did people.

Only once did Freeman agree to investigate a real case, and the reason was a commission from an editor. "The great difficulty of attempting to solve the 'unsolved mysteries' of the past." Freeman observed, "is that you have to work from the facts recorded; and they are usually wrong facts.   But they are all you have.   You can't cross-examine a law report."   He then discussed the death, in 1902, of Rose Harsent, a servant-girl in Peasenhall in Suffolk, and the two unsatisfactory trials of William Gardiner (whom Freeman, with obvious approbation, describes as "an eminently respectable master-craftsman").   Gardiner's relationship with a twenty-one-year-old servant girl, twelve years his junior, had been investigated by a church committee a year earlier after two youths had reported witnessing a meeting between the pair in an old deserted building in the village.   The investigation was inconclusive but doubts about Gardiner's character still lay heavy in the public mind when Rose Harsent was found dead on June 1st, 1902 at the foot of a staircase in the kitchen of Providence House, the home of her employers, with her throat cut and other wounds on the breast, face and hands. Her nightdress was partly destroyed by fire and her thighs and buttocks were charred.   Two items discovered nearby were traceable directly to the Gardiner household: a local newspaper found under the body and a broken medicine bottle which had latterly been used to hold paraffin (kerosene). An oil-lamp with a broken chimney also lay close to the body.

Rose's condition—she was six months pregnant—was evidently the motive for the murder, whoever the guilty man might have been.   Gardiner was the obvious suspect and, after two days of unexplained delay, he was arrested. At his first trial eleven of the twelve jurors voted for conviction, but the remaining man could not be won over. At the second, according to William Henderson,[7] the opposite position resulted, with eleven for acquittal and one for conviction. A third trial was not proceeded with and Gardiner was freed from custody after almost eight months' confinement.

At the time of the trial there were some who put forward the suggestion that the girl, alarmed by the thunderstorm that occurred that night, might have fallen down the narrow staircase and been fatally cut by glass from the bottle or lamp. In the light of all the circumstances this was so incredible that it was not even raised by the defense at the trials. To name only one objection, the dead girl had suffered numerous semi-circular cuts about her hands, suggestive of attempts to ward off blows from a knife. Nevertheless, a few defenders of Gardiner in Peasenhall put forward the accident theory, and it is this, surprisingly, that Freeman suggests as the most likely explanation of the circumstances.

If Freeman's only venture into true-life detection demonstrated a lamentable deficiency of plausibility and invention, he was doing better on the fictional front, for his next book, devised under unusual circumstances, was to become important beyond the ranks of mystery lovers. It concerns the disappearance of Daniel Penrose, an eccentric collector of archaeological and other specimens, as well as of apparent trash. The story is begun by Ernest Lockhart, a barrister, and continued by Jervis. A burglary at Penrose's house in Queen's Square raises fresh mysteries, as does the flight of an injured patient from Gravesend hospital. But the hub of the whole affair is an ancient barrow or burial mound, called Julliberrie's Grave, near Chilham in Kent. Thorndyke harbors suspicions about what it might contain but, being an ancient monument, it was protected by law and therefore immune from unofficial investigation. In this impasse, Thorndyke calls in his archaeological friend Mr. Elmhurst and backs him in an officially sanctioned and exhaustive excavation of the barrow, and in due course a grisly discovery is made.

An interesting question immediately springs to the reader's

mind.   As Julliberrie's Grave is real enough and was possibly
excavated at some time or another, just where does Freeman's
fiction end and real life begin?   A search of the archaeological
literature soon brings to light two important papers on the matter.[8]
Both were written by Ronald F. Jessup, and describe two series of
diggings in the summers of 1936 and 1937.   Jessup's first paper
begins: "The re-excavation[9] of this well known barrow was undertak-
en at the suggestion and cost of Sir Edmund Davis (upon whose
estate it is situated) after the recent publication of Dr. R. Austin
Freeman's novel. *The Penrose Mystery,* in which it largely figures."
The papers, which include a map of the area and several diagrams,
are certainly fascinating enough, but they leave an unanswered
puzzle.   How did Freeman come to write about an excavation not
yet undertaken? And what was the sequence of causation between
the book and the events which followed so closely upon its
publication?

In answer to my questions, Ronald F. Jessup, whose appearance, as "Mr. Elmhurst," is described in Chapter xii of Freeman's
novel, and to whom the work is dedicated "in grateful acknowledge-
ment of much valuable technical advice and information on matters
archaeological," kindly supplied the following account:

> Freeman and I had often had long conversations
> about the successful disposal of unwanted corpses, and
> from an archaeologist's point of view I had pointed out
> the great possibilities of dene-holes which occur frequently
> in the chalk formations of north-west and east Kent.
> They were usually to be found in remote places, and
> whatever their origin may have been—and on this, too, we
> had many discussions—unless they had been used by
> farmers for the disposal of dead cattle, a common
> practice, they were not likely to be visited, far less
> explored.   It seemed to me that a far better means of
> disposal of a human corpse would be to bury it on a site
> which had already been excavated by archaeologists. Such
> a site, especially if it were protected by the Ancient

Monuments Act, would not be touched again for very many years, if at all.

It so happened that I was recovering from a prolonged bout of pneumonia and Freeman, in his kind way, used to visit me at our house, which was called "Elmhurst," two or three times a week. As some sort of a thank-you I wrote and gave him as a Christmas present a short story based on the burial of a murdered man in the Neolithic long-barrow called Julliberrie's Grave at Chilham. Much to my surprise, but very great delight, he gave me in 1936 an advance copy of *The Penrose Mystery* with the dedication you have noticed.

By one of those coincidences which happen so often in British archaeology, I was asked to spend a week-end with the late Sir Edmund Davis at his country seat, Chilham Castle, to advise him on the nature of some curious depressions in one of his woods which he thought might be prehistoric pit-dwellings. They might well have been and their subsequent but uneventful excavation need not detain us here. At dinner on the Sunday evening I said rather boldly that I had long wanted to excavate Julliberrie's Grave, which was on his land, and talked at some length on its importance not only in British but also in Continental archaeology. Sir Edmund replied that it was a scheduled monument in the care of the Ministry of Works, and obviously it could not be touched at all. Over coffee I rather naughtily gave him a copy of *The Penrose Mystery,* and by bed-time it had been arranged that if I could secure official permission from the Ministry of Works, he himself would be responsible for the total cost of the excavation provided that any antiquities found should be deposited with him at Chilham Castle— where, incidentally, they still are, properly housed in a case and well cared for—and that a full-scale report should be prepared. Sir Edmund, a mining engineer, knew full well the importance of adequate scientific records. The Ministry of Works was fully co-operative, as I already knew it would be, and the outcome was the highly successful excavation. Since that time, many authors have used the same sort of archaeological background, but none with the accuracy and care of Austin Freeman. The archaeological details are taken from my short story, and in and out of the pages of *The Penrose Mystery,* thinly veiled, are several of my own friends, notably (Sir) Mortimer Wheeler, Veronica Seton-Williams, and Leslie McNair Scott (now Mrs. M. E. Murray-Threipland).

As a tail-piece you will be interested to know that the plane-table which I used for surveying at Chilham was made for me by Austin Freeman, and in fact he taught me the use of this little-appreciated instrument in the field. And the disappearance of the casualty from hospital was based on a true incident at Gravesend Hospital of which Freeman and I had private knowledge. The man simply walked out of hospital after recovery, in pyjamas, and was never traced. His identity was never discovered.

In the United States, Dodd, Mead and Company had, some years earlier, printed a Thorndykian quiz at the back of one or two Freeman novels,[10] and in the closing months of 1935 they reprinted the questions, with some three new ones added and one rather surprisingly omitted, in their newly launched Red Badge Bulletin. The prize offered for the three best answers to the quiz, which included such teasers as "What is Thorndyke's full name?" and "If a drop of fresh blood falls on a piece of iron, what will be its appearance in a few hours' time?" was an autographed copy of *The Penrose Mystery.* The top mark was achieved by Percival Mason Stone of Waltham, Massachusetts, his paper being judged 99% perfect. (Raymond T. Bond of Dodd, Mead, in writing to Stone, told him his answer regarding Thorndyke's method of opening an infernal machine had not been *quite* as complete as some of the others, hence his loss of one point.) In the ensuing correspondence, Stone brought forward his paper on Thorndyke's residence and was ultimately made editor of *Dr. Thorndyke's Crime File,* of which more will be heard later.

Freeman, like most authors, received a fair number of letters from admirers. He invariably answered them in his small neat script, and usually posted them himself too. His humor and self-depreciatory manner came out more clearly in his letters than in conversation, when his shyness and reserve with strangers sometimes proved an obstacle to satisfactory communication. Here is his reply[11] to a request from Walter Shewring for permission to translate a passage of a Thorndyke story into Greek:

> Rosemount,
> 94 Windmill Street,
> Gravesend.
> 2nd November 1936.

Dear Mr. Shewring,

I must thank you for your kind letter of the 28th ultimo and for your very appreciative references to my work. It is always gratifying and encouraging to learn that one's efforts to please have not entirely failed, but much more so when the reader is a scholar whose judgement and taste may be assumed to be more than commonly discriminating.

Of course, I have no objection to your incorporating the passage that you mention in your projected book. On the contrary, I am highly flattered. My books have been translated into Russian, Czechoslovakian and other heathen dialects (at the copies whereof I can only stare blankly and wonder, like the British Tar, why the devil people can't express themselves in plain, straightforward English), but classical Greek is a new honour for Thorndyke.

With reference to your very kind offer to send me a copy of the Greek, I should like it very much if the copy were duplicated or printed, but not if its production would give you trouble. I am not worth that. If I were one of your pupils, my place in the class would be a hundred below zero.

Your suggestion about the clock—stationary, but right twice a day—has possibilities. I will make a note of it according to the advice of Captain Cuttle (whose time-piece, by the way, illustrated the opposite condition) and if it is possible to use the motive, you will know in due course.

Once more thanking you for your letter, and for the suggestion,

I am,
Yours sincerely,

R. Austin Freeman.

Mr. Shewring was a Classics master at Ampleforth College, Yorkshire. The passage in question, relating to Thorndyke's collection of specimens at the zoo, duly appeared in his *Greek & Latin Versions* (London: J. M. Dent and Sons, 1938) along with its translation into Greek prose.

Not infrequently, Freeman would travel up to London to visit his old haunts. He still enjoyed walking in the City and from time to time he dined with Ronald Jessup at Simpson's Tavern. It was Jessup who related to Freeman the curious story which he used, heavily disguised, in his next book, *Felo de Se?* (published in the U. S. as *Death at the Inn*). The narrator, Robert Mortimer (like Jessup, a bank clerk) is on his way home from work when he finds a dead body on the porch of St. Michael's Church in the City. Shortly afterwards he makes the acquaintance of a strange character, John Gillum, who takes him to various disreputable places, including a gaming house. Gillum has an account at

Mortimer's bank, and a suspicious sort of account it is, for, although large regular payments are received into it, it is continually being disbursed by a multitudinous series of withdrawals by cash, rather than by check. Blackmail and gambling are the obvious explanations but are they the true ones? The banking details are authentic and, adds Jessup laconically, so are those concerning the gaming house. One unforgettable character is the creaky, antique porter of Clifford's Inn, Mr. Weech, with his frock coat, tall hat and superabundance of Latin phrases, with which he freely sprinkles his sentences. Mortimer finds Gillum dead in his apartment at the Inn, and as he was apparently penniless, for the incoming payments to his account had lately ceased while the outgoing transactions had continued, suicide seems the likely cause of death. But one of Gillum's relatives is dissatisfied by this verdict at the inquest and here Thorndyke takes over with Jervis in close attendance. One clue which comes to light early is that all the mice. up to then a great nuisance, disappeared from Gillum's chambers after he took them over. The remainder of the novel satisfactorily displays Thorndyke in top form, somewhat reminiscent of *The Mystery of 31, New Inn*; but it is a much more opaque mystery than the earlier effort, and its characterization is greatly improved.

Freeman's final residence at No. 94 Windmill Street was well equipped for handicrafts of various kinds. When Starrett called at Darnley Road, he found the workshop laboratory upstairs, but here, at "Rosemount," the heavier equipment was in the basement. Miss D. Nichols, daughter of a local optician who supplied Freeman with microscopic specimens in the late thirties, tells us that "there was a long narrow drawing room and one of the longer walls was covered with small paintings. I think now they were probably the doctor's work but at the time I had no idea he painted as well as wrote so I did not take much notice of them. The front room on the right of the hall was the doctor's museum, with a communicating door to his study behind. The front garden was heavily overgrown with trees and bushes. I do not know if this was due to a shortage of gardeners or a desire for privacy."

The present borough librarian, Mr. E. N. Moore, then a junior assistant, recalls Freeman, "a very charming man, quiet and unassuming," walking down Windmill Street from his home, only a quarter-mile away, to the library for "books on lathe-work, screw-thread cutting, key cutting and so on in order to satisfy himself that he, personally, could do whatever Dr. Thorndyke was supposed to do."

Like many shy people, Freeman was more at his ease with the young. One such youth was C. G. Bickers, an apprentice on a local newspaper, who had cause to call at Freeman's home regularly. He recalls that the doctor was "a very impressive man and, to me, quite frightening. The house where he lived had a basement full of all sorts of tools, knives, chisels, etc. He told me they were for inspiration. 'Boy,' he would say, 'when you write crime you must have the inspiration to suit the occasion!' " To me, this scene, with a mock-severe Freeman, approaching eighty, in shirt sleeves, divested of his brown walking boots in favour of carpet slippers, standing on the doorstep exercising his oratorical powers on an impressionable fifteen-year-old, is a charming picture. The inspiration he sought on this occasion may well have been for *The Stoneware Monkey* (1938). When Thorndyke called upon the potter, Peter Gannet, who was showing evident symptoms of arsenic poisoning, he observed on the bedroom mantelpiece "a number of bowls and jars and a particularly hideous figure"—a saucer eyed simian—Gannet's own work. The young physician, just out of medical school, destined to become the narrator of the major part of this novel (for Jervis takes over only for the final one-third) is James Oldfield. He it is who finds a dying constable in a wood after a diamond robbery, and not long afterwards becomes the G.P. whom Gannet calls in. His poisoning symptoms are all the more ominous because of the evident hostility shown towards him by the mysterious Boles, another member of the household, and by Bowles's attentions to the pretty Mrs. Gannet. Scenes in the large studio behind the house form the chief "atmosphere" of the book. After Gannet disappears and Oldfield discovers human remains in the still-warm pottery kiln, the house becomes quite sinister. We meet Inspector Blandy, who combines the late Badger's slyness with a courteous suavity which is most impressive. He suspects Mrs. Gannet of having had a hand in her husband's death, and Thorndyke enters the case, at Oldfield's request, partly to afford her protection from harassment. Freeman, as always, presents the clues openly and many an acute reader should be able to solve the main enigma of the case, without however reducing the story's impact. The characterization of Mr. Snuper, Thorndyke's private investigator, contributes vastly to the richness of the book's style. (In the previous novel Snuper saved Thorndyke's life, and in this one he is revealed as a collector of shellfish. "Only the day before yesterday I obtained a nearly perfect specimen of *Stenorhynchus phalangium.*" It is these touches which make a Freeman book linger in the reader's mind.)

Freeman was engaged in writing *Mr. Polton Explains* when Britain declared war on Hitler's Germany in September, 1939. Work was suspended while an air-raid shelter was constructed in his garden. Once completed, however, he found it an ideal place to write and, his health having improved after a difficult period earlier in the year, he was able to finish the book quite rapidly. When it was published early the following year the deceptive quiet of the "phony war" lay over England; surely, it was thought by many, peace would return before many months had passed. Freeman never brought either of the world wars into his fiction and this book is saturated with nostalgia, returning to the nineteenth-century London he could remember so well. It is Polton who, for the only time, is the narrator, and describes for us his early life as an orphan, separated from his sister (who turned up in *Helen Vardon's Confession*), and with an early interest in old clocks. He relates the history of how the bright young artisan, reduced to near-starvation, is rescued from an ominous destiny by the young Thorndyke, himself at the beginning of his professional career. But how to explain Polton's ill-fortune? Freeman does so by postulating certain ill-disposed persons. One of them reappears in the second part of the book (narrated by Jervis) which takes the form of an investigation into the death of Cecil Moxdale, whose apartments have been gutted by fire. The use of fire to confuse identification had been used by Freeman at least twice before, but this case does have certain unique features, including a timed incendiary device which permits Polton a hand in the detective work. The most grievous fault of the book is fundamental; Polton's age has had to be drastically altered, so that he is younger than Thorndyke. When first espied by Jervis in *The Red Thumb Mark* the faithful artificer is described as "a small elderly man" and this description is reiterated in *The Eye of Osiris*. Yet on neither occasion could Thorndyke have been past thirty. A less serious discrepancy is in Polton's initial status in Thorndyke's menage. In *Mr. Polton Explains* he describes with delight the spacious bedroom set aside for him on the top floor of No. 5A; but in *The Red Thumb Mark* it is evident that he was, at this somewhat later period, a non-resident. "That man is on wires this morning;" Thornydke remarks on the day of the big trial, "he has been wandering in and out of the rooms ever since he came, like a cat in a new house."

In the United States, P. M. Stone had been discussing with Dodd, Mead for some time the possibility of putting out an omnibus volume of Thorndyke novels, as a companion to the collected short stories published a few years earlier. At the time of the Penrose competition, Stone had shown them his pleasant little essay, "5A King's Bench Walk," dealing with the Thorndykian chambers and similar matters, for which the author had found no market in the commercial press, and Edward Dodd, Jr., now felt it could be put to good use in the forthcoming volume. "I am afraid we can't pay you for it," he wrote to Stone in April, 1940, "because the margin on such a book is a very close one. But we will of course want to give you full credit. And if the idea appeals to you we might make you editor of the whole volume. As we see it at the present time, it can contain three full-length stories and probably half a book of short stories worked in between." But later he changed his mind: "It is the opinion of several of us here that the first omnibus includes all of the short stories of Dr. Freeman," and they did not wish to repeat them, for their intention, later abandoned, was to keep the short-story omnibus in print. (Of course, they were wrong: two short stories, "Percival Bland's Proxy" and "The Missing Mortgagee," published in England in *The Great Portrait Mystery*, had never reached U. S. readers, and this would have been an excellent chance to produce them.) Stone suggested six novels, from which Dodd, Mead chose the three for which plates were available— *Frood*, *Pottermack* and *Osiris*—and elected for no apparent reason to place them in that order, thus making nonsense of any conclusions a reader might draw regarding Thorndyke's development as a detective—or Freeman's as a writer for that matter. Evidently Stone's position as editor was largely ornamental. His original ideas for the contents were not used by Dodd, Mead; his suggestions for a title were turned down, as was his wish to include an illustration; and they forgot to tell him what the final choice of title was. The large green volume, *Dr. Thorndyke's Crime File*, published on January 7th, 1941, contained not only Stone's essay and the three novels but also Freeman's magazine piece, *The Art of the Detective Story*, and his broadcast talk, *Meet Dr. Thorndyke*. The book would have benefited by the inclusion of a Freeman bibliography but Stone's intention, then and later, to compile one came to nothing.

In wartime England, Freeman at seventy-eight was losing some of his zest for writing an annual volume, and plans for yet another Thorndyke novel were slow in coming to fruition. Meanwhile, having lost the daytime air war over England in September, 1940, the Germans dispatched bombing fleets over London and other British cities after dark, and inflicted widespread damage, not only on industrial targets but on civilian areas and on such famous buildings as the House of Commons, St. Paul's Cathedral and Westminster Abbey. The Temple Church, a few yards from Thorndyke's chambers, was quite destroyed, as were two sets of chambers, Nos. 1 and 6, in King's Bench Walk itself. But this was in December. Some weeks earlier, Ronald Jessup and his wife had been bombed out of their suburban London home. Freeman was shocked by the news:

Rosemount,
94 Windmill Street,
Gravesend.
5th November, 1940

My dear Jessup,

I won't waste space by trying to tell you how deeply distressed I am to learn of the dreadful misfortune that has overtaken you and your wife. You will know that without being told. It 'must have been a soul-shaking experience, and the astounding fact that you are both alive and relatively uninjured is almost beyond belief; for the concussion from which you are suffering is a passing trouble from which no permanent effects are to be feared.

But the loss of your possessions is a grievous thing, and the more so since it includes the precious MSS of work actually completed and the unreplaceable materials for future works. Knowing you as I do and realizing your love of your household gods both domestic and literary, so carefully chosen and tenderly cared for, my heart aches to think of them and your charming home, all dissipated in a moment by the idiotic malice of our barbarous enemies.

The only gleam of consolation that I see is the fact that you are still young with a good part—the best part, I hope—of your lives before you, and I encourage myself to think that perhaps there may be some possibility of salving at least some remains from the ruins. Damaged books and MSS are better than none. But I shall hear your accounts of things when I see you. And this brings me to the final paragraph of your letter in which you suggest that I may have the privilege of repairing in some small degree a part of your loss. I think I can supply you with copies of a good many of my works, mostly, I fear, cheap reprints, but I shall try to rake up one or two first editions to give your library a fresh start.

The next question is as to the time of your visit. I think the afternoon would be best as I am nearly always at home. Next Saturday would do for me but you must consult your own convenience as to the date. If you could drop me a post-card, it would be as well; but if you can't give me notice, never mind. I shall keep you in mind on Saturday afternoons.

My wife has had a rather nasty accident in the black-out. She fell down a flight of stairs and damaged herself a good (or rather bad) deal, including a fractured radius. But I will give you details when we meet. Now, with sincere sympathy for you and your wife, to whom, and to your brother, I send warmest greetings.

Yours ever,

R. Austin Freeman

True to his promise, he dispatched what books he could, including the all-important *Penrose* (dedicated to Jessup) with a characteristic inscription: "To my friend, Mr. Elmhurst (who has been known to masquerade under the name of R. F. Jessup) with all good wishes and happy memories of the late Julieberry [*sic*]."

One of Jessup's interrupted ventures was the excavation of Loughton Camp—probably an Early Iron Age earthwork—in Epping Forest. The Essex Field Club had made four cuttings there in 1882, when some flint implements and fragments of pottery had been found. Jessup's plan to continue the exploration was halted by the war, but Freeman enjoyed hearing his friend discussing it, and together they pored over the large-scale maps of the area. Nothing was more natural than Freeman's desire to use the material in some way, but he was hard put to devise a plot which again encompassed an archaeological feature. Another hidden body seemed out of the question, but suitable alternatives failed to present themselves. What Freeman finally did was to use the earthwork as a palpable red herring, a rarity in the Thorndyke stories. *The Jacob Street Mystery* (U. S. title: *The Unconscious Witness*), Freeman's final work, takes its name from the fictitious street off the Hampstead Road in which many of Freeman's characters (including the future Mrs. Anstey in *The Cat's Eye* and Peter Gannet in *The Stoneware Monkey*) had studio-residences. This time the artist is a shy bachelor, Tom Pedley, who possesses many Freeman-esque traits, including a wariness of other people coupled with immense self-sufficiency. He is present at an impending murder in a wood but, unaware of what is afoot, continues his landscape painting undisturbed. There seems to be no connection between the incident and Lotta Schiller, an overpainted neighbor with under-developed artistic abilities who intrudes upon him repeatedly and who later disappears. Tell-tale traces of foul play are found at Loughton Camp.

Jessup tells us that under normal circumstances Freeman would undoubtedly have visited this site "as he made a point of never writing about what he had not seen for himself." As it was, he had Jessup's maps, photographs and verbal descriptions to work from, together with memories of explorations of Epping Forest in happier years. The story opens with an account, in the third person, of Tom Pedley's activities; Jervis takes over half-way through, the connecting agency, as in Penrose, being Polton who happens to be a friend of Pedley. In many ways the story, more noticeably than any previous work, is a patchwork of earlier books: water-color painting, disguise, and the preservation of a tell-tale tress in a locket. We meet Inspector Blandy and Mr. Penfield once again, and Thorn-dyke is as satisfying as ever. If Freeman's originality was beginning to fade, the charm of the writing is undiminished. Polton's dexterity, whether in restoring a pewter tankard or repairing a pedometer, makes as lively reading as ever.

Miss Nichols, the optician's daughter, was the typist of *The Jacob Street Mystery*, and when she had completed the job Freeman asked her if she thought it as good as others of his she had read and admired. "He obviously doubted that it was and, as anyone who cares to read can make comparison, I do not think I am betraying any confidences when I say that I rather agreed with him. I was too diffident to say so outright but replied that it was difficult to judge as I had read the previous books in print and whole, whereas this one I had read in manuscript and by installments. I have no doubt the absence of an enthusiastic 'yes' gave him his answer but, thinking back, I am quite sure the doctor would have preferred a blunt answer without any shilly-shallying." Miss Nichols' memory of Freeman during his last few active months were of "a big man, very robust for his age and with an old-fashioned courtesy of manner; he always treated me as a social equal rather than an employee. His great worry at the time I knew him was the impossibility of getting domestic help for Mrs. Freeman. She was a tiny creature, probably about the same age as her husband, and the house was much too big for anyone of her size and age to manage unaided. Wartime fuel shortages kept the house very chilly and I remember she was tormented by chilblains. I tried very hard to find someone to help them and their first question whenever I called was whether I had been able to discover anyone. Unfortunately I never had.

"All this was not long before the fall which I believe cracked a bone in his leg and tied him to the house and his bed. I was told by a friend of the nurse who attended him that he said he could not write in bed, but the real reason may well have been that he knew he had lost something of his power as an author. How wise he was to stop before his standard dropped too low; he had such a long record of successful achievement."

At first, no doubt, Freeman's disinclination to write was a mental and psychological fatigue: the knowledge that, however well he planned another book, it would contain no novel feature and that he could not, now, add to his reputation. Later, though, his illness began to sap his strength. After his death Mrs. Freeman wrote to Stone:

> His death was a deep loss to many, but it was a great release to him when the end came. He was lying on his back for a year, gradually losing all power of movement

and at last he could hardly speak. It was a most pathetic illness.

His mind remained active almost to the end and it is consoling to know that he still received letters from those who enjoyed his books. Some of them were new readers who had just discovered stories he had written thirty years earlier. One such reader was the late George F. G. Mills, a Manhattan business man, who took the time to send, at least twice, long cheerful letters to the writer he so much admired. Freeman was unable to pen a reply, but he had had cards of apology printed which required only a word or two inked in. He sent one to Mills at the end of February, 1943, which shows his signature to be somewhat shaky but otherwise unchanged. The last word we have from him is a dictated letter in unfamiliar handwriting:

> R. Austin Freeman,
> "Rosemount,"
> 94 Windmill Street,
> Gravesend, Kent.
> 16th May, 1943

Dear Mr. Mills,

I am not certain whether I have acknowledged already your kind and interesting letter of Jan. 18th, as I am now bedridden and unable to write my own letters. In any case I am availing myself of the kindness of a friend to tell you how greatly I was gratified by your extremely appreciative references to my works.

It is, now that I have definitely finished my life work, a very great satisfaction to know that my books have given pleasure to cultivated readers, and I thank you most warmly for your kindly meant and very greatly appreciated letter.

> Yours sincerely,
> R. Austin Freeman

Freeman's signature, a travesty of his earlier neat hand, was evidently appended with the utmost difficulty by the failing invalid's trembling fingers and is consistent with Ronald Jessup's statement that Freeman at this period had become a victim of Parkinson's disease. Richard Austin Freeman died on 28th September, 1943, and was buried in the old Gravesend and Milton Cemetery, on Old Road West, a short distance from his home and a place, according to Mr. William Lear, the superintendent, where he had spent a lot of his time during his daily walks. There is no memorial on his grave; perhaps while he continues to be remembered with affection by a multitude of devoted readers, he does not need one.

In his weekly column in the *Chicago Tribune*, Vincent Starrett wrote for all of them when he heard the sad news:[12]

There are readers who find Thorndyke too painstaking and Dr. Freeman—who has a flair for Dickensian caricature and a habit of permitting his minor figures to fall in love—too Victorian. I am not that ungrateful. Some fine detective stories are being written today; but, in general, the alcoholic blitheness and wisecracking sophistication of the current crop of fathomers is not the stuff of literature, and few of them will survive. When all the bright young things have performed their appointed task of flattering the complexes of neurotic semi-literates, and have gone their way to oblivion, the best of the Thorndyke stories will live on— minor classics on the shelf that holds the good books of the world.

CHAPTER X

The Great Fathomer

Though Dr. Joseph Bell of Edinburgh was the model on whom Sir Arthur Conan Doyle based Sherlock Holmes, the real Holmes was Conan Doyle himself. Similarly, though Freeman's intention was to create, in John Evelyn Thorndyke, an investigator without personal eccentricities of any kind, he succeeded in putting on paper an idealized Freeman, a Freeman with an augmented bonhomie and a diminished diffidence, but a recognizable Freeman all the same. And if Thorndyke's manner and methods attract us, it is because Freeman's manner and methods are inherently attractive.

The similarity between the detective and his creator does not, however, extend to physical appearance. "Probably the handsomest detective in fiction" was Dorothy Sayers' judgment, and if one word must suffice "handsome" is as apt as any. It was a word often employed by those characters who met him for the first time, most notably by Jervis in their earliest adventure together. Here is his rather fulsome tribute to his senior's appearance in the witness box:[1]

I had often noticed the quiet strength of his face, its infinite intelligence, its attractiveness and magnetism; but I had never before appreciated what now impressed me most; that Thorndyke was actually the handsomest man I had ever seen. He was dressed simply, his appearance unaided by the flowing gown or awe-inspiring wig, and yet his presence dominated the court. . . . It was not alone the distinction of his tall figure, erect and dignified, nor the power and massive composure of his face, but the actual symmetry and comeliness of the face itself that now arrested my attention; a comeliness that made it akin rather to some classic mask, wrought in the ivory-toned marble of Pentelicus, than to the eager faces that move around us in the hurry and bustle of a life at once strenuous and trivial.

Earlier in the same tale, on the occasion of the reunion of the former fellow-students, Jervis remarks on Thorndyke's "impassive and rather severe face which softened into a genial smile," but in later stories he describes his senior's appearance only briefly or not at all. Helen Vardon, seeing him first as an unidentified figure at an inquest, depicted him as a tall man with "a handsome, symmetrical face, but strangely—almost unhumanly [sic]—reposeful and impassive. Yet, though it was as immobile as a mask of stone, it conveyed an impression of intense attention—almost of watchfulness, and the clear grey eyes never moved from the face of the witness. To me there was something a little uncanny and disturbing in that immovable mask and that steady unrelaxing gaze."[2] But then, Helen had a secret which she was afraid Thorndyke might uncover at the inquest, so that the uncanny and disturbing facets of the great man's physiognomy may to some extent be discounted. The events in *Vardon* occurred back in 1908, when Thorndyke was a mere thirty-eight. In *Frood* (1924) Freeman had permitted him to advance to about fifty, at which time young Dr. Strangeways espied him—again as an unidentified stranger—entering Rochester Cathedral, and was favorably impressed:

He was obviously a personage—an unmistakable thoroughbred. He was a tall man, very erect and dignified in carriage, and in spite of his iron-grey hair, evidently strong, active and athletic. But it was his face that specially riveted my attention; not merely by reason that it was a handsome symmetrical face, inclining to the Greek type, with level brows, a fine straight nose, and a shapely mouth, but rather on account of its suggestion of commanding strength and intelligence. It was a strangely calm—even immobile—face; but yet it conveyed a feeling of attentiveness and concentration, and especially of power.[3]

Though Thorndyke was not often called upon to engage in physical combat, on one or two occasions Thorndyke tackled a malefactor barehanded, as in "The Stranger's Latchkey" and *Felo de Se?*, always giving a good account of himself. Freeman tells us that Thorndyke was created with keen eyesight, and although in middle age he adopted reading-glasses (of the pince-nez pattern),[4] he seems to have been able to dispense with them in later life.

We know nothing of Thorndyke's origins. He loved London and was probably, like Freeman, a native of that city. His creator, who should know, tells us in a brief biography[5] that he was born on July 4th, 1870, which made him more than eight years younger than Freeman. He was educated at the medical school of St. Margaret's Hospital, London, where he later became in succession Medical Registrar, Pathologist, Curator of the Museum and Professor of Medical Jurisprudence. Jervis and he were fellow students and, when the two friends met again, Thorndyke explained how he had stayed on at the hospital after the other left, taking on any small appointments that were going. "[I] hung about the chemical and physical laboratories, the museum and post mortem room, and meanwhile took my M.D. and D.Sc. Then I got called to the bar [in 1896] in the hope of getting a coronership, but soon after this, old Stedman retired unexpectedly—you remember Stedman, the lecturer on medical jurisprudence—and I put in for the vacant post. Rather to my surprise I was appointed lecturer, whereupon I dismissed the coronership from my mind, took my present chambers and sat down to wait for anything that might come."[6] His first case was for the defense in Regina *v* Gummer in 1897,[7] no detail of which has come down to us. We know little more about these early years prior to the Hornby case (1901) except that the young medical jurist employed his ample leisure hours in working out theoretical examples of the types of cases he was most likely to encounter, "and seeing that crimes against the person have nearly always a strong medical interest, I gave them special attention. For instance, I planned a series of murders, selecting royal personages and great ministers as the victims, and on each murder brought to bear all the special knowledge, skill and ingenuity at my command. I enquired minutely into the habits of my hypothetical victims; ascertained who were their associates, friends, enemies and servants; considered their diet, their residences, their modes of conveyance, the source of their clothing and, in fact, everything which it was necessary to know in order to achieve their deaths with certainty and with absolute safety to the murderer."

Having brought this to a satisfactory conclusion and after writing them up in his own private shorthand, he played the game over again "from the opposite side of the board; that is to say, I added, as an appendix to each case, an analysis with a complete scheme for the detection of the crime. I have in my safe at the present moment six volumes of cases, fully indexed; and I can assure you that they are not only highly instructive reading, but are really valuable as works of reference."

The address of Thorndyke's chambers has not been free of confusion during the unfolding of the long saga. 5A, King's Bench Walk, the address named most often in the chronicles, is based on the real No. 4 or No. 5, these being the two houses built by Christopher Wren and therefore agreeing with the various seventeenth century allusions made to the architecture by Freeman. In *The Red Thumb Mark*, Thorndyke remarks to Jervis, after their historic meeting on the sidewalk: "My chambers are some doors further down—number 6A." This was evidently a slip, for neither 6A nor the real No. 6 is ever again mentioned.

In "Meet Dr. Thorndyke,"[8] Freeman muddles the situation further by declaring, "When he made his first bow to the reading public from the doorway of Number 4 King's Bench Walk he was between thirty-five and forty." Certainly he must have been wrong about Thorndyke's age, which, at the time of the opening of the Hornby case in March, 1901, was not yet thirty-one. But as to the address, Freeman was being accurate enough, though he misled numerous readers, including P.M. Stone and Alison Hodgson. Stone, in his essay "5A King's Bench Walk,"[9] believed that Freeman was on record as claiming No. 4 as Thorndyke's chambers, and Miss Hodgson[10] states flatly that "although he gives the number as 5, No. 4 is the house described by Austin Freeman as the chambers of Dr. Thorndyke." Recently she explained to me that her identification was based on the Latin inscription on the portico describing how the building had been demolished by fire and rebuilt.

How can all these conflicting matters be resolved? Freeman undoubtedly changed his mind about Thorndyke's address after writing *The Red Thumb Mark* and for "6A" the reader should substitute "5A". Probably it was Freeman's knowledge of his slip which caused him, in his broadcast talk thirty years later, to use the locution "made his bow from the doorway of No. 4," thereby avoiding 5A or 6A at all. For Thorndyke, while residing at 5A, did indeed make his bow from No. 4, with its plaque about destruction by fire and the rest.

As *The Red Thumb Mark* opens, Jervis is studying the following inscription:

"Conflagratam An⁰ 1677. Fabricatam An⁰ 1698.
Richardo Powell Armiger Thesaurer."

This, he explains, was set out on four panels "which formed a frieze beneath the pediment of a fine brick portico. . .of one of the tall houses at the upper end of King's Bench Walk." He is about to turn away when Thorndyke in wig and gown emerges from the portico and, after a moment, the two friends recognize one another. After a short discussion on matters of mutual interest, Thorndyke invites him to his chambers that evening, upon which Jervis asks, naturally enough, "Do you reside within that noble old portico?"

"No," replied Thorndyke. "I often wish I did. It would add several inches to one's stature to feel that the mouth of one's burrow was graced with a Latin inscription for admiring strangers to ponder over. No; my chambers are some doors further down—number 6A"—and he turned to point out the house as we crossed towards Crown Office Row.

My reading of this suggests that in his first Thorndyke novel, Freeman hesitated to adopt as his hero's residence chambers so readily identifiable. Moreover, it would not have helped the case to say, "No, my chambers are next door to the right." Hence the "6A" crept in, never to be used again.

If No. 4 is to be eliminated, then the "original" of Thorndyke's house must be No. 5; and Ronald Jessup confirms this. During a walk together in the Temple, Freeman indicated No. 5 as the house which he had in mind when describing the permanent home of the two immortals, Thorndyke and Polton, and temporary shelter for Jervis, invalided Stephen Gray and incognito fugitive Humphrey Jardine.

P.M. Stone has sufficiently dwelt on the internal economy of No. 5A, so that here we shall note only a few of the more important features. The occupants of the ground floor are never described, but we may safely consider them to be a firm of barristers, who used the rooms as offices rather than as a residence.

One floor up, Thorndyke's massive outer door or "oak" was to be discovered with his name upon it in white letters. It opened outwards to disclose a baize-covered inner door, through which was a spacious wood-paneled living-room, with a broad hearth flanked by two easy chairs. In the fireplace, at least in the early days, was a gas ring on which a kettle of water could be boiled to make tea. Opening out of the living room was the rarely mentioned "office"— "hardly an office at all, excepting as a repository for documents and stationery" according to Thorndyke,[11] but we may presume it housed at least the safe containing the shorthand accounts. As Thorndyke's means improved, the little room was better stocked with books; Anstey later described it as a miniature law library.[12]

On the floor above were the laboratory and workshop, in which Nathaniel Polton worked his wonders. One entered first the workshop: "a large room—one side occupied by a joiner's [carpenter's] bench. A powerful back-geared lathe stood against one window, a jeweller's bench against the other and the walls were covered with shelves and tool-racks, filled with all sorts of strange implements. From this room we passed into another which I recognized as a chemical laboratory." All of which forced Rupert Mayfield to exclaim, "The place is like a factory!"[13]

Apart from the usual glassware and small-scale apparatus, the laboratory also boasted a cupel furnace which it was Polton's occasional practice to employ as a grill for cutlets. A smaller room set off from the main laboratory was employed for bacteriology and microscopical research.[14] On the top floor were the bedrooms, about which we know little. Probably there were three, occupied respectively by Thorndyke, Jervis (when he was in residence) and Polton, but there may have been a spare room also.

John Evelyn Thorndyke was, to Robert Anstey, K.C., most disinterested of his colleagues, "an inscrutable man; silent, self-contained, and even secretive, in spite of his genial exterior."[15]

But Thorndyke's traits were ideally suited to his calling. "He is," explained Anstey to young Strangeways, "like some highly-specialized animal, such as the three-toed sloth, for instance, which seems an abnormal sort of beast until you see it doing, with unapproachable perfection, the thing which nature intended it to do. Thorndyke is a case of perfect adaptation to a special environment."[16] From which we may conclude that Thorndyke's solitary character to some extent came upon him after he was launched in his career. Certainly a boyish, light-hearted Thorndyke was evident in the earliest adventures, when he voiced such exclamations as "yoicks!" and "Tally-ho!" though never, we may be sure, in the presence of a client. This youthful exuberance never quite returned in the latter stories, but to the end of the series Thorndyke maintained an aspect of geniality to the world. He might be suspicious of many of the phenomena presented to him, but he seldom showed it. At Scotland Yard he photographed the suspicious thumb-mark in the

Hornby case while the amused police expert looked on. "Must do something for my fee, you know," the bonhomous investigator explains. But a little earlier, with a quite different facial expression, he had warned Jervis, "Whatever you may see me do, make no comments before the officials. We are seeking information, not giving it, you understand."

Certainly he was secretive. A useful trait in a fictional detective, for it enables the narrator—Jervis or some other—to tell the reader all he knows while allowing the secrets of the investigation to remain relatively intact to the end of the story, when they may be exhibited all at once by the detective himself. But the impression persists that Thorndyke was more secretive than other investigators, more than Holmes, or Wimsey or Sergeant Cuff in *The Moonstone*— but then Cuff's conclusions were largely wrong anyway, so he gave no secrets away! Thorndyke's secretiveness, like Freeman's shyness, is consistent with his other characteristics, even with his didacticism, as when he enlarges on Mendelism in *A Silent Witness* or on dactylography in *Felo de Se?* While appearing to explain all, much remains hidden, and Thorndyke, after some qualms about it in the earliest adventures, is quite at ease in leaving Jervis in the dark. And yet, while the practice was well suited to Thorndyke's introversion, it was also imprudent, for had he been killed during an investigation, for example in the poison chamber in *The Cat's Eye*, it would have been impossible to have brought the criminals to justice. Thorndyke kept a diary, but it was highly condensed[17] and not likely to be of great value to subsequent investigators.

If Thorndyke is not disposed to discuss the progress of an unfinished case, what *does* he talk about: The answer is, plenty! And it is not exactly small talk either. Thorndyke is not only the best-looking detective in fiction; he is also the best informed. Two of his favorite topics of conversation, London lore and medical curiosities, are neatly and amusingly combined at the beginning of an early tale, "A Message from the Deep Sea." The narrator, as usual is Jervis:

We had been to the London Hospital to see a remarkable case of acromegaly, and, as we returned, we discussed this curious affection, and the allied condition of gigantism, in all their bearings, from the origin of the "Gibson chin" to the physique of Og, King of Bashan.

"It would have been interesting," Thorndyke remarked as we passed up Aldgate High Street, "to have put one's finger into His Majesty's pituitary fossa—after his decease, of course. By the way, here is Harrow Alley; you remember Defoe's description of the dead-cart waiting out here, and the ghastly procession coming down the alley."

Thorndyke's procedures, though eminently reasonable to the scientific observer, frequently caused bewilderment among lawyers and policemen. As he once explained to Anstey, "The lawyer's investigations tend to proceed along the line of the information wanted: the scientist's tend to proceed along the line of information available. The business of the man of science is impartially to acquire all the knowledge that is obtainable: the lawyer tends to concern himself only with that which is material to the issue."[18]

This avoidance of selection from among the known facts, especially at the opening of a case, was not unique with Thorndyke. Holmes had insisted on it too, and in more recent years it has become an axiom familiar to all detective story readers. At the beginning of the century, however, it still had some of the force of novelty. "Don't be sketchy, Jervis." was Thorndyke's plea in *The Mystery of 31, New Inn.* "To be sketchy is to be vague. Detail, my child, detail is the soul of induction. Let us have all the facts. We can sort them out afterwards." Upon which Jervis, in retaliation, attempted to overdo the recounting of minutiae, but in vain. In the very earliest tales Thorndyke was in danger of being classed with the theatrical Sherlock; thus, he was surely excessive in proclaiming: "I had six possible theories of the cause of death worked out before I reached Halbury, and it only remained to select the one that fitted the facts."[19] (No disclosure of the remaining theories, of course, was forthcoming.) But even in those early days, Freeman's great detective showed signs of not taking himself too seriously. Once Jervis complained to him that he was hopelessly baffled by a case:[20]

"I've read all the documents and boiled all the evidence down to a stiff jelly, and I am in a worse fog than ever."

"There seems to be a slight mixture of metaphors in my learned friend's remarks. But never mind the fog, Jervis. There is a certain virtue in fog. It serves, like a picture frame, to surround the essential with a neutral zone that separates it from the irrelevant."

"That is a very profound observation, Thorndyke," I remarked ironically.

"I was just thinking so myself," he rejoined.

"And if you could contrive to explain what it means—"

"Oh, but that is unreasonable. When one throws off a subtly philosophical obiter dictum one looks to the discerning critic to supply the meaning."

Thorndyke, as he never hesitated to explain to eager clients, was not an advocate. If he took up a case, it was at the client's own risk; for if the evidence he unearthed was unfavorable to the latter's case and a felony had been committed, he would be obliged to disclose his findings to the authorities. In one case, indeed, as set forth in *As a Thief in the Night*, his discoveries were of an exceedingly unpleasant kind, and brought to the person who had commissioned his services much pain. But then, never was anyone more severely warned before the event than Rupert Mayfield.

Thorndyke's procedures are nothing if not convincing; rarely is a chemical test, mechanical device or pathological condition referred to without being fully described; nor are they descriptions of the kind which are copied from text books. Whenever possible, Freeman carried through laboratory processes himself to see how they went; collected and photographed marine shells and industrial dust; built see-behind spectacles and periscope walking-sticks; all so that his characters could engage in realistic activities. Never do his characters employ deadly poisons of unknown composition, or invisible inks made from unnamed ingredients. If Thorndyke appears to know an infinitude of wayward facts, at least he has learned them the hard way. When he visited the London Zoo for another purpose, he improved the occasion by adding to his collection of hairs and feathers; he "gathered up each with care, wrapped it in its separate paper on which was written its description, and deposited it in his collecting-box."[21] True, he can describe the fibers in a mixed fabric;[22] but then he maintains a collection of such fibers, mounted on slides, assembled by Polton from dressmakers' cuttings.[23]

As a sound jurist, Thorndyke is aware of the value of corroborative evidence from an expert, even in those cases when he is confident of his own knowledge, which is by no means always the case. Thus, he turns to the indispensable Mr. Elmhurst on archaeological matters in much the same way that Freeman turned to the real Elmhurst. In *The Cat's Eye* he obtains appropriate help in identifying a vertebra of the porcupine ant-eater; in *The Shadow of the Wolf* a petrologist is consulted; and in *A Silent Witness* a complete professional team pulls together in the final stages of the investigation to make one of the most convincing workshop scenes in all detective fiction. And always Thorndyke would read up on a subject in which he was rusty, just like any other professional man, although our credibility is sometimes stretched by the comprehensiveness of his private library, which included, we are told, not only a list of members of the London Stock Exchange,[24] but even the Old Testament in Russian and Yiddish on facing pages.[25]

Of the host of details which make the Thorndyke canon distinctive, perhaps the first to come to mind is the Doctor's famous traveling research case covered with green Willesden canvas. In the very earliest stories the little case, "only a foot square by four inches deep," had not yet been devised. In "The Old Lag," Thorndyke sets forth with "his queer outfit—something like that of a field geologist"; it is more fully described in "A Message from the Deep Sea" as consisting of a small metal box containing "such requisites as cover-slips, capillary tubes, moulding wax, and other 'diagnostic materials'," as well as seed envelopes; in other words, nothing much more than a collecting box. The green research case, a much more sophisticated affair, was first glimpsed by the reader as it rested on the hat-rack of a train in "The Case of Oscar Brodski." By this time the detective never traveled from home without it; it was indispensable. Everything in it was minuscule—"little reagent bottles, tiny test-tubes, diminutive spirit-lamp, dwarf microscope and assorted instruments on the same Lilliputian scale." Asked whether the microscope is efficient, Thorndyke replies, convincingly enough: "Perfectly efficient at low and moderate magnifications. It looks like a toy, but it isn't one; the lenses are the best that can be had. Of course, a full-sized instrument would be infinitely more convenient— but I shouldn't have it with me, and should have to make shift with a pocket-lens. And so with the rest of the undersized appliances; they are the alternative to no appliances." Not only did the contents of the green case, which could be varied by Thorndyke according to the probable requirements of the situation, permit him to examine clues under the microscope, but also to employ other of his favorite techniques, among them the preservation of foot- and hand-prints in soft earth. "I now make a rule of securing a plaster cast of any object that I cannot retain in my possession," he once declared;[26] and he used this method for bone fragments and the ant-eater's vertebra as well as foot-prints. An excellent example of Thorndyke's versatility is afforded by two incidents described by Freeman within a few months of one another in 1922. In *The Cat's Eye*, Thorndyke employs his normal method of copying footprints with plaster; all the details are there—dusting of dry plaster over the prints to avoid disturbing the earth; use of a ball-spray diffuser for gentle addition of water; prior addition of alum to the plaster of Paris for quicker setting; and so on. Freeman suspended the writing of the novel to produce a series of stories for magazine publication, and in one of them, "The Touchstone," Thorndyke makes a cast of a toeprint half-way down a cliff. This time, though, he uses shredded wax and a blow-lamp. The only reason for the change in method would appear to be Freeman's dislike of repeating himself, and certainly, each method has its advantages.

Over and over again, Thorndyke's thoroughness, his sheer professionalism, overawe us. "All right," we may sometimes be tempted to say to ourselves, "Thorndyke's case is watertight: so why does he have to continue his explanation long after we are satisfied?" This, as we noted in an earlier chapter, is H. Douglas Thomson's view: "The trouble with Dr. Freeman is just this: he takes too much pains. . ."

My own view is that Thorndyke's insistence on the need for an overwhelming case for presentation to a *jury* is in line with real-life practice and can hardly be criticized. Moreover, Thorndyke's summation of the case is usually the most satisfying part of the story. Thorndyke's opinions as they are exhibited to us are largely Freeman's opinions, slightly modified here and there. Thorndyke, like Freeman, was a nineteenth-century man adapting with difficulty to the twentieth. He loved London as it had been in his youth, not as it later became;[27] and most other Freeman characters felt the same way. Thorndyke is on record as having said that "had he not been a man of science he would, by choice, have been a skilled craftsman;" and the same is certainly true of Freeman. But Thorndyke *is* a man of science; for over half a century he has been the very personification of the scientific method to thousands who would otherwise have felt little sympathy with the term or the cold, stark attitude of mind it has sometimes been thought to represent. Thorndyke not only possesses an efficient reasoning faculty fed by an active observation but, alongside this, a lively sympathy for those suffering misfortune. Two occasions in which his warmth of personality especially evinced itself were his condolences on the breakdown of Jervis's romance with Juliet in *The Red Thumb Mark* and his sympathy for Rupert Mayfield's much greater misfortune in *As a Thief in the Night*. His benevolence stopped short of criminals, however, especially of blackmailers, and more than once he expressed the opinion that, because the law could afford no protection against them, their victims were perfectly justified in killing their tormentors. This theme, in fact, is at the heart of *Mr. Pottermack's Oversight*, one of the most successful Thorndyke tales. Towards other types of criminals also, Thorndyke exhibited a remorselessness which could at times be startling. In *The Cat's Eye*, Anstey pleads with Thorndyke to save the lives of two murderers who have fallen into the fatal trap which they had set for the two investigators. Thorndyke refuses and at that moment Anstey found in his "quiet, unconcerned manner something inhuman and repelling." Jervis never went so far in criticism of his senior.

An implication met with in the few criticisms of Thorndyke to be found in historical reviews of detective fiction and the like is that his knowledge was just too encyclopedic to be genuine. It is certainly true that his apparent openness with the non-specialist reader often leaves the mystery as obscure as before, and this, of course, is intentional on Freeman's part, for a premature uncovering of the mystery would destroy the story, and the reader would be the first to complain. All the same, Dorothy Sayers[28] was correct in observing:

> "Thorndyke can cheerfully show you all the facts. You will be none the wiser, unless you happen to have an intimate acquaintance with the fauna of local ponds; the effect of belladonna on rabbits; the physical and chemical properties of blood; optics; tropical diseases; metallurgy; hieroglyphics; and a few other trifles."

Actually, Freeman would have scored high in an examination on any of these subjects, but it is one thing to possess Freeman's wide knowledge and another to harness it to the requirements of detective fiction. It is here that Freeman demonstrated remarkable ingenuity, constructing short stories, six at a time, dependent for their denouements on, respectively, such arcane matters as the specific gravity of lead and gold; the existence of four British species of duckweed; parallax; the narrowly circumscribed habitat of a land mollusc; and the respective dyeing characteristics of methylene blue on cellulose and oxycellulose. Rereading the stories, one is impressed by the incidental detail, characterization and additional detective interest. More than one critic has remarked on the richness of the short stories —their concentrated character; often they contain sufficient incident and detection to be extended to book-length, as did indeed happen with *The Shadow of the Wolf.*

One result of this method of construction, with its emphasis on scientific fact rather than characterization or thrilling incident, is the frequent appearance of oddities and freaks, many of them—in the case of the Thorndyke stories—of a medical nature. The earliest Thorndyke tale to be conceived and drafted was *The Mystery of 31, New Inn,* devised by its author while working in the Westminster

Ophthalmic Hospital; the story introduces, not surprisingly, such tidbits as a tremulous iris and a divergent squint, though not, fortunately, in the same individual. Lotta Schiller (in Freeman's last book) possessed a small Darwinian tubercle on her right ear; Nicholas Frood had clubbed fingers; Mr. Pottermack's undoing was a small port-wine mark; and ringed hair and speckled teeth also play their part in the saga. It is this sort of abnormality which contributes to the special flavor, most appreciated by male readers, of the stories. Thorndyke, in addition to being a mine of information on obscure medical aberrations, was also a member of the Bar and could quote technicalities by the yard. ("If Mr. Weiss has administered poison. . . he. . . is liable under the Consolidation Acts of 1861 to ten years penal servitude.")[29] And indeed, one always feels as secure with Thorndyke's law as with his science, a tribute to the care with which Freeman would ascertain, from his barrister friends and elsewhere, the precise state of the law touching on any of the situations described in his stories. Thorndyke the metallurgist is to be found in *Dr. Thorndyke Intervenes*, and his more-than-nodding acquaintance with typewriters is revealed in *The Red Thumb Mark*. Again, his knowledge of walking-stick lore is nothing short of fabulous, encompassing as it does not only the recognition of impressions made by a stick having a knob (rather than a crook) at the top,[30] but even the detection of marks made by a walking-stick which does not belong to the man using it.[31]

Knowledge is one thing; wisdom is quite another. If Thorndyke had nothing to offer but quick-fire scientific diagnosis he would lack the preeminence as an investigator he has justly attained. The almost mystical quality of Thorndyke, the aura of omnipotence he exudes, is an exceedingly difficult thing to communicate to the reader unfamiliar with Freeman's books. It is a quality more evident in the novels than in the short stories, and largely accounts for Alfred C. Ward's remark, in his admirable comparison of Thorndyke with Sherlock Holmes, previously set out at length, that whereas "story for the sake of story is more generously given by Conan Doyle than by Austin Freeman [in the] short tales,. . . in the novels the position is probably reversed."

Largely, the reason is that Conan Doyle's inventive powers failed him when lengthy descriptions of the domestic life of Holmes and Watson was called for. Thus, if we eliminate *The Sign of Four* which is generally regarded as being inferior, two of the remaining long Holmes stories, *A Study in Scarlet* and *The Valley of Fear*, have recourse to lengthy American episodes. Nothing more alien to the tastes of true Sherlockians can possibly be imagined. They love nothing better than the cosy scenes between Holmes and Watson upstairs in their living room at No. 221B Baker Street, with a real London "particular" swirling outside and the muffled sounds of hansom cabs dimly heard through tightly shut windows.

Freeman's creative powers were under no such strain; he could have filled many volumes with the talk of Thorndyke, Jervis, Polton, Inspector Miller and the rest. And the reason, of course, is simple enough: having, in one master-stroke, created the great investigator, Freeman's major work was done. All Thorndyke's future actions flowed freely from the original conception; his creator needed only guide him through a series of diverse scientific investigations, the raw material for which, being almost entirely within Freeman's professional experience, was readily and convincingly at hand.

This, of course, fails to explain why Thorndyke, conceived as a matter-of-fact medical jurist without oddities of character, should exert such an impact on the reader. The answer can only be that Freeman was eminently successful in creating, in Thorndyke, a noble, highly convincing and thoroughly consistent character who was precisely fitted to his role.

What a superb executor Thorndyke would have made! He was not only capable, as a lawyer, in dealing with all one's business and legal affairs; but would have been the ideal person to detect any irregularities associated with one's demise. What a pity he is unavailable!

CHAPTER XI

Thorndyke's Circle

Among the select group who play a part in Thorndyke's magnificent career, pride of place, chronologically as well as in importance,
belongs to Nathaniel Polton, genial artificer and jack-of-all-trades,
crinkly-faced guardian angel of Thorndyke's bachelor establishment
in King's Bench Walk. Evidently, his facial crinkles were often mistaken for wrinkles, so that he looked more than his age. Such is the
only interpretation that seems to fit the facts. For Polton was a mere
undernourished youth when Thorndyke, some years his senior,
helped restore him to health and gave him employment;[1] yet Jervis,
only six years after he had left the medical school he had attended
with Thorndyke, described Polton as "a small elderly man."[2] Thorndyke himself is sometimes deceived in this matter: "What a wonderful old man he is," he once confided to a companion,[3] and "old"
here is unlikely to have been meant merely as a term of endearment.
Readers must simply swallow the apparent age discrepancy as one

Dr. Thorndyke comes to TV. Peter Copley as Thorndyke in the 1964 series. (Photo by Nicholas Acraman. Courtesy of BBC-TV, London.)

No. 5 King's Bench Walk, doorway of Thorndyke home as it was in 1966. (Courtesy of Mrs. Marilyn Peterson.)

more of Freeman's slips, along with Thorndyke's inability to grow older after he became fifty[4] and inconsistent dates in several of the books.

Polton and his sister Margaret were orphans, raised in separate households miles apart. He became apprenticed to a watch-maker and later worked as a maker of optical instruments before ill fortune drove him into unemployment and near-starvation. No wonder that, in the years that followed, he became utterly devoted to the man who had saved him. He was given a spacious bed-sitting room on the floor of No. 5A but his main stamping ground was the laboratory and workshop on the floor below, where he worked his many wonders. For instance, there were the magic spectacles:

> "As you see, [said Thorndyke to Anstey] they consist of a rigid spectacle-frame fitted with dummy glasses—clear, plain glass—at the outer edge of which is fixed a little disc of speculum metal worked to an optically plane surface and set at a minute angle to the glass. As the disc is quite close to the eye, it enables the wearer, by the very slightest turn of the head, to get a clear view directly behind him."[5]

Other Polton inventions were the periscope walking-stick used to good effect by Thorndyke to spy on Mr. Pottermack, and the device for photographing through a keyhole in *When Rogues Fall Out.* (All of these ingenious instruments were actually fabricated by Freeman for his own satisfaction.)

Nathaniel Polton (Thorndyke once grievously referred to him as Francis!)[6] from the beginning was employed as domestic servant as well as technician. The matter was agreed upon at the time of his engagement, when he and his future master sat beside the microtome in the laboratory of St. Margaret's Hospital one morning around 1895:

> "Mine will be a bachelor establishment [Thorndyke explained]. I want no servants; so that, if you come to me,

you would have to render a certain amount of personal and domestic services. You would keep the little household in order and occasionally prepare a meal. In fact, you would be in the position of my servant as well as laboratory assistant. Would you object to that?"

Would I object! I could have fallen down that instant and kissed his boots. What I did say was that I should be proud to be his servant and only sorry that I was not more worthy of that honourable post.

"Then," said he, "the bargain is struck; and each of us must do his best to make it a good bargain for the other."[7]

So Polton, in later life, is as often as not found, laboratory apron removed, serving tea or something a little stronger to the Doctor and his friends. He was also an excellent cook, though of unusual methods, for there was no kitchen at No. 5A, only the workshop and laboratory. "These cutlets were probably grilled in the cupel furnace," Thorndyke once remarked to Stephen Gray, "but I have known him to do a steak with the brazing jet."[8]

Young Dr. Strangeways thought so much of Polton's culinary skill that he suggested to Thorndyke he ought to have been a chef. The great man was shocked at the idea:[9]

"Do you suggest that a man who can make anything from an astronomical clock to a microscope objective; who is an expert in every branch of photographic technique, a fair analytical chemist, a microscopist, and general handicraftsman, should be degraded to the office of a mere superintendent cook? It is a dreadful thought."

In later years, his domestic burdens were shared, off-stage, by an obscure character named William, so that he was able to enjoy increased leisure. His devotion to "the Doctor"—to Polton there was only one person deserving of the capital letter—never diminished. It may be overlooked by many readers that, before Mr. Snuper's arrival on the scene, Polton on at least one occasion acted as Thorndyke's private investigator, donning the disguise of a nautical man and sallying forth to a nearby sea-port, under the assumed name of Simmons,[10] and in a later case he was willing even to snip off his eyelashes to bring a murderer to book.[11]

It is only just that gradually during the saga he is elevated from the role of Thorndyke's employee to that of partner and confidant. When we last see him he is enjoying a pinch of snuff and settling down with Thorndyke's guests to enjoy his master's review of the final recorded case, a bottle of lemonade placed before him in lieu of something more potent.

Freeman in his BBC talk explained that Polton was not "drawn from any real person" but "he is associated in my mind with two actual individuals. One is a Mr. Pollard, who was the laboratory assistant in the hospital museum when I was a student and who gave me many a valuable tip in matters of technique. . . . The other was a watch- and clock-maker—familiarly known as Uncle Parsons, who had premises in a basement near the Royal Exchange, and who was a man of boundless ingenuity and technical resource. But [Polton's] personality is not like either. His crinkly countenance is strictly his own copyright."[12]

Polton's sister Margaret, we learn in *Helen Vardon's Confession,* became a nurse; her brother, whom she called Nat, later set her up in charge of a boarding-house for sailors and being, like him, a highly capable, ingenious person, she took up weaving as a hobby. Later still her sailor boarders were replaced by "a little family of women who also work at handicrafts for a living." It was to this sorority in Wellclose Square, near London's docks, that Helen Vardon went in an effort to make her own way after her father's death.

Christopher Jervis is to Thorndyke what Watson is to Holmes: the not-too-intelligent companion and biographer who is at one and the same time essential to the story and irritating to the reader. Freeman described him in his broadcast talk as being an "expert misunderstander. His job is to observe and record all the facts and to fail completely to perceive their significance." At times, certainly, his wits seem to slow down so far as to be in danger of atrophy, but at least he does not make the mistake of overpraising Thorndyke's feats as Watson did Holmes's. Quite the reverse, in fact. Thorndyke was apparently so impressed by his friend's performance as his temporary assistant in *The Red Thumb Mark* that he begged him to come back on a permanent basis. "I must have a junior with my increasing practice, and you are the junior I want. . . . You are the best man for the job that I know."[13] Thereafter he makes a point of overvaluing his junior's feeble flashes of intelligence. A good example of this occurs in "Anthropologist at Large:" "Jervis, you are a treasure," cries Thorndyke when his right-hand man succeeds in identifying mother-of-pearl under the microscope. Their partnership is a strange one, for Jervis is inevitably left in the dark throughout each investigation, and, while Thorndyke is apologetic about his secrecy at first, he soon changes his attitude. In *The Mystery of 31, New Inn*, after the two men have questioned a house-agent's clerk, Jervis asks, "What did you learn from him," only to receive the strange reply, "Oh come, Jervis, is that a fair question under the present circumstances?"

Professor John Adams, in an early appraisal of Freeman's books,[14] found Jervis "certainly not as dull as Dr. Watson, for his creator has had the advantage of Sir Arthur Conan Doyle's experience, and makes his secondary character much more an active partner in the detection of crime. But, after all, Jervis is as inferior to Thorndyke as Watson was to Holmes. It must be acknowledged, however, that Jervis stands out more as an individual than does Watson." Strangely enough, Thorndyke's presence greatly inhibits the Jervis mentality. When the great man is absent a transformation often takes place, and scintillating intelligence, acute observation and shrewd comportment become manifest. Thus it is in the opening chapters of *The Mystery of 31, New Inn* when Jervis, not yet in partnership with Thorndyke, is conveyed to the bedside of a mysterious patient in such a way that he is unable to determine the route taken or the whereabouts of his destination. His perceptiveness inside and outside the sickroom is admirable, and the data he has gathered are of great assistance to Thorndyke after the latter has been called into the case. At this stage, however, Jervis's customary obtuseness sets in with lightning rapidity and rarely leaves him again throughout his long association with the Doctor.

We first meet him standing at the door of No. 4 King's Bench Walk, a few yards from his future home, admiring the historic doorway. His meeting with Thorndyke, the first in six years, follows, and we learn that he had been on his way to see Turcival, the medical agent—for he is unemployed—when he had providentially paused a few moments in the Temple. The meeting results in the younger man—Thorndyke was somewhat the senior in age as well as position, although they had been fellow students—being taken on as a resident assistant for the Hornby case. This affair, described in *The Red Thumb Mark*, leads to his engagement to Juliet Gibson but not, it transpires, to a permanent position in Thorndyke's employ. This does not come about until *The Mystery of 31, New Inn* (1912) though it is anticipated in some of the short stories published earlier. Jervis's marriage is implied in "The Stranger's Latchkey," where a wife is alluded to, although *New Inn* has him still single. Much of the confusion over this and other matters is undoubtedly due to the delay—a matter of years—in the publication of *New Inn,* the first Thorndyke story to be written; but the details are hardly worth unravelling now.

The skill with which Freeman delineated his investigator stands in marked contrast to the neglect poor Jervis suffered. Sometimes in the earliest novels he is present when not needed as narrator (this happens in *The Eye of Osiris* and *A Silent Witness)* and we then get a rare glimpse of him as seen by others. Humphrey Jardine describes him as "a rather tall gentleman of some thirty years of age." At other times he is present or absent according to the dictates of the novel in hand. (He is present, however, in every short story, except for four, in which Jardine or Anstey is used.)[15] Freeman's favorite device, of course, is to have the first part of the novel "written" by an innocent participant, often a young doctor lately out of medical school. Then Thorndyke is called in, and at this point Jervis usually becomes the narrator.[16]

This use of Jervis with "on again, off again" irregularity is usually unexplained, and consequently his life and career take on a spotty and uneven texture, beginning with a long period when he is, or is not, married to Juliet; followed by a longer period when he is, or is

not, living at No. 5A rather than at home; and finally by an indeter-
minate period when he is being tempted away from Thorndyke's
service but returning inevitably to the well-loved chambers.[17]

His wife, Juliet, is absent from most of the later cases. She was
an orphan of fifteen when she went to live in Kensington with her
aunt, the woolly-minded Mrs. Hornby of *The Red Thumb Mark*. Before meeting Jervis six years later, she had come into some money—
600 pounds a year—of her own. Her engagement is prolonged, for
Jervis is in poor financial shape until his employment by Thorndyke.
Shortly thereafter we must suppose the marriage took place. We
meet Juliet again years later in *When Rogues Fall Out*, and for the
last time in the pleasant domestic scene with the Pippets at the close
of *Dr. Thorndyke Intervenes*.

If Jervis is the most important of Thorndyke's colleagues—after
Polton, of course—Robert Anstey, King's Counsel, is the most interesting. Though he develops some self-confidence in the later stories
and is able to twit his senior from time to time, Jervis is never Thorndyke's equal in the same sense that Anstey, already a successful barrister, is. Jervis liked him immediately and found "his whimsical,
facetious manner covered a nature (as it often does) that was serious
and thoughtful; and I found him not only a man of considerable
learning, but one also of a lofty standard of conduct. His admiration
for Thorndyke was unbounded, and I could see that the two men
collaborated with the utmost sympathy and mutual satisfaction."

Anstey shows no awe at Thorndyke's mysteries, referring irrev-
erently to the great man's laboratory investigations as "parlour magic
upstairs," and when Jervis offers him one of Thorndyke's special
cigars he eloquently declines: "What! Those foul Trichinopolies?
Not while brown paper is to be obtained at every stationer's; I'd
rather smoke my own wig."[18]

He practised law at an address in King's Bench Walk[19] but, like
most professional inhabitants of the Inner Temple, he maintained
only an office there; his lodgings, before his marriage, were in Hampstead. Whereas discussion between Thorndyke and Jervis are those
of one medical man with another, Anstey brings a welcome outsider's
viewpoint to pathological affairs. Thus, his reaction to the "curious

aroma, half spirituous, half cadaveric" upstairs at the College of
Surgeons differs markedly from Thorndyke's.

"Yes," said Thorndyke, sniffing appreciatively, "the
good old museum bouquet. You smell it in all curators'
rooms and though, I suppose, it is not physically agreeable,
I find it by no means unpleasant The effects of odours
are largely a matter of association."

"The present odour," said [Anstey], "seems to suggest the association of a very overripe Duke of Clarence
and a butt of shockingly bad malmsey."[20]

We are constantly reminded of Anstey's independence and his
resistance to any domination by Thorndyke's personality. "I was
secretly impressed," he once wrote regarding a particularly ingenious
discourse by the medical jurist, "by the way in which Thorndyke had
'placed' Mr. Halliburton in respect of the inquiry, but, of course, it
wouldn't do to say so. It was necessary to assert my position."[21]

He is invariably more critical of Thorndyke than Jervis is. When
the investigator fails to take it for granted that Anstey will accom-
pany him on a mission to Aylesbury, the barrister is piqued; and
when he does go, and the pair are locked by the criminals in a booby-
trapped chamber with a flask of deadly hydrocyanic acid delicately
poised above their heads, Anstey's thoughts are rich in unspoken
eloquence as Thorndyke improves the perilous moments with a characteristic discourse on the elaborate mechanism by which their enemies have imprisoned them. "In my heart I cursed his inquiring
spirit, for I wanted to get out of this horrible trap. But I offered no
objection, standing by sullenly while he proceeded with calm interest
to complete his experiment."[22]

Most striking of all are the contrasted reactions of the two
investigators to the fate of the criminals who, after the escape of
Thorndyke and Anstey, are themselves entombed in the poison-filled
room. Anstey wants to attempt their rescue; Thorndyke opposes the
idea: the men are certainly dead and, anyway, "I would not risk a
hair of my head to save their lives." Anstey glanced at Thorndyke's

calm face as they strode away from the death-trap "and found in his quiet unconcerned manner something inhuman and repelling. It is true that those two wretches who now lay stark and dead on the floor of that dreadful chamber deserved no sympathy. They had digged a pit for us and fallen into it themselves. But still, they were human lives; but Thorndyke seemed to value them no more than if they had been a couple of rats."[23]

Winifred Blake, who was to become Mrs. Anstey at the end of *The Cat's Eye,* appeared first in *Helen Vardon's Confession* as one of the group of woman artists presided over by Margaret Polton. In this earlier story she bears the nickname of Lilith and, like her famous forebear, William Blake, shows strong leanings towards the psychic and supernatural. Robert Anstey, in *The Cat's Eye,* saves the life of Winifred and her younger brother, Percy, whom she has supported for several years by her artistry. We hear of her once more when her talents are strangely put to use by Thorndyke in unravelling the Frood case.

Although the *British Medical Journal,* in its obituary notice, made the remarkable claim that Freeman seldom introduced any love interest into his stories, it is a fact that, in his novels at any rate, he almost invariably did so. This is the reason, of course, for the introduction of a series of young medicos and other eligible suitors to act as narrators and to be appropriately married off to the current heroine. These young ladies are, more often than not, artists or craftsmen in their own right. Sylvia Vyne, who marries Humphrey Jardine, is a landscape painter in water-colors; strong-willed Helen Vardon is a worker in precious metals; Marion D'Arblay, whose beau is Stephen Gray, is a waxwork artist. On the other hand, Angelina Frood, with whom John Strangeways falls in love before her dramatic disappearance, is an actress, a profession dictated by requirements of the plot.

Another common ingredient of Freeman's stories is the crusty old lawyer. Mr. Brodribb is the almost invariable choice for the short stories; he is "rosy-gilled, portly and convivial, to whom a mass of bushy, white hair, an expansive double chin, and a certain prim sumptiousness of dress imparted an air of old-world distinction."[24]

In the novels we meet others of his profession. In *The Mystery of 31, New Inn* it is Mr. Marchmont, an "elderly, professional-looking man, a typical solicitor of the old school; fresh-faced, precise, rather irascible, and conveying a not unpleasant impression of taking a reasonable interest in his diet."

Perhaps the pick of the bunch are frosty, argumentative Mr. Jellicoe of *The Eye of Osiris* and, from the same mold, Mr. Penfield, who first meets Thorndyke as an antagonist in *The Shadow of the Wolf* but becomes a friend and ally in later novels. In particular, the casuistical duel between Jellicoe and Jervis is a veritable gem of Freeman craftsmanship.

Thorndyke's relationship with the police is nominally a friendly one; actually there is a good deal of reserve on both sides. More than once the medical jurist warns his assistants: "Remember, we are seeking information, not giving it," and on their side Scotland Yard are frequently secretive. A good example is Superintendent Miller's failure, in *The Cat's Eye,* to tell Thorndyke that the prime suspect has a perfect alibi, having been in prison at the time of the murder. Miller, who continues to appear throughout Thorndyke's long series of cases, is an example of a "good" policeman, though evidently below the minimum standards of intelligence of the metropolitan police. Though warned of Walter Hornby's criminality in *The Red Thumb Mark* he permits him to escape and, shortly afterwards in "The Old Lag," seems to have forgotten everything he learned in that earlier case. Less benevolent members of the force also make their appearance, notably ill-fated foxy-featured Inspector Badger who, as a practical joke, sends the benevolent director of a cats' home to Thorndyke with a collection of pick-pocket's leavings in "A Sower of Pestilence." Thorndyke takes his revenge in "The Stolen Ingots" by sending Badger to sea on a wild-goose chase. But all this is forgiven and forgotten when he meets his death in a railway carriage in *When Rogues Fall Out (Dr. Thorndyke's Discovery).*

Inspector Blandy's deviousness is of a subtler character than Badger's; he is "a rather remarkable-looking gentleman, slightly bald, with a long placid face and a still longer, and acutely pointed nose, and an expression in which concentrated benevolence beamed on an undeserving world."[25] He acted with polite viciousness on occasion, but once faced point-blank gunfire with great bravery.

Altogether, Freeman's subsidiary characters are not unworthy of the great man whose exploits they embellish. Of course, without him they would amount to little; Thorndyke's absence leads, at best, to a story like *The Unwilling Adventurer* which, even with its memorable pirate captain, Parradine, is of little popular appeal to modern readers. Freeman was a more-than-adequate story-teller; his prose, though quiet in tone, is full of interest. But his great achievement was the invention of a totally convincing scientific investigator who is also a well-rounded human being.

CHAPTER I

[1] Richard Austin Freeman, *Travels and Life in Ashanti and Jaman* (Westminster: Constable & Co., 1898), p. 6.

[2] *Ibid.*, pp. 13-14.　[3] *Ibid.*, pp. 2-3.

[4] "Variations in *Talpa europœa*" in *Naturalist's World*, (Feb. 1886), p. 40.

[5] He was registered May 20, 1887 as Member of the Royal College of Surgeons and as Licentiate of the Royal College of Physicians.

[6] *West Africa*, 5 January 1924; pp. 1622-24. *West Africa* was a weekly newspaper published in London for Englishmen with an interest in that part of the world. The unsigned article, entitled "R. Austin Freeman, Coaster and Author," is undoubtedly by Freeman himself.

[7] *Ibid.*

[8] Freeman, *Ashanti*, pp. 19-20.

[9] *Ibid.*, pp. 35-36.　[10] *Ibid.*, pp. 42-43.　[11] *Ibid.*, pp. 46-48.

[12] *Royal Geographical Society Supplementary Papers*, 3 (1893): 117-46.

[13] Freeman, *Ashanti*, p. 58.

[14] By Frank Cass & Co., London, 1967. The book also contains numerous drawings by Freeman and interesting chapters on native clothing and customs.

[15] Freeman, *Ashanti*, p. 88.　[16] *Ibid.*, pp. 92-93.

[17] *Ibid.*, pp. 100-103. For an account of the enstooling of Prempeh III in 1970, see *Time*, Aug. 10, 1970, p. 26.

[18] K.A. Busia, *The Position of the Chief in the Modern Political System of Ashanti* (Oxford University Press, 1951).

[19] R.A. Rattray, *Ashanti* (Oxford University Press, 1923), pp. 9-10, 187-93.

[20] To the Ashantis, this British interference in native justice was an intimation of their loss of independence, and thus humiliation was added to the national grief (Busia, *loc.cit.*, pp. 113-17).

[21] Freeman, *Ashanti*, pp. 135-36.

[22] *Ibid.*, pp. 144-45.　[23] *Ibid.*, pp. 156-59.　[24] *Ibid.*, pp. 168-69.

[25] *Ibid.*, p. 181.

[26] W. Walton Claridge, *A History of the Gold Coast and Ashanti* (London: John Murray, 1915), II, 334.

CHAPTER II

[1] Richard Austin Freeman, *Travels and Life in Ashanti and Jaman* (Westminster, Constable & Co., 1898), p. 227.

[2] *Ibid.*, pp. 235-36.   [3] *Ibid.*, pp. 261-63.   [4] *Ibid.*, pp. 246-47.

[5] *Ibid.*, pp. 268-69.   [6] *Ibid.*, pp. 296-98.   [7] *Ibid.*, p. 303.

[8] *Ibid.*, pp. 349-50.   [9] *Ibid.*, p. 352.

[10] G.K. French, *National Geographic Magazine*, 8 (1897): 1-15.

[11] *Royal Geographical Society, Supplementary Papers*, 3 (1893): 117-46.

[12] *Field*, 3 November 1894.

[13] The first story, "The Resurrection of Matthew Jephson," is a nautical adventure about an abandoned ship. See also p. 264.

[14] "Collecting Detective Fiction" in *New Paths in Book Collecting* (London: Constable & Co., 1934).

CHAPTER III

[1] Ellery Queen, *Queen's Quorum* (Boston: Little, Brown & Co., 1951), pp. 46-48.

[2] Six are identified by Ellery Queen (*loc.cit.*), a seventh is in the possession of the co-author's family and an eighth was sold by Mr. David Symberlist at Sotheby's in October, 1966. A facsimile edition was issued by Oswald Train in Philadelphia in 1968.

[3] *Cassell's Magazine*, iv 10 (1902):   54-62, 185-94, 271-80, 380-89, 503-12, 590-99.

[4] This information reached Stone 28 August 1946. Mrs. Freeman died at her home 22 April 1948.

[5] Pitcairn's widow asked her daughter Winifred Mary (Mrs. T.H. Johns) to correspond with Stone. Mrs. Pitcairn died in 1956, aged ninety-eight; Stone died in 1965.

[6] *Chicago Sunday Tribune Magazine of Books,* 1 February 1948.

[7] The Queen collection, containing Freeman's own copy of *Pringle,* is now owned by the University of Texas; the catalog omits mention of Pitcairn.

[8] *British Medical Journal,* 14 July 1888, p. 75; 22 September 1888, p. 691.

[9] The post was so ephemeral that no record exists of it, according to a letter from the Prison Commissioners to P.M. Stone in 1947.

[10] "By the Black Deep," by R. Austin Freeman and Ashdown Piers, in *Windsor Magazine,* May 1903, pp. 677-86.

[11] *Cassell's Magazine,* June-November 1903. They were not issued in volume form until 1970 (by the Philadelphia book-seller Oswald Train).

[12] Richard Church, *Kent* (London: Robert Hale, 1948), p. 236.

[13] See the dedication in Freeman's *A Silent Witness,* (*cf.* pp. 240-41).

[14] Information on this obscure period of Freeman's life was kindly supplied by the Bishops' daughter, Mrs. Dorothy Moriarty.

[15] A.D.C. Peterson, *A Hundred Years of Education* (London: Duckworth, 1952), p. 125.

[16] *Eugenics Review,* 21 (1929): 292-95. (My italics.).

[17] See Sir E. Ruggles-Brise, *The English Prison System* (London: Macmillan & Co., 1921).   The term 'Borstal' for this reformatory system has persisted through the years for want of a more suitable name, although institutions were soon built in other parts of the country, including one exclusively for girls at Ayllsbury. As medical officer, Pitcairn's role was, of course, very important.

[18] Ellery Queen, *The Detective Short Story: a bibliography* (Boston: Little, Brown & Co., 1942).

CHAPTER IV

[1] *Raymond Chandler Speaking,* edited by Dorothy Gardiner and Kathrine Sorley Walker (Boston: Houghton Mifflin Company, 1962).

[2] Dorothy L. Sayers in the introduction to *Great Short Stories of Detection, Mystery and Horror* (London: Gollancz, 1928).

[3] *British Medical Journal,* 12 June 1880, pp. 905-6.

[4] *Illustrated London News*, 15 and 22 March 1845; *Times* (London) 13-15 March 1845; A.S. Taylor, *Principles and Practice of Medical Jurisprudence*, 2nd. U.S. ed., p. 38.

[5] The reader will find a full account in *The Trial of William Palmer*, edited by George H. Knott (Edinburgh: W. Hodge & Co., 1912). A singularly sympathetic treatment of Palmer is provided by Robert Graves in his *They Hanged My Saintly Billy* (New York: Doubleday & Co., 1957).

[6] The authoritative account is *The Trial of Thomas Smethurst*, edited by Leonard A. Parry (Edinburgh: W. Hodge & Co., 1931).

[7] *The Cat's Eye*, xi.

[8] *The Eugenics Review*, October 1943, p. 52.

CHAPTER V

[1] Now owned by the University of Texas, Austin, and quoted by permission.

[2] In rarity it is second only to *The Adventures of Romney Pringle*.

[3] The matter is thrashed out rather fully by G.W. Wilton (a Faulds champion) in his *Fingerprints: History, Law and Romance* (Edinburgh: W. Hodge & Co., 1938).

[4] Francis Galton, *Finger Prints* (London: Macmillan & Co., 1892)

[5] Anne P. Wigger, in *American Literature*, 28 (1957): 517-20, discusses the Galton—Twain relationship.

[6] *Criminal Appeal Reports*, III 74 (1909). The sentence was three years' penal servitude.

[7] It was to this Freeman novel, or maybe to *Croker*, that Lord Atkin alluded in an address to the Medico-Legal Society; see the Society's *Transactions*, 24 (1931): 95.

[8] *The Red Thumb Mark*, xvi. Thorndyke's views are given *in extenso* but without comment in the large standard work on fingerprints, R. Heindl's *Daktyloskopie* (1927).

[9] *Finger Prints*, pp. 112-13. (My italics.)

[10] Thorndyke's evidence in *The Red Thumb Mark*, xvi.

[11] Douglas G. Browne and Alan Brock, Fingerprints: *Fifty Years of Scientific Crime Detection* (New York: E.P. Dutton & Co., 1954), p. 74.

[12] Wilton, *loc.cit.*, p. 231.

[13] 25 January 1938, p. 9.

[14] B.C. Bridges, *Practical Fingerprinting* (New York: Funk & Wagnalls Co., 1942), pp. 293-98.

[15] *The Red Thumb Mark*, xvi.

[16] H. Cummins, "Counterfeit Finger Prints" in *J. Criminal Law and Criminology*, 25 (1934): 666-71.

[17] The editor of the journal submitted the test-card to "six qualified individuals, one of whom is in charge of a police finger-print bureau, and the percentage of accuracy approximates that obtained by Dr. Cummins."

[18] C.D. Lee, "Finger-Prints Can be Forged" in *J. Criminal Law and Criminology*, 25 (1934): 671-74.

CHAPTER VI

[1] *Aspects of the Modern Short Story* (University of London Press, 1924), pp. 211-26.

[2] *The Singing Bone*, preface.

[3] A device used around the same date by Arnold Bennett in *Clayhanger* and *Hilda Lessways*, with similarly dramatic results.

[4] *Strand*, 73 (1927): 90-91. Freeman forgot his use of R. v. Castleton in *Danby Croker* (1916). Later he was to use another true case in *Dr. Thorndyke Intervenes* (1933).

[5] Alfred Swaine Taylor, *Principles and Practice of Medical Jurisprudence* (London: J. & A. Churchill, 1883) I, 541-43; see also the *Times* (London), 19-20 November 1866; 16-18 March, 1867.

[6] *Bookman* (London), April 1913, pp. 6-7.

[7] Introduction to *Great Short Stories of Detection, Mystery and Horror* (London: Gollancz, 1928).

[8] *Masters of Mystery* (London: Collins, 1931), pp. 168-76.

[9] From a letter quoted by "R.B." in the introduction to *The Golden Pool*, edited and abridged for class use with the approval of the author (University of London Press, 1939).

[10] Vincent Starrett, *Books and Bipeds* (New York: Argus Books, 1947), pp. 257-58.

[11] *Pearson's Magazine*, April 1917, pp. 276-88.

[12] E.M. Wrong, in the introduction to *Crime and Detection* (London: Oxford University Press, 1926).

CHAPTER VII

[1] *Eugenics Review*, October 1943, 35, 52.

[2] This chapter, "The Brazen Serpent," has been anthologized in Ellery Queen's *Rogues' Gallery* (Boston: Little, Brown, 1945).

[3] "Percival Bland's Proxy" appeared in *Ellery Queen's Mystery Magazine*, Vol. 3, pp. 5-24.

[4] For example, Kwaku Essien in "The Trail of Behemoth" and Vanderpuye in *The Unconscious Witness*.

[5] *Eugenics Review*, 13, 414-16 (1921).

[6] *Ibid.*, 23, 383-92 (1931).

[7] *International Journal of Ethics*, 33, 347-68 (1923).

[8] "Segregation of the Fit" in the *Eugenics Review*, 23, 207-13 (1931).

[9] But not quite! See the *Eugenics Review*, 25, 273-74 (1934).

CHAPTER VIII

[1] *Journal of Conchology*, 18, 340 (1929).

[1a] An example of such a case is reported in the *Times* (London), 11 October 1927, p. 7.

[2] For illustrations see Thompson's *Light, Visible and Invisible*, 2nd ed. (London: Macmillan, 1928), pp. 50-54.

[3] *Times* (London), 13 November 1922, et seq.; George Dilnot, *The Story of Scotland Yard* (Boston: Houghton, Mifflin Co., 1927), pp. 152-53.

[4] *The D'Arblay Mystery*, v.   [5] *Dickensian*, 24, 223-24 (1928).

[6] Thorndyke cites Alfred Lucas's experiments, which were described in his *Forensic Chemistry* (London: Arnold, 1921).

[7] *Dickensian*, 26, 70-71 (1930).

[8] For example, Richard M. Baker, *The Drood Murder Case* (Univ. of California Press, 1951); Felix Aylmer, *The Drood Case* (London: Hart-Davis, 1964). Both treatments of the case are quite satisfying, yet completely at variance with one another.

[9] *Born in a Bookshop* (Norman: Univ. of Oklahoma Press, 1965).

[10] *Ibid.,* p. 255.

[11] *Books and Bipeds* (New York: Argus Books, 1947), pp. 108-11.

[12] *Pearson's Magazine,* 34, 354-64, 556-68 (1922).

[13] "Petrographical and Mineralogical Techniques in Forensic Science" in *British Academy of Forensic Sciences,* Teaching Symposium No. 1—Soil, pp. 37-46.

[14] "Gleanings from the Wreckage" never appeared in *Pearson's.*

CHAPTER IX

[1] *Masters of Mystery* (London: Collins, 1931), pp. 168-76.

[2] My friend Dr. James E. Rush points out that Freeman punned, perhaps unconsciously, in naming this character, for indeed Hornby "*did* bury Toke."

[3] For the exhumation proceedings see the *Times* (London), 31 December 1907, p. 10. The entire affair is fully recounted in Theodore Besterman's *The Druce-Portland Case* (London: Duckworth, 1935).

[4] *The Great Platinum Robbery* seems to have been considered as a possible U.S. title for the work; in the end the London title was retained.

[5] The scientifically-inclined reader will find the appropriate phase-diagram for the two metals in *Zeitschrift für anorganische Chemie,* 54, 333-66 (1907).

[6] *Dr. Thorndyke Intervenes,* xi.

[7] *Trial of William Gardiner,* edited by W. Henderson (Edinburgh: Hodge & Co., 1934). Freeman's discussion is in *Great Unsolved Crimes* (London: Hutchinson, 1935).

[8] *Antiquaries Journal,* xvii, 122-37 (1937); xix, 260-81 (1939).

[9] It was tentatively explored in 1702 by Heneage Finch.

[10] See the U.S. editions of *As a Thief in the Night* and *Mr. Pottermack's Oversight.*

[11] Reproduced by permission of James Keddie, Jr.

[12] *Books and Bipeds* (New York: Argus Books, 1947), p. 111.

CHAPTER X

[1] *The Red Thumb Mark*, xvi

[2] *Helen Vardon's Confession*, ix

[3] *The Mystery of Angelina Frood*, v

[4] *Ibid.*, xvii.

[5] Kenneth MacGowan (Ed.), *Sleuths* (New York: Harcourt, Brace), p. 202.

[6] *The Red Thumb Mark*, i.

[7] *Sleuths*, p. 202.

[8] Reprinted in *Dr. Thorndyke's Crime File.*

[9] *Ibid.*

[10] "Writers in the Temple" in the *Lady*, 1 October 1959, p. 265.

[11] *The Red Thumb Mark*, v.

[12] *The Cat's Eye*, xi.

[13] *As a Thief in the Night*, x.

[14] *The Red Thumb Mark*, v.

[15] *The Cat's Eye*, xi.

[16] *The Mystery of Angelina Frood*, xvi.

[17] *Pontifex, Son and Thorndyke*, vii.

[18] *The Cat's Eye*, vi.

[19] "The Blue Sequin"

[20] *The Mystery of 31, New Inn*, xi.

[21] "The Old Lag"

[22] "The Case of Oscar Brodski"

[23] *The D'Arblay Mystery.*

[24] *The Mystery of 31, New Inn,* vi

[25] "A Message from the Deep Sea"

[26] *The Cat's Eye,* vi.

[27] For a nostalgic apologia by Freeman, see the *Eugenics Review,* 25, 117 (1933).

[28] Introduction to *Great Short Stories of Detection, Mystery and Horror* (London: Gollancz, 1928).

[29] *The Mystery of 31, New Inn,* ii.

[30] "The Stranger's Latchkey"

[31] "The Seal of Nebuchadnezzar"

CHAPTER XI

[1] *Mr. Polton Explains.*

[2] *The Red Thumb Mark,* i.

[3] *The Mystery of 31, New Inn,* ii

[4] An age he reached in *The Mystery of Angelina Frood.*

[5] *The Cat's Eye,* xv.

[6] *Helen Vardon's Confession,* xxviii.

[7] *Mr. Polton Explains,* ix.

[8] *The D'Arblay Mystery,* xi.

[9] *The Mystery of Angelina Frood,* xvi.

[10] "The Mystery of the Nailed Shoes."

[11] *The D'Arblay Mystery.*

[12] "Meet Dr. Thorndyke" in *Meet the Detective* (London: Allen and Unwin, 1935), a collection of talks by detective-story writers broadcast in the Empire Service of the BBC.

[13] *The Mystery of 31, New Inn,* ii.

[14] *Bookman* (London), April, 1913, pp. 6-7.

15 Jardine in "The Mysterious Visitor" and "Rex v. Burnaby"; Anstey in "The Seal of Nebuchadnezzar" and "A Mystery of the Sandhills."

16 In *The Cat's Eye*, Robert Anstey describes the entire story, first as participant, later as Thorndyke's companion. The narrative style is employed throughout *A Certain Dr. Thorndyke, The Shadow of the Wolf* and *Mr. Pottermack's Oversight*, the second and last of these being the only Thorndyke novels of the inverted type.

17 In *The Cat's Eye*, Jervis is said to be "enjoying a sort of professional holiday in New York," acting as consultant in "the Rosenbaum case"; in *A Certain Dr. Thorndyke* he has left Thorndyke's employ for insurance work, but he returns, without explanation, in later stories.

18 *The Red Thumb Mark*, vi.

19 In "The Moabite Cipher" this is said to be two doors *above* No. 5A, i.e. at No. 3 or No. 4; but by the time of *The Cat's Eye*, his office has moved down to No. 8A.

20 *The Cat's Eye*, vi.

21 *Ibid.*, v.   22 *Ibid.*, xvii   23 *Ibid.*, xviii

24 "The Mandarin's Pearl."

25 *The Stoneware Monkey*, ix.

R.A. FREEMAN: A CHECKLIST

Date of London publication is on the left, U.S. publication on the right. Thorndyke books are marked by an asterisk; Thorndyke short stories bear the notation "ss."

The serial numbers on the left afford a key to the bibliography which follows.

1.	1898	Travels and Life in Ashanti and Jaman	-
2.	1902	Adventures of Romney Pringle, by Clifford Ashdown *pseud.* (i.e., R.A. Freeman and J.J. Pitcairn.)	-
3.	1905	The Golden Pool	-
4.	1907	*The Red Thumb Mark	1911
5.	1909	ss*John Thorndyke's Cases (U.S. title: Dr. Thorndyke's Cases)	1931
6.	1911	*The Eye of Osiris (original U.S. title: The Vanishing Man)	1912
7.	1912	ss*The Singing Bone	1923
8.	1912	*The Mystery of 31, New Inn	1913
9.	1913	The Unwilling Adventurer	-
10.	1920	The Uttermost Farthing (U.S.) (Published six years later in London as A Savant's Vendetta)	1914
11.	1914	*A Silent Witness	1915
12.	1916	The Exploits of Danby Croker	-
13.	1918	ss*The Great Portrait Mystery	-
14.	1921	Social Decay and Regeneration	1921
15.	1922	*Helen Vardon's Confession	-
16.	1923	ss*Dr. Thorndyke's Case Book (U.S. title: The Blue Scarab)	1924

17.	1923	*The Cat's Eye	1927
18.	1924	*The Mystery of Angelina Frood	1925
19.	1925	ss*The Puzzle Lock	1926
20.	1925	*The Shadow of the Wolf	1925
21.	1926	*The D'Arblay Mystery	1926
22.	1927	ss*The Magic Casket	1927
23.	1927	The Surprising Experiences of Mr. Shuttlebury Cobb	-
24.	1927	*A Certain Dr. Thorndyke	1928
25.	1928	Flighty Phyllis	-
26.	1928	*As a Thief in the Night	1928
27.	1929	ss*Dr. Thorndyke Omnibus [London] ("The Famous Cases of Dr. Thorndyke - 37 of his criminal investigations. . ." All the Thorndyke short stories except three of those published in John Thorndyke's Cases.)	-
28.	1930	*Mr. Pottermack's Oversight	1930
29.	1931	*Pontifex, Son and Thorndyke	1931
30.	-	ss*Dr. Thorndyke Omnibus [U.S.] ("38 of his criminal investigations. . ." All the Thorndyke short stories except the two published in The Great Portrait Mystery.)	1932
31.	1932	*When Rogues Fall Out (U.S. title: Dr. Thorndyke's Discovery)	1932
32.	1933	*Dr. Thorndyke Intervenes	1933
33.	1934	*For the Defence: Dr. Thorndyke (U.S. title: For the Defense: Dr. Thorndyke)	1934
34.	1936	*The Penrose Mystery	1936

35.	1937	*Felo De Se (U.S. title: Death at the Inn)	1937
36.	1938	*The Stoneware Monkey	1939
37.	1940	*Mr. Polton Explains	1940
38.	-	*Dr. Thorndyke's Crime File (contains three novels: Osiris, Frood and Pottermack; and three short pieces: Meet Dr. Thorndyke and The Art of the Detective Story, both by Freeman, and 5A King's Bench Walk by P.M. Stone)	1941
39.	1942	*The Jacob Street Mystery (U.S. title: The Unconscious Witness)	1942

Note: *Dr. Thorndyke Investigates* (Univ. of London Press, Ltd., 1930) contains five short stories: The Blue Sequin, The New Jersey Sphinx, The Magic Casket, The Pathologist to the Rescue and The Touchstone.

R. AUSTIN FREEMAN: A BIBLIOGRAPHY

1.   *Travels and Life in Ashanti and Jaman*   1898

First edition

TRAVELS AND LIFE/IN ASHANTI AND JAMAN/BY/Richard Austin Free-
man/Late Assistant Colonial Surgeon, and Anglo-German/Boundary Commissioner of the Gold Coast/WITH ABOUT ONE HUNDRED ILLUSTRATIONS
BY/THE AUTHOR AND FROM PHOTOGRAPHS/AND   TWO MAPS/WEST-
MINSTER/ARCHIBALD CONSTABLE & CO/2 WHITEHALL GARDENS/
1898

The words "IN ASHANTI AND JAMAN" and "WESTMINSTER" are in red, the
remainder in black.

9¼ x 6 1/8 in. pp. [i-vii] viii-xi [xii-xiii] xiv-xvi [xvii] xviii-xx, [1] 2-551 [552-
5] 556-9 [560]; [ ] ^{10} 1-35^8; 290 leaves.

[i] Half-title; [ii-iii] blank; [iv] frontispiece (after a photograph); [v] title; [vi]
blank; [vii]-xi Contents; [xii] blank; [xiii]-xvi list of illustrations; [xvii]-xx
Introduction; [1]-551 text; [552] blank; [553] INDEX (half-title); [554]
blank; [555]-559 index; [560] blank.

Map in color tipped in between pp. xx and [1]; folding map in color tipped in
after p. [560].

Issued in orange cloth with linen finish; top edge trimmed, gilt; fore and lower
edges uncut; front cover and spine have gilt lettering; front cover shows (in gilt)
two devices; a Sakrobundi mask (*cf.* p. 152 of the book), and an Ashanti stool
(*cf.* p. 101).

2.   *The Adventures of Romney Pringle*   1902

First edition.

THE ADVENTURES OF/ROMNEY PRINGLE/BY/CLIFFORD ASHDOWN/
"But a double life was the life he led,/* * * */That pettifogger from Furnival's
Inn."/*Longfellow*/ILLUSTRATIONS BY FRED PEGRAM/LONDON/WARD,
LOCK & CO., LIMITED/NEW YORK AND MELBOURNE/1902

7 5/8 x 5 in. pp. [1-5] vi [7-9] 10-198 [199-202]

[1] Half-title; [2] blank; [3] title; [4] blank; [5]-vi Preface; [7] Contents; [8]
blank; [9]-198 text; 199-200 advertisements; 201-2 blank.

Frontispiece is tipped in to face title; there are three other illustrations. The adventures are entitled The Assyrian Rejuvenator; The Foreign Office Despatch; The Chicago Heiress; The Lizard's Scale; The Paste Diamonds; The Kailyard Novel.

Issued in blue or red cloth; front cover has pictorial design in white in lower right corner; front cover and spine have lettering in gold; back cover plain; all edges trimmed.

(Additional information from E.T. Guymon, Jr., and University of Texas Library.)

NOTE: The first U.S. edition, issued by the Philadelphia bookseller, Oswald Train, in 1968 is a facsimile (so far as the text is concerned) of the above; the preliminaries have been rearranged and the title page is new; there are no illustrations. For *The Further Adventures of Romney Pringle,* see item 40, p. 263.

3.   *The Golden Pool*   1905

First edition.

THE GOLDEN/POOL/A STORY OF A/FORGOTTEN MINE/BY/R. AUSTIN FREEMAN/CASSELL AND COMPANY, LIMITED/LONDON, PARIS, NEW YORK/AND MELBOURNE, MCMV/All Rights Reserved.

7 9/16 x 5 in. pp. [i-v] vi-vii [viii], [1] 2-341 [342-344]; A^4 B-U^8 V^{12} (leaf V^a_s has sig. V*)

[i] Half-title; [ii] blank; [iii] title; [iv] blank; [v]-vii Contents; [viii] blank; [1]-341 text; [342] Epilogue; at foot of p. 342 (below rule): PRINTED BY CASSELL & COMPANY LIMITED, LA BELLE SAUVAGE, LONDON, E.C. [343-344] blank.

Issued in blue-green cloth; all edges trimmed; black lettering and black and cream landscape on front cover; gilt lettering on spine; back cover has circular device within square, all in black. Author's name on front cover and spine given as "AUSTIN FREEMAN" without initial.

4.   *The Red Thumb Mark*   1907

a) *First edition.*

THE/RED THUMB MARK/BY/R. AUSTIN FREEMAN/*Author of "The Golden Pool*," &c./COLLINGWOOD BROS., 65-66, CHANCERY LANE, W.C.

7 9/32 x 4 3/4 in. [i-viii], [1] 2-232; [A]^4 B-H^{16} I^4; 120 leaves.

[i] Half-title; [ii] advertisement for *The Golden Pool*; [iii] title; [iv] BRAD-BURY AGNEW & CO. LD. PRINTERS/LONDON AND TONBRIDGE [v] Pre-face; [vi] blank; [vii] Contents; [viii] blank; [1]-232 text; frontispiece (a drawing by T.E. Francis of the hypodermic missile incident) is pasted in oppo-site the title.

Issued in smooth black cloth, front cover has The Red [two leaf designs] Thumb Mark at the top and By/R. Austin/Freeman at the bottom left. This lettering is in white. In the center is an enlarged thumb print in red. The spine has THE/RED/THUMB/MARK/R.A./FREEMAN/COLLINGWOOD/BROS in white. All edges trimmed, unstained; back cover plain.

b) *First Hodder & Stoughton edition.*

THE/RED THUMB MARK/BY/R. AUSTIN FREEMAN/AUTHOR OF "THE GOLDEN POOL," ETC./HODDER AND STOUGHTON/WARWICK SQUARE, LONDON, E.C./1911

7¼ x 4 3/4 in. pp. [i-v] vi-viii, [1] 2-248; [A]^4 B-Q^8 R^4; 128 leaves.

[i] Half-title; [ii] publisher's advertisement of "The Golden Pool"; [iii] title; [iv] RICHARD CLAY & SONS, LIMITED/BREAD STREET HILL, E.C., AND/BUNGAY, SUFFOLK. [v]-vi Preface; vii-viii Contents; [1]-248 text; p. 248 has (below text): [rule] *Richard Clay & Sons, Ltd., London and Bungay.*

Issued in deep red cloth, all edges trimmed, unstained; black lettering on front cover, gilt lettering on spine; back cover plain.

c) *First U.S. edition.*

THE/RED THUMB MARK/BY/R. AUSTIN FREEMAN/AUTHOR OF "THE GOLDEN POOL," ETC./NEW YORK/DONALD W. NEWTON/1911

7 3/8 x 4 15/16 in. pp. [i-v] vi-viii, [1] 2-248; [A]^4 B-Q^8 R^4; 128 leaves.

[i] Half-title; [ii] blank; [iii] title; [iv] blank; [v]-vi preface; vii-viii contents; [1]-248 text.

Issued in red cloth, all edges trimmed, unstained; gilt lettering at head of front cover and on spine; back cover plain.

5.   *John Thorndyke's Cases*   1909

a) *First edition.*

JOHN THORNDYKE'S/CASES/RELATED BY/CHRISTOPHER JERVIS, M.D./ AND EDITED BY/R. AUSTIN FREEMAN/AUTHOR OF "THE GOLDEN POOL," ETC./ [circular publisher's device with letters CW]/WITH SIX ILLUS- TRATIONS BY H.M. BROCK, AND/NINE FROM PHOTOGRAPHS, ETC./ LONDON/CHATTO & WINDUS/1909

7 3/8 x 4 11/16 in. pp. [i-iv] v [vi] vii-ix [x] xi [xii], 1-288; [ ]^6 1-18^8; 150 leaves.

[i] Half-title; [ii] blank; [iii] title; [iv] *All rights reserved* v TO MY FRIEND/ FRANK STANDFIELD/IN MEMORY OF MANY A PLEASANT EVENING/ SPENT WITH MICROSCOPE AND CAMERA/THIS VOLUME IS DEDICATED [vi] blank vii-viii Preface ". . . I may add that the experiments described have in all cases been performed by me, and that the micro-photographs are, of course, from the actual specimens. . . ." ix Contents; [x] blank; xi List of [15] illustrations; [xii] blank; 1-288 text. On p. 288 below rule: BILLING AND SONS, LTD., PRINTERS, GUILDFORD

There are four photographs pasted in, as follows: 1. Fluff from key-barrel; 2. Transverse sections of human hair; 3. The sand from the murdered wom- an's pillow; 4. Human hair, showing roots.

There are five sketches in the text, as follows: 1. Plan of St. Bridget's Bay (p. 9); 2. The Sergeant's sketch of the nailed shoes (p. 41); 3. The Moabite cipher (p. 156); 4. The Professor's analysis of the cipher (p. 171); 5. The aluminium dagger (p. 240).

Issued in yellowish-brown cloth, all edges trimmed, unstained; front cover has (at top) book title in pink letters outlined in black and (at bottom) author's name in black with (between) a sketch in pink of dead woman being discovered in railway carriage (a copy of H.M. Brock's sketch, which is also used within the book); spine is lettered in gold: JOHN/THORNDYKE'S/CASES/R. AUSTIN/ FREEMAN/CHATTO & WINDUS; back cover plain.

Contents: The man with the nailed shoes—The Stranger's Latchkey—The An- thropologist At Large—The Blue Sequin—The Moabite Cipher—The Mandarin's Pearl—The Aluminium Dagger—A Message from the Deep Sea.

b) *First U.S. edition (Dr. Thorndyke's Cases).*

DR./THORNDYKE'S/CASES/BY/R. AUSTIN/FREEMAN/NEW YORK/DODD, MEAD/& COMPANY/1931

Title page has vertical multiple rule on left of title page; silhouette of man with raised walking-stick in lower right.

7 3/8 scant x 5 1/8 in. pp. [i-vi] vii [viii], 1-312.

[i] Half-title; [ii] list of books by the author; [iii] title; [iv] PUBLISHED, 1931/BY DODD, MEAD & COMPANY INC./PRINTED AND BOUND IN THE U.S.A./BY CHAS. H. BOHN & CO., INC., N.Y.C. [v] *To My Friend/FRANK STANDFIELD/in memory of many a pleasant evening/spent with microscope and camera/this volume is* dedicated [vi] blank; vii Contents; [viii] blank; 1-312 text.

Issued in green cloth; lower edge trimmed, fore edge cut, top edge trimmed and stained red; black ornamental title and black silhouette (*cf.* title-page) on front cover; black lettering on spine; back cover plain. End papers cream-colored with green abstract pattern.

6.   *The Eye of Osiris*   1911

a) *First edition.*

THE EYE OF OSIRIS/A DETECTIVE ROMANCE/BY/R. AUSTIN FREEMAN/ AUTHOR OF "THE RED THUMB MARK," ETC./HODDER AND STOUGH-TON/LONDON NEW YORK TORONTO

7 3/32 x 4 25/32 in. pp. [i-v[vi-vii [viii] [1] 2-303 [304]; [A]^4 B-U^8; 156 leaves

[i] Half-title; [ii] advertisement for "The Red Thumb Mark"; [iii] title; [iv] TO MY FRIEND/A.E.B.; [v]-vii Contents; [viii] blank; [1]-303 text; [304] PRINTED BY/WILLIAM BRENDON AND SON LTD./PLYMOUTH

Issued in orange-brown cloth, all edges trimmed unstained; black lettering on front cover, gilt lettering on spine; back cover plain.

[According to John Carter, an earlier issue had brown cloth with "Egyptian-style decoration and lettering." Some copies have 8 pp. of publisher's advertisements sewn in.]

b) *First U.S. edition (The Vanishing Man).*

THE/VANISHING MAN/*A Detective Romance*/BY/R. AUSTIN FREEMAN/ Author of/"The Red Thumb Mark," etc./[publisher's device]/NEW YORK/ DODD, MEAD AND COMPANY/1912

7 5/16 x 4 7/8 in. pp. [i-viii], [1] 2-351 [352]

[i] Half-title; [ii] blank; [iii] title; [iv] COPYRIGHT, 1911, BY/DODD, MEAD AND COMPANY [v] TO MY FRIEND/A.E.B. [Gothic Type] [vi] blank; [vii] Contents; [viii] blank; [1]-351 text; [352] blank.

Issued in dark blue-green cloth, all edges trimmed, unstained. Front cover shows three silhouetted men, one of them shining a torch. Red lettering on front cover and spine; back cover plain.

7. *The Singing Bone* 1912

a) *First edition.*

THE SINGING BONE/BY/R. AUSTIN FREEMAN/AUTHOR OF/'JOHN THORNDYKE'S CASES," "THE RED THUMB MARK, ETC./HODDER AND STOUGHTON/LONDON NEW YORK TORONTO

[Note the misprinted quotation marks at the beginning and near the end of the fifth line.]

7 3/16 scant x 4 13/16 in. pp. [i-v] vi [vii-viii], [1] 2-312; [A]^4 B-U^8 X^4; 160 leaves.

[i] Half-title; [ii] *WORKS BY THE SAME AUTHOR* [Advertisements for "The Eye of Osiris" and "The Red Thumb Mark" set in single-rule frame]; [iii] title; [iv] TO/MY WIFE; [v]-vi Preface; [vii] Contents: [viii] blank; [1]-312 text. At foot of p. 312, below rule: *Richard Clay & Sons, Limited, London and Bungay.*

Issued in crimson cloth, all edges trimmed, unstained; front cover has THE SINGING/BONE at top, and R. AUSTIN FREEMAN at bottom in black lettering; spine has gilt lettering: THE/SINGING/BONE/R. AUSTIN/FREEMAN and, at foot, HODDER & STOUGHTON; back cover plain.

Contents: The Case of Oscar Brodski—A Case of Premeditation—The Echo of a Mutiny—A Wastrel's Romance—The Old Lag.

b) *First U.S. edition*

THE/SINGING BONE/BY/R. AUSTIN FREEMAN/AUTHOR OF "JOHN THORNDYKE'S CASES," "THE RED THUMB/MARK," "THE VANISHING MAN," ETC./[publisher's device]/NEW YORK/DODD, MEAD AND COMPANY/1923

The whole title page is enclosed in a single-rule border.

7 3/8 x 5 in. pp. [i-vi] vii-viii [ix-xii], 1-256 [257-260]; 136 leaves.

[i] Half-title; [ii] blank; [iii] title; [iv] PUBLISHED IN U.S.A. 1923,/BY DODD, MEAD AND COMPANY INC./PRINTED IN U.S.A. BY The Quinn & Company [company name in Gothic Type]/BOOK MANUFACTURERS/RAHWAY NEW JERSEY [v] TO/MY WIFE [vi] blank; vii-viii Preface; [ix] Contents; [x] blank; [xi] half-title; [xii] blank; 1-256 text; [257-260] blank.

Contents: The Case of Oscar Brodski; A Case of Premeditation; The Echo of a Mutiny; A Wastrel's Romance; The Old Lag.

Issued in tan cloth, top edge only trimmed, unstained; lettering on spine and front cover in orange; blind stamping in center of front cover; back cover plain.

(Information from E.T. Guymon, Jr.)

c) *Special edition of one story from The Singing Bone.*

THE CASE OF/OSCAR BRODSKI/*By*/R. AUSTIN FREEMAN/[device]/DE-TECTIVE STORY CLUB, Inc./11 East Forty-Fourth Street/NEW YORK

7 5/16 x 4 3/4 in. pp. [i-iv], 1-63 [64-68]

[i] [Introductory] [ii] blank; [iii] title; [iv] PUBLISHED IN U.S.A., 1923/BY DODD, MEAD AND COMPANY, INC./[*rule*]/REPRINTED BY PERMISSION OF/DODD, MEAD & COMPANY/FROM THE SINGING BONE/BY R. AUSTIN FREEMAN/PRINTED IN U.S.A.; 1-63 text; [64] blank; [65] advertisement; [66-68] blank.

Issued in pale-green boards; black printing on front cover with single-rule border; spine and back cover plain.

8.   *The Mystery of 31 New Inn*   1912

a) *First edition.*

THE MYSTERY OF/31 NEW INN/BY/R. AUSTIN FREEMAN/AUTHOR OF/ "THE RED THUMB MARK," "THE EYE OF OSIRIS," ETC./HODDER AND STOUGHTON/LONDON NEW YORK TORONTO

7 3/8 x 4 7/8 in. pp. [i-vi] vii-viii [ix-x] xi [xii], [1] 2-311 [312-314].

[i] Half-title; [ii] works by the same author: [iii] title; [iv] PRINTED IN 1912; [v] TO/MY FRIEND/BERNARD E. BISHOP; [vi] blank; vii-viii Preface; [ix] sketch of doorway by the author; [x] blank; xi-[xii] Contents; [1]-311 text; [312] RICHARD CLAY & SONS, LIMITED,/BRUNSWICK STREET, S.E.,/ AND BUNGAY, SUFFOLK; [313-314] blank.

Issued in dark-green cloth, top and fore-edge trimmed, bottom untrimmed, all unstained; front cover lettered in white with dark stamping of doorway (as on p. [ix]); spine has gilt lettering; back cover plain.

b) *First U.S. edition.*

THE MYSTERY OF/31, NEW INN/BY/R. AUSTIN FREEMAN/AUTHOR OF "THE RED THUMB MARK," "THE EYE OF OSIRIS," ETC./*Illustrated by*/ EDWIN J. PRITTIE/PHILADELPHIA/THE JOHN C. WINSTON COMPANY/ 1913

7 5/8 x 5 in. pp. [1-8] (ix) x (xi) [12-14] (15) 16-332 [333-336].

[1-2] Blank; [3] half-title; [4] blank; [5] title; [6] COPYRIGHT, 1913, BY THE JOHN C. WINSTON CO./COPYRIGHT, 1911, BY THE RIDGWAY COMPANY [7] TO/MY FRIEND/BERNARD E. BISHOP [8] blank; (ix)-x Preface; (xi) Contents; [12] blank; [13] Illustrations; [14] blank; (15)-332 text; [333-336] blank.

Issued in dark-green smooth cloth; front cover has gold lettering and design in white enamel and blind of doorway bearing numerals "31"; spine has white lettering; back cover plain.

9.   *The Unwilling Adventurer*   1913

First edition.

THE UNWILLING/ADVENTURER/BY R. AUSTIN FREEMAN/AUTHOR OF/ "THE EYE OF OSIRIS," "THE MYSTERY OF 31 NEW INN,"/THE SINGING BONE"/HODDER AND STOUGHTON/LONDON   NEW YORK   TORONTO

7 7/16 x 4 7/8 in. pp. [1-4] 5-389 [390-2]

[1] Half-title; [2] works by the same author; [3] title; [4] TO MY SONS/ JOHN AND LAWRENCE 5-8 Contents; 9-389 text; [390] blank; [391] PRINTED AT / THE NORTHUMBERLAND PRESS/WATERLOO HOUSE, THORNTON STREET/NEWCASTLE-UPON-TYNE [392] blank. Frontispiece: sketch of "THE ISLAND OF MY IMPRISONMENT" tipped in opposite title.

Issued in pale-brown cloth with single-rule border in black; mermaid design below title on front cover is in black, title and author's name in gilt; gilt lettering on spine; back cover plain.

10.   *The Uttermost Farthing: A Savant's Vendetta*   1914

a) *First edition.*

THE UTTERMOST/FARTHING/A SAVANT'S VENDETTA/BY/R. AUSTIN FREEMAN/Author of "The Mystery of 31, New Inn," etc./ILLUSTRATED BY/ H. WESTON TAYLOR/[short rule]/PHILADELPHIA/THE JOHN C. WINSTON COMPANY/PUBLISHERS

7 9/16 x 5 1/8 in. pp. [(1)-(4)] (5) [(6)] (7) [(8)] (9) 10-296; [1]^8 2-18^8 19^4; 148 leaves.

[(1)] Half-title; [(2)] blank; frontispiece tipped in here; [(3)] title; [(4)] Copyright, 1914, by THE JOHN C. WINSTON CO. (5) Contents; [(6)] blank; (7) list of illustrations; [(8)] blank; (9)-296 text.

Plates tipped in to face pp. 50, 124 and 292.

Issued in orange-red cloth, all edges trimmed, unstained; front cover has gilt lettering on upper part, lower part has checkered pattern representing 25 men's faces (the savant's victims) in black, with the central head framed in gilt; single black rule encloses front cover; spine has gilt lettering and black and gilt device; back cover plain.

b) *First British edition (A Savant's Vendetta).*

A SAVANT'S/VENDETTA/BY/R. AUSTIN FREEMAN/AUTHOR OF "JOHN THORNDYKE'S/CASES," "THE RED THUMB/MARK," ETC./ [circular publisher's device]/LONDON/ C. ARTHUR PEARSON LTD.

6 3/4 x 4¼ in. pp. [1-10] 11-252 [253-258]

[1-4] Blank; [5] half-title; [6] blank; [7] title; [8] FIRST CHEAP EDITION 1920 [9] Contents; [10] blank; 11-252 text; [253-255] advt. for "Pelmanism"; [256-258] blank.

Issued in light-red cloth, all edges trimmed, unstained; front cover has decorative blind-stamping with title and author's name also blind-stamped; spine has black lettering: A/SAVANT'S/VENDETTA/R. AUSTIN/FREEMAN/PEARSON; back cover shows an advertisement for "Fry's Breakfast Cocoa."

(Based on information supplied by E.T. Guymon, Jr., whose copy lacks pp. [1-2], actually front end-paper, which, like that at the back, was evidently tipped in.)

11.   *A Silent Witness*   1914

a) *First edition.*

A SILENT WITNESS/BY/R. AUSTIN FREEMAN/AUTHOR OF "THE RED THUMB MARK"/"THE UNWILLING ADVENTURER"/"THE EYE OF OSIRIS"/ETC./HODDER AND STOUGHTON/LONDON NEW YORK TORONTO/MCMXIV

7 5/16 scant x 4 3/4 in. pp. [i-v] vi-vii [viii], [9] 10-328; [A]^8 B-U^8 W^4; 164 leaves.

[i] Half-title; [ii] list of works by the author; [iii] title; [iv] DEDICATION/ TO DOROTHY, CUTHBERT, CARTERET AND GERALD BISHOP IN MEMORY OF LABOURS THAT ARE PAST AND IN TOKEN OF FRIENDSHIP THAT ENDURES; [v]-vii Contents; [viii] blank; [9]-328 text.

Issued in deep red cloth, all edges trimmed, unstained; front cover and spine have black lettering; front cover has drawing (in black) of a pendant on chain, bearing the letters AMDG along one side. (A variant binding has gilt lettering.)

b) *First U.S. edition*

A SILENT/WITNESS/By/R. AUSTIN FREEMAN/Author of "The Mystery of 31, New Inn,"/"The Uttermost Farthing," etc./Illustrated by/H. WESTON TAYLOR/PHILADELPHIA/THE JOHN C. WINSTON COMPANY/PUBLISHERS

The whole title page is enclosed in a double-rule border.

7 11/16 x 5¼ in. pp. [1-6] (7) [8] (9) [10] (11)-382 [383-384]; [1]⁸ 2-24⁸; 194 leaves.

[1] Half-title; [2] blank; [3] title; [4] Copyright, 1915, by/THE JOHN C. WINSTON COMPANY [5] To DOROTHY, CUTHBERT, CARTERET AND GERALD BISHOP/IN MEMORY OF LABORS THAT ARE PAST AND IN/ TOKEN OF FRIENDSHIP THAT ENDURES. [6] blank; (7) Contents; [8] blank; (9) list of illustrations; [10] blank; (11)-382 text; [383-384] blank. Frontispiece faces title; three other illustrations.

Issued in deep-blue cloth, all edges trimmed, unstained; figure of man holding lighted match on front cover in black with yellow highlights, yellow lettering below, black border; spine has gilt lettering and locket bearing initials AMDG; back cover plain.

12.   *The Exploits of Danby Croker*   1916

First edition.

THE EXPLOITS/OF DANBY CROKER/BEING EXTRACTS FROM A SOME-WHAT/DISREPUTABLE AUTOBIOGRAPHY/BY/R. AUSTIN FREEMAN/"For though myselfe be a ful vicious man/A moral tale yet I yow telle can/Which I am wont to preche for to winne./Now holde your pees, my tale I wol be-ginne."/*Prologe of the Pardoner.*/[intricate rectangular publisher's device bearing the word 'DESORMAIS']/LONDON/DUCKWORTH & CO./3 HENRIETTA STREET, COVENT GARDEN

7 7/16 x 4 9/16 in. pp. [i-iv] v-vi [vii-viii], [1] 2-307 [308-328].

[i] Half-title; [ii] blank; [iii] title; [iv] TO/MY FRIEND/PROFESSOR JOHN ADAMS/*First published 1916* v-vi Preface; [vii] Contents; [viii] blank; [1]-307 text; [308] PRINTED BY WILLIAM BRENDON AND SON, LTD./PLY-MOUTH, ENGLAND [309-312] advertisements; [313-328, i.e., [1]-16] adver-tisements; [329-330] blank.

Issued in light-red cloth, top and fore-edge trimmed, bottom untrimmed, all unstained; front cover blind-stamped with title and author's and publisher's names; back cover plain.

(Information from E.T. Guymon, Jr.)

13.   *The Great Portrait Mystery*   1918

First edition

THE/GREAT PORTRAIT MYSTERY/BY/R. AUSTIN FREEMAN/AUTHOR OF "JOHN THORNDYKE'S CASES," ETC./HODDER AND STOUGHTON/ LONDON NEW YORK TORONTO

7 5/16 x 4 3/4 in. pp. [1-6] 7-111 [112] 113-137 [138-139] 140-183 [184-185] 186-245 [246-247] 248-285 [286] 287-318 [319-320]; [A]8 B-U8; 160 leaves.

[1] Half-title; [2] list of five books by the author; [3] title; [4] blank; [5] contents; [6] blank; 7-318 text.

Contents: The Great Portrait Mystery; The Bronze Parrot; The Missing Mortgagee; Powder Blue and Hawthorn; Percival Bland's Proxy; The Attorney's Conscience; The Luck of Barnabas Mudge

After end of text on p. 318: [rule]/Printed in Great Britain by Wyman and Sons Ltd., London and Reading.

Issued in pale blue linen-grained cloth; paper of inferior quality, all edges trimmed, unstained; black lettering on front cover and spine; simple oval device on front cover; back cover plain.

14.   *Social Decay and Regeneration*   1921

First edition

SOCIAL DECAY AND/REGENERATION/BY/R. AUSTIN FREEMAN/WITH AN INTRODUCTION BY/HAVELOCK ELLIS/"Ill fares the land, to hast'ning ills a prey,/Where wealth accumulates and men decay."/LONDON/CONSTABLE AND COMPANY LTD./1921

8 11/16 x 5½ in. pp. [i-iv] v-xx [xxi-xxii], 1-345 [346]

[i] Half-title; [ii] TO/MRS. BERNARD BISHOP/THIS BOOK IS DEDICATED IN GRATEFUL ACKNOWLEDGMENT/OF THE KINDLY AND HELPFUL INTEREST THAT/SHE HAS TAKEN IN ITS MAKING; [iii] title; [iv] *Printed in Great Britain*; v-x Introduction; xi-xii Preface; xiii-xx Synopsis of Contents; [xxi] PART ONE/ANALYTICAL; [xxii] blank; 1-345 text; [346] blank; p. 345 has, below the text: PRINTED IN GREAT BRITAIN BY/BILLING AND SONS, LTD., GUILDFORD AND ESHER

Issued in maroon cloth, all edges trimmed, unstained; front cover has triple blind-stamped lines top and bottom, no lettering; spine has triple gilt lines top and bottom and gilt lettering; back cover has blind stamping as front, otherwise plain.

(The "U.S. edition" (printed in Britain) is identical, except for substitution of "BOSTON AND NEW YORK HOUGHTON MIFFLIN CO. 1921" for the British imprint on the title page; p. iv is blank. Issued in purple-brown cloth, all edges trimmed, unstained; gilt lettering at top of front cover and on spine; back cover plain.)

15.   *Helen Vardon's Confession*   1922

First edition.

HELEN VARDON'S/CONFESSION/[rule]/BY/R. AUSTIN FREEMAN/AUTHOR OF/"THE EYE OF OSIRIS," "THE RED THUMB MARK," ETC./ [rule]/[space]/[rule]/HODDER AND STOUGHTON LTD./TORONTO LONDON NEW YORK

The whole title-page is enclosed in a single-rule border

7 7/16 x 4 7/8 in. pp. [1-8] 9-335 [336] ;[1]^8 2-21^8; 168 leaves

[1] Half-title; [2] blank; [3] title; [4] blank; [5-6] Contents; [7-8] Prologue; 9-335 text; [336] Epilogue, with [below rule]: Printed in Great Britain by Ebenezer Baylis & Son, Trinity Works, Worcester.

Issued in bright blue cloth, upper and fore edges trimmed, lower edge cut, untrimmed; black lettering (large fount) on front cover with single-rule frame blindstamped on it; black lettering on spine; back cover plain.

16.   *Dr. Thorndyke's Case-Book*   1923

a) *First edition.*

DR. THORNDYKE'S/CASE-BOOK/[double rule]/BY/R. AUSTIN FREEMAN/ AUTHOR OF/"HELEN VARDON'S CONFESSION," ETC./[double rule]/ [space]/[double rule]/HODDER AND STOUGHTON LTD./TORONTO LONDON NEW YORK

The whole title page is enclosed by a double-rule border

7 5/16 x 4 13/16 in. pp. [1-4] v [6-8] 9-62 [63-64] 65-80 [81] 82-100 [101] 102-106 [107-108] 109-150 [151-152] 153-188 [189-190] 191-229 [230-232] 233-273 [274-276] 277-317 [318-320] ; [A]^8 B-U^8; 160 leaves.

[1] Half-title; [2] list of novels by the author, within single-rule frame; [3] title; [4] [below 2 15/16 inch rule:] Made and Printed in Great Britain by Wyman & Sons Ltd., London, Reading & Fakenham. [5] Contents; [6] blank; [7]-317 text; [318-320] blank

Issued in pale blue cloth; lettering on front cover in pale blue on black rectangular ground with multiple border; black lettering on spine; back cover plain.

Contents: The case of the white foot-prints—The blue scarab—The New Jersey sphinx—The touchstone—A fisher of men—The stolen ingots—The funeral pyre.

b) *First U.S. edition (The Blue Scarab).*

THE BLUE/SCARAB/BY/R. AUSTIN FREEMAN/AUTHOR OF/"THE SING-ING BONE," ETC./[long double rule]/[publisher's device]/NEW YORK/DODD, MEAD AND COMPANY/1924

The whole title page is enclosed by a double-rule border.

7 5/16 in. pp. [i-viii], 1-276.

[i] Half-title; [ii] blank; [iii] title; [iv] COPYRIGHT, 1923,/BY DODD, MEAD AND COMPANY, INC./PRINTED IN THE U.S.A. BY/The Quinn & Boden Company [company name in Gothic Type]/[rule]/BOOK MANUFACTURERS/RAHWAY NEW JERSEY; [v] Contents; [vi] blank; [vii] half-title; [viii] blank; 1-276 text.

Contents: The Blue Scarab; The Case of the White Foot-Prints; The New Jersey Sphinx; The Touchstone; A Fisher of Men; The Stolen Ingots; The Funeral Pyre.

Issued in blue-grey rough cloth, top and bottom edges trimmed, unstained; fore-edge cut. Front cover has blue ornamental lettering, quintuple rules across top and bottom, picture of scarab in blue in lower right corner; blue lettering on spine; back cover plain.

17.   *The Cat's Eye*   1923

a) *First edition.*

THE CAT'S EYE/[rule]/BY/R. AUSTIN FREEMAN/[rule]/[space]/[rule]/HODDER AND STOUGHTON/LIMITED LONDON

The whole title page is enclosed by a single-rule border.

7¼ scant x 4 7/8 in. pp. [i-vi] vii [viii-xii], [1] 2-304; [a]⁴ b² A-T⁸; 158 leaves.

[i] Blank; [ii] list of nine novels by the author, set in single rule border; [iii] half-title; [iv] drawings of "the locket" and "Mr. Halliburton's mascot"; [v] title; [vi] Made and printed in Great Britain. T. and A. Constable Ltd., Printers, Edinburgh [vii] preface, dated Gravesend, 19th June 1923; [viii] blank; [ix-xi] Contents; [xii] blank; [1]-304 text.

Issued in pale green cloth, all edges trimmed, unstained. Lettering on front cover green on black rectangular ground; lettering on spine in black.

b) *First U.S. edition*

THE CAT'S EYE/BY/R. AUSTIN FREEMAN/[triangular (point downwards) publisher's device in green]/DODD, MEAD AND COMPANY/NEW YORK— 1927

The whole title page is enclosed by a double-rule green border.

7 3/8 x 5 1/16 in. pp. [i-vi] vii [viii], 1-334 [335-336].

[i] Half-title; [ii] list of books by the author (enclosed in frame); [iii] title; [iv] PUBLISHED IN U.S.A., 1927,/BY DODD, MEAD AND COMPANY, Inc./ PRINTED IN THE U.S.A. BY/The Quinn & Boden Company [company name in Gothic Type]/[rule]/BOOK MANUFACTURERS/RAHWAY NEW JERSEY; [v] Preface; [vi] blank; vii Contents; [viii] drawings (as in English edition); 1-334 text; [335-336] blank.

Issued in dark blue cloth; front cover has orange ornamental lettering, and two overlapping elliptical shapes (cat's eyes) in green and orange, single-rule border stamped in blind; spine has orange lettering and single circular device in green and orange; back cover plain.

18.   *The Mystery of Angelina Frood*   1924

a) *First edition.*

THE MYSTERY OF/ANGELINA FROOD/BY R. AUSTIN FREEMAN/[ornamental rule]/[space]/[ornamental rule]/HODDER AND STOUGHTON/LIMITED [publisher's device] LONDON

The whole title-page is enclosed within frame of single ornamental rules consisting of small leaves.

7¼ scant x 4¾ in. pp. [1-4] v-vi [7-8] 9-320; [A]^{16} B-K^{16}; 160 leaves.

[1] Half-title; [2] list of novels and stories by the author; [3] title; [4] [rule]/ *Made and Printed in Great Britain by Wyman & Sons Ltd., London, Reading and Fakenham*; v-vi Contents; [7] half-title: *PART I;* [8] blank; 9-320 text; [179] half-title; *PART TWO.*

Issued in bright orange cloth, all edges trimmed, unstained; front cover has black lettering, with double rules near top and lower edges, black lettering on spine, with publisher's monogram near foot; back cover plain.

b) *First U.S. edition.*

THE MYSTERY OF/ANGELINA FROOD/BY/R. AUSTIN FREEMAN/Author of "THE SINGING BONE," THE BLUE SCARAB,"/THE RED THUMB MARK," etc./[device]/NEW YORK/DODD, MEAD AND COMPANY/1925

7½ x 5 1/16 in. pp. [i-vi], [1-2] 3-312 [313-314]

[i] Half-title; [ii] blank; [iii] title; [iv] COPYRIGHT, 1925,/BY DR. R. AUS-
TIN FREEMAN/PRINTED IN U.S.A./THE VAIL-BALLOU PRESS/BINGHAM-
TON AND NEW YORK; [v] Contents; [vi] blank; [1] PART I; [2] blank; 3-
312 text; [313-314] blank.

Issued in purple rough-grained cloth with yellow lettering on front cover and
spine; oval device in blind in center of front cover; top edge trimmed, unstained;
fore and lower edges cut.

19.   *The Puzzle Lock*   1925

a) *First edition.*

The Puzzle Lock/[rule]/*By R. AUSTIN FREEMAN*/[rule]/*Hodder and Stoughton*/*Limited London*

The whole title page is enclosed within a single-rule border.

7¼ scant x 4 7/8 in. pp. [1-6] 7 [8] 9-320; [1]^8 2-20^8; 160 leaves.

[1] Half-title (between rules); [2] list of novels and stories by the author (in
frame); frontispiece photograph of "Mr. Luttrell's Seal" tipped in; [3] title; [4]
(at foot): Made and Printed in Great Britain. Butler and Tanner Ltd., Frome and
London; [5] TO/VINCENT STARRETT; [6] blank; 7 Contents; [8] blank;
9-320 text. p. 320 (below text): Printed in Great Britain by Butler and Tanner
Ltd., Frome and London

Issued in pale blue rough-grained cloth; all edges trimmed, unstained; lettering
on front cover and spine in black; single-rule border stamped in blind on front
cover; back cover plain.

Contents: The puzzle lock—The green check jacket—The seal of Nebuchadnezzar—Phyllis Annesley's peril—A sower of pestilence—Rex v. Burnaby—A mystery
of the sand-hills—The apparition of Burling Court—The mysterious visitor.

b) *First U.S. edition.*

THE / PUZZLE LOCK /BY/ R. AUSTIN FREEMAN / [device] / NEW YORK/
DODD, MEAD AND COMPANY/1926

The whole title page is enclosed in a single-rule border.

7 5/16 x 5 1/16 in. pp. [i-viii] 1-327 [328]

[i] Half-title; [ii] list of books by author, within single-rule frame; [iii] title; [iv] COPYRIGHT 1924, 1925, BY R. AUSTIN FREEMAN/PRINTED IN U.S.A./THE VAIL-BALLOU PRESS/BINGHAMTON AND NEW YORK; [v] TO/VINCENT STARRETT; [vi] Contents; [viii] blank; 1-327 text; [328] blank.

Issued in black cloth, with rough grain, except for rectangular smooth panel on upper left of front cover within which blue lettering is set; spine has blue lettering; back cover plain; top and lower edges trimmed, unstained, fore-edge cut.

20.   *The Shadow of the Wolf*   1925

a) *First edition.*

The Shadow of the/Wolf/[rule]*/By/R. Austin Freeman/*[rule]*/*[space]*/*[rule]*/ Hodder and Stoughton/Limited London.*

The whole title page is enclosed in a single-rule border.

7¼ x 4¾ in. pp. [1-4] 5-320; [1]⁸; 160 leaves.

[1] Half-title; [2] list of novels and stories by the author; [3] title; [4] MADE AND PRINTED IN GREAT BRITAIN BY/BILLING AND SONS, LTD., GUILDFORD AND ESHER; 5-6 Contents; 7-320 text.

Issued in smooth scarlet cloth, all edges trimmed, unstained; single rule border stamped in blind on front cover; black lettering on front cover and spine; back cover plain.

b) *First U.S. edition.*

THE SHADOW/OF THE WOLF/BY/R. AUSTIN FREEMAN/*Author of/*"The Red Thumb Mark," etc./[device]/NEW YORK/DODD, MEAD AND COMPANY/1925

The whole title page is enclosed by a double-rule border.

7 13/32 x 5 in. pp. [i-vi], 1-297 [298]

[i] Half-title; [ii] list of books within single-rule frame; [iii] title; [iv] COPYRIGHT, 1925, BY DODD, MEAD AND COMPANY, INC./PRINTED IN THE U.S.A. BY/The Quinn & Boden Company [company name in Gothic Type]/ [rule]/BOOK MANUFACTURERS/RAHWAY NEW JERSEY; [v] Contents; [vi] blank; 1-297 text; [298] blank.

Issued in black cloth; top and lower edges trimmed, top edge stained red; fore-edge cut; front cover has red lettering in upper left, device (as on title page) stamped blind in lower right; spine has red lettering, back cover plain.

21.   *The D'Arblay Mystery*   1926

a) *First edition.*

The / *D'Arblay Mystery* /[rule]/BY/ R. AUSTIN FREEMAN / [rule]/[space]/ [rule]/HODDER AND STOUGHTON/LIMITED LONDON

The whole title page is enclosed in a double rule border.

7 5/16 scant x 4 15/16 scant in. pp. [1-4] 4-312 [313-320]; [D'A.M.-1]^8 D'A.M.-2–D'A.M.20^8; 160 leaves.

[1] Half-title; [2] list of novels and stories by the author; [3] title; [4] [short rule with paragraph symbol set sideways at each end] Made and Printed in Great Britain by Hazell, Watson & Viney Ld. London and Aylesbury; 5-6 Contents, 7-312 text; [313-320] publisher's advertisements.

Issued in blue cloth, all edges trimmed, unstained; front cover blind stamped with frame of rules; black lettering on front and spine; author's monogram in lower right corner of front cover; publisher's monogram near foot of spine.

b) *First U.S. edition.*

THE D'ARBLAY/MYSTERY/BY/R. AUSTIN FREEMAN/[triangular device (point downwards) in orange]/DODD, MEAD AND COMPANY/NEW YORK 1926

Whole title page is enclosed by double-rule border.

7 11/32 x 5 1/16 in. pp. [i-vi], 1-291 [292-294]

[i] Half-title; [ii] list of books by the author; [iii] title; [iv] COPYRIGHT, 1926/BY R. AUSTIN FREEMAN/PRINTED IN THE U.S.A. BY/The Quinn & Boden Company [company name in Gothic Type]/[rule]/BOOK MANU-FACTURERS/RAHWAY NEW JERSEY; [v] Contents; [vi] blank; 1-291 text; [171] has half-title; *BOOK II THE INVESTIGATOR*; [292-294] blank.

Issued in dark blue cloth; lettering and design (of a man with knife attacking a woman at foot of stairs) in blind; lettering on spine in orange; back cover plain.

22.   *The Magic Casket*   1927

a) *First edition.*

The Magic Casket/BY/R. AUSTIN FREEMAN/[rule]/[space]/[rule]/HODDER AND STOUGHTON/LIMITED LONDON

The whole title page is enclosed by a double-rule border.

7 5/32 x 4 7/8 in. pp. [1-4] 5 [6] 7-309 [310-320];[1]^8 2-20^8; 160 leaves.

[1] Half-title; [2] list of novels and stories by the author; [3] title; [4] *Made and Printed in Great Britain. Hazell Watson &* Viney, Ld., London and Aylesbury; 5 Contents; [6] blank; 7-309 text; [310] blank; [311-318] publisher's advertisements; [319-320] blank

Issued in bright blue cloth, all edges trimmed, unstained; black lettering on front cover and spine; single-rule border blind-stamped on front cover; author's monogram in lower right corner of front cover, publisher's monogram near foot of spine; back cover plain.

Contents: The magic casket—The contents of a mare's nest—The stalking horse—The naturalist at law—Mr. Ponting's alibi—Pandora's box—The trail of Behemoth—The pathologist to the rescue—Gleanings from the wreckage.

b) *First U.S. edition.*

The Magic Casket/[rule]/BY R. AUSTIN FREEMAN/[rule]/[space]/[rule]/ DODD, MEAD & COMPANY/ NEW YORK 1927

Title in green; other lettering in black. The whole title page is enclosed by a double-rule border.

7 9/32 x 5 3/32 in. pp. [1-4] 5 [6] 7-288

[1] Half-title; [2] list of books by the author; [3] title; [4] COPYRIGHT, 1926, 1927,/BY DODD, MEAD AND COMPANY, INC./PRINTED IN U.S.A./ MANUFACTURED IN THE UNITED STATES OF AMERICA/BY THE VAIL-BALLOU PRESS, INC., BINGHAMTON, N.Y.; 5 Contents; [6] blank; 7-288 text.

Issued in black cloth; top and lower edges trimmed; top edge stained red; fore edge cut; red lettering on front cover and spine; single-rule border on front cover stamped in blind; back cover plain.

23.   *The Surprising Experiences of Mr. Shuttlebury Cobb*   1927

First edition.

The/Surprising Experiences/of/Mr. Shuttlebury Cobb/[rule]/BY/R. AUSTIN FREEMAN /[rule]/[space]/[rule]/ HODDER AND STOUGHTON / LIMITED LONDON

The whole title-page is enclosed by a double-rule border.

7¼ x 4 7/8 in. pp. [1-9] 10-281 [282], 1-4 [5-6] ;[A]⁸ B-S⁸; 144 leaves.

[1] Half-title; [2] frontispiece (by the author) with caption: THE SIGN OF THE MERMAID; [3] title; [4] list of novels and stories by the author, and (at foot, below rule): *Printed in Great Britain by Wyman and Sons, Ltd., London, Fakenham and Reading.* [5] Contents; [6] blank; [7] half-title: THE GIFTED STRANGER; [8] blank; [9]-281 text; [282] blank; half titles for chapters other than the first are on pp. [53], [97], [141], [185] and 229, the versos being blank. Supplementary pp. 1-[6] contain publisher's advertisements.

Issued in reddish brown cloth, all edges trimmed, unstained; front cover has lettering (in black) and rectangular mermaid device (in black and yellow) in upper right; author's signature printed in black over yellow oval at top of spine, with black lettering below; back cover plain.

24. *A Certain Dr. Thorndyke* 1927

a) *First edition.*

A Certain/Dr. Thorndyke/[rule]/BY/R. AUSTIN FREEMAN/AUTHOR OF/ "THE D'ARBLAY MYSTERY," ETC./[rule]/[space]/[rule]/HODDER AND STOUGHTON/PUBLISHERS LONDON

The whole title page is enclosed in a double-rule border.

7¼ x 4 7/8 in. pp. [1-4] 5 [6] 7 [8] 9-175 [176] 177 [178] 179-310 [311-320] ;[1]⁸ 2-20⁸; 160 leaves.

[1] Half-title; [2] list of novels and stories by the author; [3] title; [4] Made and Printed in Great Britain for Hodder and Stoughton Limited by Hazell, Watson & Viney, Ld., London and Aylesbury; 5 Contents; [6] blank; 7 BOOK I THE ISHMAELITE; [8] blank; 9-175 text; [176] blank; 177 BOOK II THE INVESTIGATOR; [178] blank; 179-310 text; [311-318] publisher's advertisements.

Issued in pale blue cloth, all edges trimmed, unstained.

Front cover unlettered, blind stamped with frame of rules. Spine lettered in gilt with publisher's monogram at foot. Back cover plain.

b) *First U.S. edition.*

A CERTAIN/DR. THORNDYKE/BY R. AUSTIN FREEMAN/[publisher's device]/[rule]/DODD, MEAD AND COMPANY/NEW YORK—1928

The whole title page is enclosed by double-rule border.

7 3/8 x 5 in. pp. [i-vi], [1-2] 3-304 [305-306]

[i] Half-title; [ii] list of books by the author; [iii] title; [iv] COPYRIGHT, 1928,/BY DODD, MEAD AND COMPANY, INC./PRINTED IN THE U.S.A. BY/ The Quinn & Boden Company [company name in Gothic Type]/[rule]/BOOK MANUFACTURERS/RAHWAY NEW JERSEY; [v] Contents; [vi] blank; [1] *BOOK I THE ISHMAELITE* [2] blank; 3-304 text; [305-306] blank.

Issued in dark green cloth, upper and lower edges trimmed, fore edges cut, upper edges stained red. Front cover has double wide rule in blind top and foot, narrow blind rule near binding edge; lettering on front and spine in orange, with device incorporating a narrow-necked cylindrical bottle; back cover plain.

25.   *Flighty Phyllis*   1928

First edition.

Flighty Phyllis/[rule]/By/R. AUSTIN FREEMAN/[rule]/[space]/[rule]/Hodder and Stoughton/Publishers London

The whole title page is enclosed by a single-rule border.

7 7/32 x 4 25/32 in. pp. [1-4] 5 [6-8] 9-39 [40-42] 43-72 [73-74] 75-101 [102-104] 105-135 [136-138] 139-170 [171-172] 173-210 [211-212] 212-315 [316-320] last leaf pasted down to make end-paper. [A]^8 B-V^8; 160 leaves.

[1] Half-title; [2] list of novels and stories by the author; [3] title; [4] Made and Printed in Great Britain for Hodder and Stoughton, Limited,/by C. Tinling & Co., Ltd. Liverpool, London and Prescot; 5 Contents; [6] blank; [7] half-title; [8]-315 text; [316-318] blank; [319-320] is pasted down.

Issued in blue cloth; all edges trimmed and unstained; front cover has black lettering in upper right corner with picture stamped in black immediately below representing a woman boarding a taxi-cab; black lettering on spine; back cover plain.

26.   *As a Thief in the Night*   1928

a) *First edition.*

AS A THIEF/IN THE NIGHT/[rule]/BY/R. AUSTIN FREEMAN/[rule]/ [space]/[rule]/HODDER AND STOUGHTON/LIMITED LONDON

The whole page is enclosed in a double rule border.

7¼ x 4 7/8 in. pp. [1-7] 8-320; [A$_N$]^8 B$_N$-U$_N$^{8}, 160 leaves.

[1] Half-title; [2] List of novels and stories by the author; [3] title; [4] Made and printed in Great Britain by The Camelot Press Limited, London and Southampton; [5] Contents; [6]-320 text.

Issued in pale blue cloth, all edges trimmed, unstained. Lettering on front cover and spine in black. Publisher's monogram at foot of spine; author's monogram in lower right corner of front cover.

b) *First U.S. edition.*

AS A THIEF/IN THE NIGHT/R. AUSTIN FREEMAN/[ornament]/*New York*/ DODD, MEAD & COMPANY/1928

The whole title page is enclosed in a double rule border.

7 3/8 x 5 in. pp. [i-viii], 1-312 [313-316].

[i] Half-title; [ii] books by the author; [iii] title; [iv] COPYRIGHT, 1928,/By DODD, MEAD & COMPANY, INC./PRINTED IN THE U.S.A. BY/The Quinn & Boden Company [company name in Gothic Type]/[rule]/BOOK MANU-FACTURERS/RAHWAY NEW JERSEY; [v] Contents; [vi] blank; [vii] half-title (repeated); [viii] blank; 1-312 text (p. 306 consists of charts).

Issued in orange-red cloth; front cover has lettering in black with ornamental brackets to left and right of title, and publisher's device stamped in blind in lower right corner; single-rule border in blind on front cover; black lettering on spine; back cover plain. White end-papers covered by repeated publisher's device in green; upper and lower edges trimmed, fore edges cut; upper edge stained red.

27.   *The Dr. Thorndyke Omnibus (London)*   1929

First edition.

THE FAMOUS CASES OF/DR. THORNDYKE/*Thirty-seven of his criminal*/ *investigations as set down by*/R. AUSTIN FREEMAN/[publisher's circular monogram, white on black]/HODDER & STOUGHTON, LONDON

7 3/8 x 4 7/8 in. pp. [i-iv] v-viii, [1-2] 3-1080; [1]^{16} 2-34^{16}; 544 leaves.

[i] Half title; [ii] blank; [iii] title; [iv] *Made and Printed in Great Britain for*/ *Hodder and Stoughton Limited by*/*Hazell, Watson & Viney, Ltd., London and* *Aylesbury;* v-vi PREFACE, dated GRAVESEND, 3rd April, 1929; vii-viii; [1] THE FAMOUS CASES OF/DR. THORNDYKE/[rule]/[on left:] GROUP/ONE [on right:] INVERTED/STORIES; [2] blank; 3-1080 text; p. [232] is blank; p. [233] has THE FAMOUS CASES OF/DR. THORNDYKE/[rule]/[on left:] GROUP/TWO [on right:] DIRECT/STORIES; p. [234] is blank.

Issued in bright blue cloth, all edges trimmed, unstained; top and bottom edges of front cover and spine have dark blue, crimson and dark blue rules. Title near top of front cover and spine: [in crimson] DR. THORNDYKE/[in dark blue] HIS FAMOUS CASES/[in crimson] AS DESCRIBED BY/[in dark blue] R. AUSTIN FREEMAN. Publisher's rectangular monogram in dark-blue near foot of spine with publisher's name in crimson below it. Back cover plain. (For contents see p. 170 of *In Search of Dr. Thorndyke*.)

28.   *Mr. Pottermack's Oversight*   1930

a) *First edition.*

MR. POTTERMACK'S/OVERSIGHT/BY/R. AUSTIN FREEMAN/HODDER AND STOUGHTON / LIMITED LONDON / ST. PAUL'S HOUSE / WARWICK SQUARE/E.C./4

7 3/16 x 4¾ in. pp. [1-6] vii [8] 9-319 [320];[A]⁸ B-U⁸; 160 leaves.

[1] Half-title; [2] list of novels and stories by the author; [3] title; [4] Made and Printed in Great Britain for HODDER AND STOUGHTON LTD./by T. and A. CONSTABLE LTD. Printers, Edinburgh; [5] TO MY FRIEND/THE HONOURABLE LADY LYNDEN-BELL; [6] blank; vii Contents; [8] blank; 9-319 text; [320] blank.

Issued in bright orange cloth, all edges trimmed, unstained; front cover has black double rule along top and bottom edges; black lettering on front cover and spine; back cover plain.

b) *First U.S. edition.*

MR. POTTERMACK'S/OVERSIGHT/[rule]/A DETECTIVE STORY BY/R. AUSTIN FREEMAN/[rule]/[stooping figure with electric torch]/[rule]/NEW YORK MCMXXX/DODD, MEAD & COMPANY [Thick rules run across title-page above and below the lettering.]

7 5/16 x 5 in. pp. [i-x], 1-338 [339-342]

[i] Half-title; [ii] list of books; [iii] title; [iv] COPYRIGHT, 1930,/BY DODD, MEAD AND COMPANY, INC./All rights reserved—. . ./. . ./. . ./PRINTED IN THE U.S.A. BY/The Quinn & Boden Company [company name in Gothic Type]/[rule]/BOOK MANUFACTURERS/RAHWAY, NEW JERSEY; [v] TO/THE HONOURABLE LADY LYNDENBELL; [vi] blank; [vii] Contents; [viii] blank; [ix] half-title; [x] blank; 1-10 Prologue; 11-338 text; [339] woodcut after a photograph of the author; [340-342] A Dr. Thorndyke examination and notices of Thorndyke stories.

Issued in deep-red cloth; top and lower edges trimmed; fore-edge cut; top edge stained blue; black lettering on spine; back cover plain. End-papers have green rectangular pattern.

29.   *Pontifex, Son and Thorndyke*   1931

a) *First edition.*

PONTIFEX, SON/AND/THORNDYKE/BY/R. AUSTIN FREEMAN/HODDER AND STOUGHTON/LIMITED [publisher's monogram, white on black] LONDON/1931

Title and author's name in ornamental capitals.

7 5/16 x 4 7/8 in. pp. [1-7] 8-320; [A] ^{8} B-U^8; 160 leaves.

[1] Half-title; [2] list of novels and stories by the author; [3] title; [4] To my friend,/BERTHA FOWLE/In commemoration of many industries/and pleasant labours/First Printed October 1931; [5] Contents; [6] blank; [7]-320 text; p. 320 has, below text: [rule] *Printed in Great Britain for Hodder & Stoughton, Limited,/by Wyman & Sons, Ltd., London, Fakenham and Reading.*

Issued in pale blue cloth, all edges trimmed, unstained; black lettering on front cover and spine; author's monogram, in black, in lower right corner of front cover; publisher's monogram at foot of spine; back cover plain.

b) *First U.S. edition.*

[double rule]/PONTIFEX, SON/& THORNDYKE/[double rule]/BY R. AUSTIN FREEMAN/[circular device]/*New York*/[double rule]/DODD, MEAD & COMPANY/[double rule]/1931

The whole title page is enclosed by a single-rule border with a circular device within each corner

7 11/32 x 5 in. pp. [i-viii] 1-303 [304]

[i] Half-title, blurb, and list of author's books; [ii] publisher's announcement; [iii] title; [iv] COPYRIGHT, 1931,/BY DODD, MEAD AND COMPANY, INC./ All rights reserved—. . ./. . ./. . ./PRINTED IN THE U.S.A. BY/The Quinn & Boden Company [company name in Gothic Type]/[rule]/BOOK MANUFAC-TURERS/RAHWAY NEW JERSEY; [v] blank; [vii] half-title; [viii] blank; 1-303 text; p. 303 has emblem below text; 304 blank.

Issued in bright orange cloth with ornamental lettering on front cover and spine, ornamental rule on front cover; top and lower edges trimmed, top edge stained orange; fore-edge cut. Buff end papers with "lightning" design and "Red Badge Books" emblem.

30.   *The Dr. Thorndyke Omnibus* (New York)   1932

First edition.

THE / DR. THORNDYKE / OMNIBUS / 38 / OF HIS CRIMINAL / INVESTI-
GATIONS / AS SET DOWN / BY / R. AUSTIN / FREEMAN / DODD, MEAD &
COMPANY / NEW YORK 1932

["DR. THORNDYKE" is curved, with ends up; "OMNIBUS" is curved, with
ends down.]

8 x 5 3/16 in. [1 leaf] [i-iv] v-xv [xvi] xvii-xviii [1 leaf] 1-256 [1 leaf] 1-
312 [1 leaf] 7-288 [1 leaf] 1-327 [328] [1 leaf] 1-276 [277-280]

v-xv "R. Austin Freeman," an unsigned study of the author and his works.

Contents: The Singing Bone; Dr. Thorndyke's Cases; The Magic Casket; The
Puzzle Lock; The Blue Scarab.

Issued in bright orange cloth, all edges trimmed, unstained; front cover has black
lettering with title curved as on title page, enclosed by single rule stamped in
blind; spine has black lettering; back cover plain.

31.   *When Rogues Fall Out*   1932

a) *First edition.*

WHEN/ROGUES FALL OUT/BY/R. AUSTIN FREEMAN/[publisher's mono-
gram]/LONDON/HODDER AND STOUGHTON LIMITED/1932

Title and author's name in ornamental capitals

7 3/8 x 4 7/8 in. pp. [1-6] 7 [8-10] 11-320, [1]^8 2-20^8; 160 leaves.

[1] Half-title; [2] Novels and stories by the author; [3] title; [4] FIRST
PUBLISHED 1932 *Made and Printed in Great Britain. Hazell, Watson & Viney,
Ltd., London and Aylesbury* [5] TO MY FRIEND/LADY ADAMS/FOR AULD
LANG SYNE; [6] *The characters in this book are entirely imaginary/and have
no relation to any living person;* 7 Contents; [8] blank; [9] BOOK I/THE
THREE ROGUES; [10] blank; 11-320 text; [77] BOOK II/ INSPECTOR BAD-
GER DECEASED: p [179] BOOK III/THE MISSING COLLECTOR.

Issued in pale blue glazed cloth with linen finish, all edges trimmed, unstained;
front cover and spine have black lettering; back cover plain.

b) *First U.S. edition (Dr. Thorndyke's Discovery).*

DR./THORNDYKE'S/DISCOVERY/BY/R. AUSTIN/FREEMAN/NEW YORK/
DODD, MEAD/& COMPANY/1932

The title page has vertical triple rule on left. The title is in solid black ornamental capitals. In lower left is silhouette of man in hat and coat with raised
walking-stick.

7 11/32 x 5 1/8 in. pp. [i-iv] v [vi], 1-2, 3-312 [313-314]

[i] Half-title and blurb; list of books by the author; [ii] publisher's announcement; [iii] title; [iv] COPYRIGHT, 1932/BY DODD, MEAD AND COMPANY INC./ALL RIGHTS RESERVED/. . ./. . ./PRINTED IN THE UNITED STATES OF AMERICA/BY THE VAIL-BALLOU PRESS, INC., BINGHAMTON, N.Y.; v Contents; [vi] blank; [1] BOOK I/MR. DIDBURY TOKE [2] blank; 3-312 text; p. [69] BOOK II/INSPECTOR BADGER DECEASED; p. [70] blank; p. [170] blank; p. [171] BOOK III/THE MISSING COLLECTOR; p. [172] blank.

Issued in black cloth, top and bottom edges trimmed, unstained, fore-edge cut; green lettering on front cover and spine, green silhouette in lower right corner of front cover of man in top hat with walking-stick (different from that on title page); back cover plain.

32.   *Dr. Thorndyke Intervenes*   1933

a) *First edition.*

DR. THORNDYKE / INTERVENES /BY/ R. AUSTIN FREEMAN / LONDON/ HODDER AND STOUGHTON, LTD./1933

7 5/32 x 4 25/32 in. pp. [1-4] v [6] 7-317 [318-320] ; [A] ^{8} B-T^8; 160 leaves.

[1] Half-title; [2] list of books by the author; [3] title; [4] *The characters in this book are entirely imaginary and have no relation to any living person.* First printed October 1933/PRINTED IN GREAT BRITAIN FOR HODDER AND STOUGHTON, LTD.,/BY RICHARD CLAY AND SONS, LTD., BUNGAY, SUFFOLK; v Contents; [6] blank; 7-317 text; [318–320] blank.

Issued in blue cloth with linen texture. Front cover has black lettering at head, otherwise plain. Black lettering and publisher's monogram on spine. Back cover plain.

b) *First U.S. edition.*

DR./THORNDYKE/INTERVENES/BY/R. AUSTIN/FREEMAN/NEW YORK/ DODD, MEAD/& COMPANY/1933

Title page has vertical triple rule on left of title page; a silhouette of a man with a raised stick is seen on the lower right.

7 11/32 x 5 in. pp. [i-iv] v [vi-viii], 1-344.

[i] Half-title and summary of the plot, followed by a list of the author's books; [ii] drawing of tombstone with epitaph and humorous verse; [iii] title; [iv] COPYRIGHT, 1933/BY DODD, MEAD AND COMPANY, INC./ALL RIGHTS RESERVED/NO PART. . ./. . ./PRINTED IN THE UNITED STATES OF AMERICA/BY THE VAIL-BALLOU PRESS, INC., BINGHAMTON, N.Y.; v

Contents; [vi] blank; [vii] half-title; [viii] blank; 1-344 text; p. 344 has, below text, the words (set within a shield): DODD, MEAD/449.4A/[rule]/*Red Badge Books*/[rule]/MYSTERY/DETECTIVE.

Issued in bright orange cloth; buff end-papers; front cover has black lettering and thick dotted line, surrounded by single rule frame stamped in blind; black lettering on spine, with title running from top to bottom; back cover plain.

33.   *For the Defence: Dr. Thorndyke*   1934

a) *First edition.*

FOR THE DEFENCE:/DR. THORNDYKE/BY/R. AUSTIN FREEMAN/LONDON/HODDER AND STOUGHTON/1934

7½ x 4 29/32 in. pp. [1-8] 9-319 [320]; [1]^8 2-20^8; 160 leaves.

[1] Half-title; [2] list of novels and stories by the author; [3] title; [4] *First printed. . . Sept.* 1934/MADE AND PRINTED IN GREAT BRITAIN FOR HODDER AND/STOUGHTON LIMITED, BY EBENEZER BAYLIS AND SON/LIMITED, THE TRINITY PRESS, WORCESTER, AND LONDON; [5] Contents; [6]. blank; [7] To/MY BROTHER ROBERT; [8] blank; 9-319 text; [320] blank.

Issued in gray-blue linen weave cloth; all edges trimmed and unstained; lettering on front cover and spine in black; publisher's monogram near foot of spine; back cover plain.

b) *First U.S. edition (For the Defense: Dr. Thorndyke).*

FOR THE DEFENSE:/DR. THORNDYKE/[device]/R. AUSTIN FREEMAN/ [device: Red Badge Detective, Dodd Mead]/DODD, MEAD & COMPANY/NEW YORK 1934

Title page has ornamental triple rule top and bottom.

7 11/32 x 5 1/8 in. pp. [i-vi] vii [viii], 1-310 [311-312]

[i] Half-title and blurb; [ii] publisher's announcement; [iii] title; [iv] COPYRIGHT, 1934/BY DODD, MEAD AND COMPANY, INC./ALL RIGHTS RESERVED/. . ./. . ./PRINTED IN THE UNITED STATES OF AMERICA/BY THE VAIL-BALLOU PRESS, INC., BINGHAMTON, N.Y. [v] *To my Friend,*/ LADY ADAMS/*For Auld Lang Syne;* [vi] blank; vii Contents; [viii] blank; 1-310 text; p. 310 has, below text, a "Red Badge Detective" emblem. [311] publisher's advertisement; [312] blank.

Issued in bright blue cloth; top and lower edges trimmed, top edge stained blue; fore-edge cut; the black lettering is characterized, on the front cover only, by the use of the Greek "e"; single-rule border on front cover stamped in blind; spine has black lettering with double rule between title and author's name; back cover plain.

a) *First edition.*

THE PENROSE MYSTERY/BY R. AUSTIN FREEMAN/LONDON/HODDER
AND STOUGHTON LIMITED

7½ x 5 in. pp. [1-11] 12-317 [318-320]; [A]^8 B-U^8; 160 leaves.

[1] Half-title; [2] list of books by the author; [3] title; [4] *The characters in
this book. . ./. . ./First Printed. . . .* 1936/*Printed in Great Britain for Hodder and
Stoughton, Limited/by Wyman & Sons Ltd. London ·Fakenham and Reading.*
[5] TO MY FRIEND,/ RONALD F. JESSUP, F.S.A./in grateful acknowledge-
ment of much/valuable technical advice and information/on matters archæological; [6] blank; [7-8] Contents; [9] BOOK 1/Being the Narrative of Ernest
Lockhart,/Barrister at Law; [10] blank; [11]-317 text; p. [51] has BOOK II/
Narrated by Christopher Jervis, M.D.; p. [52] is blank; [318-320] publisher's
advertisements.

Issued in pale blue cloth, all edges trimmed, top edge stained blue; black lettering
on front cover and spine; back cover plain.

b) *First U.S. edition.*

R. AUSTIN FREEMAN / THE / PENROSE / MYSTERY / [publisher's device] /
DODD, MEAD & COMPANY/NEW YORK 1936

Title page is set in heavy-face type: two double rules run the length of the page
on the left.

7 3/8 x 5 in. pp. [i-vi] vii-viii, [1-2] 3-300 [301-304].

[i] Half-title and summary [ii] publisher's advertisement; [iii] title; [iv] Copyright, 1936,/BY DODD MEAD AND COMPANY, Inc./All rights reserved—. . ./
. . ./. . ./PRINTED IN THE U.S.A. BY/The Quinn & Company [company name
in Gothic Type]/[rule]/BOOK MANUFACTURERS/RAHWAY, NEW JERSEY;
[v] TO MY FRIEND/RONALD F. JESSUP, F.S.A./IN GRATEFUL ACKNOWL-
EDGEMENT OF MUCH/VALUABLE TECHNICAL ADVICE AND INFOR-/
MATION ON MATTERS ARCHÆOLOGICAL; [vi] The characters in this
book. . .vii-viii Contents; [1] *Book I/Being the Narrative.* . . . [2] blank;
3-300 text; [301-304] blank

End papers bear "Red Badge Detective" shield emblem in red; p. 300 carries the
same emblem in black below the text.

Issued in rough dull orange cloth; top and lower edges trimmed, fore-edge cut,
untrimmed, upper edge stained orange-red. Front cover and spine have obliquely
set lettering in brown; back cover plain.

35. *Felo de Se?* 1937

a) *First edition.*

FELO DE SE? / BY / R. AUSTIN FREEMAN / LONDON / HODDER AND STOUGHTON

7 9/32 x 4 7/8 in. pp. [1-11] 12-315 [316-320] ; [A]^8 B-U^8; 160 leaves.

[1] Half-title; [2] list of novels and stories by the author; [3] title; [4] *The characters in this book are entirely imaginary/and have no relation to any living person./*First Printed. . . 1937/Printed in Great Britain for Hodder and Stoughton, Limited.,/by Wyman & Sons, Ltd., London, Fakenham and Reading; [5] TO/MY BROTHER ROBERT; [6] blank; [7-8] Contents; [9] PART I/THE GAMBLER/*Narrated by Robert Mortimer;* [10] blank [11]-315 text

Issued in pale blue linen-textured cloth; top edge stained light blue; all edges trimmed; blue end-papers; lettering in black capitals near top edge of front cover; black lettering and publisher's monogram on spine; back cover plain.

b) *First U.S. edition (Death at the Inn).*

DEATH [*set to the right, ornamental capitals*]/AT THE INN [*set to the left*]/ A DR. THORNDYKE DETECTIVE STORY [*running perpendicularly upwards on the left*]/R. AUSTIN FREEMAN/[*long rule*]/DODD, MEAD & COMPANY/ NEW YORK 1937

7 11/32 x 5 in. pp. [i-vi] vii [viii], [1-2] 3-312.

[i] Half-title and blurb; [ii] publishers' announcement; [iii] title; [iv] COPY-RIGHT, 1937/BY DODD, MEAD & COMPANY/All rights reserved—. . ./. . ./. . ./ PRINTED IN THE U.S.A. BY/The Quinn & Company [company name in Gothic Type]/[rule]/BOOK MANUFACTURERS/RAHWAY, NEW JERSEY; [v] TO/ MY BROTHER/ROBERT; [vi] blank; vii Contents; [viii] blank; [1] PART I/ THE GAMBLER/*Narrated by/Robert Mortimer;* [2] blank; 3-312 text, p. [126] blank; [127] PART II/THE CASE OF JOHN GILLUM, DECEASED/*Narrated by/Christopher Jervis, M.D.*; [128] blank.

Issued in olive-green cloth, top and bottom edges trimmed, fore-edge cut, top edge stained red; red lettering on front cover resembling title page but with oval device added in center; red lettering on spine; book cover plain. Yellow end-papers bearing "Red Badge Detective" emblems and "lightning" design.

36. *The Stoneware Monkey* 1938

a) *First edition.*

THE / STONEWARE MONKEY /BY/ R. AUSTIN FREEMAN / LONDON / HODDER AND STOUGHTON

7¼ x 4 7/8 in. pp. [1-4] 5 [6-8] 9-288; [1]^8 2-18^8, 144 leaves.

[1] Half-title; [2] list of books by the author (with some omissions and inaccuracies); frontispiece (photograph of the stoneware monkey) tipped in here; [3] title; [4] *The characters in this book. . ./. . ./First Printed. . . 1938*/MADE AND PRINTED IN GREAT BRITAIN/FOR HODDER AND STOUGHTON LIMITED/BY JARROLD AND SONS LTD. NORWICH; 5 Contents; [6] TO/ MY FRIEND/W.P. WATT/IN COMMEMORATION OF MANY YEARS/OF HAPPY AND HARMONIOUS COLLABORATION; [7] BOOK I *Narrated by James Oldfield M.D.* [8] blank; 9-288 text; p. [197] is blank; p. 198 BOOK II *Narrated by Christopher Jervis M.D.*

Issued in rough blue cloth, all edges trimmed, unstained; end papers blue; front and back covers plain; lettering and publisher's monogram on spine in dull gilt.

b) *First U.S. edition.*

THE STONEWARE/MONKEY/By/R. AUSTIN FREEMAN/Author of/"The Penrose Mystery"/"Death at the Inn"/Etc./DODD, MEAD & COMPANY/NEW YORK 1939

The title page has a wavy double rule near the upper and lower edges.

7 11/32 x 5 inches pp. [i-vi], [1-2] 3-312 [313-314]

[i] Half-title; [ii] publisher's announcement; [iii] title; [iv] COPYRIGHT, 1939,/BY R. AUSTIN FREEMAN/All rights reserved–. . ./. . ./. . ./PRINTED IN THE U.S.A. [v-vi] Contents; [1] BOOK 1/*Narrated by James Oldfield, M.D.;* [2] blank; 3-312 text; [313-314] blank. A frontispiece is tipped in opposite the title page: a photograph of "the stoneware monkey"; p. 211 has BOOK 2/ *Narrated by Christopher Jervis, M.D.*

Issued in pale yellow cloth, showing only a drawing in red of the monkey on the front cover, with no lettering; spine has red lettering; back cover plain. Top and lower edges trimmed, top edge stained red; fore-edge cut. Buff end papers with "Red Badge Detective" emblem in red.

37.   *Mr. Polton Explains*   1940

a) *First edition.*

MR. POLTON EXPLAINS/BY/R. AUSTIN FREEMAN/LONDON/HODDER AND STOUGHTON LIMITED

7¼ x 4¾ in. pp. [1-4] v [6-8] 9-285 [286-288]; [A]^8 B-S^8; 144 leaves.

[1] Half-title; [2] list (inaccurate and incomplete) of books by the author; [3] title; [4] TO LIEUT.-COM. RUPERT T. GOULD/R.N. (Retd.)/THE DISTINGUISHED HOROLOGIST,/THIS STORY OF A SIMPLE CLOCK-/MAKER

IS DEDICATED BY HIS OLD/FRIEND, THE AUTHOR/*First printed 1940;*
v Contents; [6] The characters in this book.../.... [7] PART I/THE ANTECE-
DENTS; [8] blank; 9 text begins, headed INTRODUCTORY OBSERVATIONS
BY MR. POLTON; 13-285 text; 149 PART II/THE CASE OF MOXDALE DE-
CEASED/*Narrated by Christopher Jervis M.D.*; [286] PRINTED AND BOUND
IN GREAT BRITAIN/FOR HODDER AND STOUGHTON, LIMITED,/BY
RICHARD CLAY AND COMPANY LTD.,/BUNGAY, SUFFOLK; [287-288]
blank

Issued in bright green cloth, edges trimmed, unstained; front cover plain, unlettered; black lettering on upper third of spine within frame of double rules;
back cover plain.

b) *First U.S. edition.*

A Dr. Thorndyke Mystery/MR. POLTON/EXPLAINS/By/R. Austin Freeman/
Dodd, Mead & Company/New York 1940

Title page is lettered in ornamental script.

7 3/8 scant x 5 in. pp. [i-vi] vii-viii, [1-2] 3-290 [291-296]

[i] Half-title; [ii] publisher's announcement; [iii] title; [iv] COPYRIGHT,
1940,/BY R. AUSTIN FREEMAN/All rights reserved—.../.../.../PRINTED IN
THE U.S.A. BY/The Quinn & Company [company name in Gothic Type]/[rule]/
BOOK MANUFACTURERS/RAHWAY, NEW JERSEY; [v] dedication; [vi]
blank; vii-viii Contents; [1] PARTI/THE ANTECEDENTS/Introductory Observations by Mr. Polton [2] blank; 3-290 text; p. 290 bears (below text) the "Red
Badge Detective" emblem; [291-296] blank.

Issued in red cloth; top and lower edges trimmed, unstained; fore-edge cut; no
lettering on front cover but "Red Badge" emblem in center in black; spine has
black lettering; back cover plain.

38. *Dr. Thorndyke's Crime File*   1941

First edition.

DR. THORNDYKE'S/CRIME FILE/*A Selection of his most celebrated cases/
containing, also, hitherto unpublished/material about the famous detective/and
his methods/By*/R. AUSTIN FREEMAN/*Edited by*/P.M. STONE/[device bearing
words "RED BADGE DETECTIVE DODD MEAD"]/DODD, MEAD & COM-
PANY/NEW YORK 1941

7 29/32 x 5 5/16 in. pp. [i-viii] ix-xv [xvi]; [i-iv], 1-344; [1-2] 3-16; [i-iv],
[1-2] 3-312; [1-2] 3-18; [i-vi], 1-338 [339-340].

[i] DR. THORNDYKE'S/CRIME FILE; [ii] publisher's announcements; [iii]
title; [iv] DR. THORNDYKE'S CRIME FILE/COPYRIGHT, 1925,/BY DR. R.
AUSTIN FREEMAN/COPYRIGHT, 1911, BY DODD, MEAD AND COMPANY/

COPYRIGHT, 1930, 1940, 1941,/BY DODD, MEAD AND COMPANY, INC./ ALL RIGHTS RESERVED/NO PART OF THIS BOOK MAY BE REPRODUCED IN ANY FORM/WITHOUT PERMISSION IN WRITING FROM THE PUB-LISHER/PRINTED IN THE UNITED STATES OF AMERICA/BY THE VAIL-BALLOU PRESS, INC., BINGHAMTON, N.Y.; [v] Contents (six items); [vi] blank; [vii] MEET DR. THORNDYKE/By/R. AUSTIN FREEMAN; [viii] blank; ix-xv text; [xvi] blank; [i] THE EYE OF OSIRIS; [ii] blank; [iii] Contents; [iv] blank; 1-344 text; [1] THE ART OF THE DETECTIVE STORY/BY/R. AUSTIN FREEMAN; [2] blank; 3-16 text; [i] THE MYSTERY OF ANGELINA FROOD; [ii] blank; [iii] Contents; [iv] blank; [1] PART I; [2] blank; 3-312 text; [1] 5A KING'S BENCH WALK/By/P.M.STONE; [2] blank; 3-18 text; [i] MR. POTTERMACK'S OVERSIGHT [ii] blank; [iii] TO/THE HONOURABLE LADY LYNDEN-BELL; [iv] blank; [v] Contents; [vi] blank; 1-338 text; [339-340] blank.

Issued in green cloth; front cover plain, except for "RED BADGE DETECTIVE" emblem in black; spine has black lettering; back cover plain; all edges trimmed, top edge stained green.

39.   *The Jacob Street Mystery*   1942

a) *First edition.*

R. AUSTIN FREEMAN/[long rule]/*The*/JACOB STREET/MYSTERY/London HODDER AND STOUGHTON/Limited.

7 3/16 x 4¾ in. pp. [1-4] 5-286 [287-288] [1]-18^8 [sig. No. 3 omitted]; 144 leaves.

[1] Half-title; [2] advert; [3] title; [4] The characters in this book. . ./. . ./ [rule]/First printed. . . March 1942/MADE AND PRINTED IN GREAT BRI-TAIN/FOR HODDER AND STOUGHTON LIMITED/BY JARROLD AND SONS LTD. NORWICH 5 Contents; 6 DEDICATION/[rule] TO/P.M. STONE/ BEST AND KINDEST OF MY MANY KIND AND/GENEROUS AMERICAN FRIENDS; 7-286 text; [287-288] adverts.

Issued in bright blue cloth; front cover blank; black lettering and publisher's device on spine; back cover plain.

b) *First U.S. edition (The Unconscious Witness).*

THE UNCONSCIOUS/WITNESS/By/R. AUSTIN FREEMAN/["Red Badge De-tective" device]/This is a Red Badge Book/DODD, MEAD & COMPANY/NEW YORK 1942

The title page has a single rule near top and bottom edges with one serrated edge.

7 11/32 x 5 in. pp. [i-iv] v-vi [vii-viii] [1-2] 3-303 [304]

[i] Half-title; [ii] publisher's announcement; [iii] title; [iv] COPYRIGHT, 1942/R. AUSTIN FREEMAN/ALL RIGHTS RESERVED/NO PART. . ./. . ./ PRINTED IN THE UNITED STATES OF AMERICA; v-vi Contents; [vii] Half-title; [viii] blank; [1] *PART I*/A PLOT IN THE MAKING [2] blank; 3-303 text; p. 303 below text has the "Red Badge Detective" emblem; p. [177] has *PART II*/THE UNKNOWN FACTOR/NARRATED BY CHRISTOPHER JERVIS M.D.

Issued in dull yellow rough cloth, with only "Red Badge Detective" emblem (in black) stamped on front cover; spine has black lettering and design incorporating a skull and a question mark; back cover plain.

40. *The Further Adventures of Romney Pringle* 1970

First edition.

The Further Adventures/of/Romney Pringle/By/"Clifford Ashdown"/[R. Austin Freeman & John J. Pitcairn]/Introduction by August Derleth/Oswald Train, Publisher/Philadelphia

Title page is set in ornamental hand-written characters.

7¼ x 4 13/16 in. pp. [1-6] 7-216 [217-222]

[1] Half-title; [2] blank; [3] title; [4] Copyright 1969 by Oswald Train/All rights reserved/FIRST EDITION/Printed in the United States of America; [5] Contents; [6] blank; 7-11 OF ROMNEY PRINGLE (p. 11 has signature: August Derleth/Sauk City, Wisconsin/29 January 1969); [12] blank; 13-20 CLIFFORD ASHDOWN: A RETROSPECT/By Norman Donaldson; [21] THE FURTHER ADVENTURES OF/ROMNEY PRINGLE; [22] blank; 23-216 text; [217] advertisement for *The Adventures of Romney Pringle* (U.S. edition); [218-222] blank.

NOTE: Production of the book was delayed; it was published in May or June, 1970.

Contents: The Submarine Boat—The Kimberley Fugitive—The Silk Worms of Florence—The Box of Specie—The Silver Ingots—The House of Detention.

Issued in bright red smooth cloth; all edges trimmed; front and back covers plain; spine has FREEMAN/AND/PITCAIRN at head, title lengthwise, TRAIN at foot, all in gilt.

EARLY ARTICLES AND SHORT STORIES BY R. AUSTIN FREEMAN IN CASSELL'S MAGAZINE (1898–1906)

The Resurrection of Matthew Jephson (story)	October 1898, pp. 534-42
Caveat Emptor: The Story of a Pram (story)	August 1900, pp. 247-52
A Victim of Circumstance (story)	March 1901, pp. 360-65
The Costume Model (story)	January 1902, pp. 233-37
The Great Tobacco "Plant" (story)	March 1902, pp. 417-20
Beyond the Dreams of Avarice (story)	May 1902, pp. 685-91
The Coastwise Lights of England (article)	December 1902, pp. 624-31
The Ebb Tide (story)	February 1903, pp. 352-56
The Royal Yacht (article)	April 1903, pp. 499-507
A Thames Sailing Barge Match (article)	September 1903, pp. 411-16
Ye Olde Spotted Dogge (Story)	April 1904, pp. 591-98
Small Yacht Racing (article)	May 1904, pp. 661-68
Bird of Passage (story)	June 1904, pp. 212-17
A Suburban Autolycus (story)	November 1904, pp. 652-57
Down the River (article)	June 1906, pp. 50-57

The three "Clifford Ashdown" serials also appeared in *Cassell's Magazine* during this period as follows:

The Adventures of Romney Pringle, June-November 1902

The Further Adventures of Romney Pringle, June-November 1903

From a Surgeon's Diary, December 1904–May 1905

Many years later the following single story appeared:

A Question of Salvage   September 1916, pp. 33-38

INDEX

Real persons are shown in Roman type thus: Jessup, Ronald F.
Fictional characters are shown in italics thus: *Vardon, Miss Helen.*
Short stories are shown thus: "Case of Oscar Brodski, The."
Books are shown in italics thus: *Cat's Eye, The.*
Freeman's works are listed individually by name, not under Freeman.